Theology Through Creative Practice

Engagements with the Work of Heather Walton

— EDITED BY —

DOUG GAY

ALISON JASPER

DAVID JASPER

Sacristy Press

Sacristy Press
PO Box 612, Durham, DH1 9HT

www.sacristy.co.uk

First published in 2025 by Sacristy Press, Durham

Copyright © Sacristy Press 2025
The moral rights of the author have been asserted.

All rights reserved, no part of this publication may be reproduced or transmitted in any form or by any means, electronic, mechanical photocopying, documentary, film or in any other format without prior written permission of the publisher.

Scripture quotations, unless otherwise stated, are from the New Revised Standard Version Bible: Anglicized Edition, copyright © 1989, 1995 National Council of the Churches of Christ in the United States of America. Used by permission. All rights reserved worldwide.

Every reasonable effort has been made to trace the copyright holders of material reproduced in this book, but if any have been inadvertently overlooked the publisher would be glad to hear from them.

Sacristy Limited, registered in England & Wales, number 7565667

British Library Cataloguing-in-Publication Data
A catalogue record for the book is available from the British Library

ISBN 978-1-78959-398-3

For Heather Walton, Friend, Teacher and Colleague

Contents

Preface *(Doug Gay, Alison Jasper, David Jasper)* v
Acknowledgements. vii
Contributors viii

Chapter 1. Lingering at the crossroads: Practical theology between imagination and empiricism *(Elaine Graham)*.......... 1
Chapter 2. Hello darkness, my old friend: Generating theology from loss and waste *(Frances Ward)*. 17
Chapter 3. A writing life: On leaving nothing out *(Nicola Slee)*...... 29
Chapter 4. No answers—Four poems and a midrash *(Ariel Zinder)* . 46
Chapter 5. Theology through creative listening *(Andrew W. Hass)*... 50
Chapter 6. Theology in the making: A glossary of theopoetic practices (for relating to oneself, others, materials, traditions and the Sacred) *(Wren Radford)*.............................. 65
Chapter 7. "Thank the Goddess there is a book": Reading Alice Walker's *The Color Purple* as a gift of return *(Fiona Darroch)*.... 95
Chapter 8. The making and unmaking of methodological habits *(Tone Stangeland Kaufman and Simon Hallonsten)*............ 116
Chapter 9. Tiresias *(Pádraig Ó Tuama)*......................... 135
Chapter 10. Creative Black theological writing: Explorations in being yourself *(Anthony Reddie)*........................... 137
Chapter 11. Life in the liminal: The ecotonal theology of Heather Walton *(L. Callid Keefe-Perry)* 154
Chapter 12. It's another day to love you *(Pamela Couture)*......... 175
Chapter 13. The great derangement in literature and practical theology: Following fiction into the other-than-human world *(Bonnie J. Miller-McLemore)*................................ 197

Selected bibliography of Heather Walton's published writings .. 214

Preface

Heather Walton has been teaching at the University of Glasgow for nearly 30 years. Before that, she taught in Northern Baptist College, Manchester and Westminster College, Oxford, studying for her doctorate first at the University of Durham and completing it in Glasgow. The friends and colleagues who have gathered to write in the present volume all have reason to be grateful to Heather for her scholarship and teaching but above all for her gift for friendship. What we celebrate here is the multifaceted academic contribution of Heather, remarkable for the range of its scholarship and creative energy.

We celebrate a friend and scholar who teaches and writes in a liminal space, between the wonder and horror of life, in a place that is between the heart and the head, between academic disciplines seeking articulation in a world that is torn by ecological threat and threatened by waste and devastation, and yet remains beautiful and creative if we would but listen and remain creative. Heather offers us a theopoetics that is at once joyous and challenging—and we hope that this book reflects both of those gifts to its readers.

Even Heather's earliest theological work displayed the feminist, anti-racist passion for justice and liberation, the concern for reflexivity and method and the deep interest in ethnography which would persist through all of her later scholarship and writing. Her earliest publications (1985–7) included a study of "Black People in British Methodism", "An Ethnographic Study of a Moss Side Pub", a reflection on "White Researchers and Racism", and *My Mother is Ill: An Experiment in Feminist Research*. Her doctoral research was on the uses of women's literature within theological reflection, and she has continued to work on the relation between theology and creative writing ever since. She did a further degree in Creative Writing at Goldsmiths and is a "life writer" who has pioneered the uses of autoethnography as a theological resource.

In the 1990s, she published on the use of the Bible in feminist pastoral care and on women's distinctive voice in preaching.

In 2000, she edited, with Andrew Hass of the University of Stirling, *Self, Same, Other: Re-visioning the Subject in Literature and Theology,* and later took over from Andrew the editing of the journal *Literature and Theology*. Books on literature and theology continued to appear until her important edited volume of essays, *Literature and Theology: New Interdisciplinary Spaces* (2011). She also served as editor of the journal *Theology and Sexuality* and has written with great pathos and honesty about her personal experience of infertility.

Heather's interests at that time were ranging broadly into the field of practical theology as well as literature and spirituality. Her literary energies, at the same time, were moving towards exploring models of theological reflection as expressed in her books, written with Elaine Graham and Frances Ward, *Theological Reflection: Methods* (2005) and *Theological Reflection: Sources* (2007), and her teaching in life writing and spirituality. She authored a seminal essay on "Poetics" for the 2011 Wiley Blackwell *Companion to Practical Theology* edited by Bonnie Miller-McLemore.

This interest in creative writing is described at length in her book *Not Eden: Spiritual Life Writing for this World* (2015). Her international reputation as a feminist practical theologian led to her serving as President of the International Academy of Practical Theology (2015–17).

Students at the University of Glasgow, both undergraduate and postgraduate, have long appreciated Heather's genius for teaching at the Centre for Literature, Theology and the Arts, in the Professional Doctorate in Practical Theology Consortium and most recently in the pioneering Doctoral Programme in Theology through Creative Practice. This last degree, which is very much the product of Heather's own vision, perhaps best expresses her love of theopoetics and their outcome in creative, artistic practice in poetry, writing and the visual arts.

The essays in the present book are written, each in their own way, in profound gratefulness for Heather as a teacher, as a colleague and as a friend. They are in the form of a conversation with her many interests and as expressions of gratitude for all that she has done for the academy and the world of theology in our time. Apart from the university, Heather has continued to serve the church as an elder in the Church of Scotland and has lived in accordance with passionately held political views, from her time in South Africa, to her work in inner-city Manchester, her activism at Greenham Common, and her growing concern for environmental issues. Her life and scholarship have displayed a rich and deep integrity, and we honour that in this volume.

Doug Gay, Alison Jasper, David Jasper

Acknowledgements

Thanks are due to the Drummond Trust, Kelvin West Church of Scotland and Trinity College, Glasgow for their generous assistance with funding for the publication of this book.

The editors gratefully acknowledge permission to reproduce the following images:

Chapter 6. Figures 1 – 9: Original Artwork and Photographs, Courtesy of Wren Radford.

Chapter 12. Figure 1: Zen Series – River Bottom Mosaic, Ceramic Tiles, Courtesy of the Artist, Sheryl Turoila Jorgensen. Figure 2: Iris, Opeongo Sunset, Seasonal Work, Giclée Prints, Courtesy of the Artist, John Ovcacik. Figure 3: Hand-Painted Ceramic Botanical Series, Courtesy of Potterswork, Muizenerg, Cape Town, South Africa. Figure 4: Glass Artwork, Courtesy of Peter Krauski, Krauski Art Glass. Figure 5: Our Rochester home: Gifts from our International Friends, Original Photograph Courtesy of Pamela Couture.

Contributors

Pamela D. Couture, before her retirement in 2023, held the Geoffrey and Jane Martin Chair in Church and Community at Emmanuel College of Victoria University in the University of Toronto. She has been Executive Director of the Toronto School of Theology.

Fiona Darroch is a lecturer in Religion at the University of Stirling and editorial board member for the journal *Literature and Theology* (Oxford University Press). She works in the field of postcolonial literature, critical religion and gender theory.

Doug Gay is Senior Lecturer in Practical Theology at the University of Glasgow, where he has been a close colleague of Heather Walton since 2005. He combines interests in homiletics and liturgy with work in ecclesiology and political theology. His creative practice includes preaching, liturgical writing, hymnwriting and songwriting. Publications include *Remixing the Church: The Five Moves of Emerging Ecclesiology* (2009), *Honey from the Lion: Christianity and the Ethics of Nationalism* (2014), and *God Be in My Mouth: 40 Ways to Grow as a Preacher* (2018). With Heather Walton, he set up and leads the groundbreaking Glasgow doctoral and master's programmes in Theology Through Creative Practice.

Elaine Graham is Professor Emerita of Practical Theology at the University of Chester and author of a number of works including *Transforming Practice* (1996), *Representations of the Post/Human* (2002), and with Heather Walton and Frances Ward, *Theological Reflection: Methods* (2nd edn, 2018). In 2021, she was elected a Fellow of the British Academy.

Simon Hallonsten is a Lecturer in Practical Theology at University College Stockholm and the Coordinator for the Center for Theology, Ecology, and Culture. His research in Christian religious education integrates participatory action research with creative methodologies, aiming to explore new approaches to continuous formation and theological engagement.

Andrew W. Hass is Reader in Religion at the University of Stirling. His interests and publications operate at the intersection of religion, philosophy, theology, literature and art, with particular interest in the idea of negation and German Idealism. His latest book is the co-authored *The Music of Theology: Language—Space—Silence* (Routledge, 2024). He is the General Secretary of the International Society for Religion, Literature and Culture.

Alison Jasper is currently an honorary research fellow in the Faculty of Social Sciences at Stirling University, where she is working in partnership with colleagues in Education. She was, until 2019, a Senior Lecturer in the Faculty of Arts and Humanities at Stirling, where she taught in the subject areas of both religion and gender studies.

David Jasper is Emeritus Professor at the University of Glasgow, where he was formerly professor of Literature and Theology. He has been Principal of St Chad's College, University of Durham, and Chang Yiang Chair Professor at Renmin University of China, Beijing. His recent publications include *Scripture and Literature: A David Jasper Anthology* (Baylor University Press, 2023). He is a Fellow of the Royal Society of Edinburgh.

Tone Stangeland Kaufman is Professor of Practical Theology at MF Norwegian School of Theology, Religion and Society and Visiting Professor at University College Stockholm. She is also chief editor of the ecclesial journal *Luthersk Kirketidende*. Her publications and research interests include spirituality, homiletics, ecclesiology, youth ministry and disciplinary and methodological contributions to practical theology and qualitative research, including work on normativity, reflexivity and action research.

Callid Keefe-Perry is Assistant Professor of Contextual Education and Public Theology at Boston College's Clough School of Theology and Ministry.

Bonnie Miller-McLemore is E. Rhodes and Leona B. Carpenter Professor of Religion, Psychology, and Culture Emerita at the Divinity School and Graduate Department of Religion of Vanderbilt University, Nashville, Tennessee. She was also a Henry Luce Fellow for the year 1999–2000 and a resident scholar at the Collegeville Institute in 2014.

Pádraig Ó Tuama is an Irish poet, theologian and conflict mediator. From 2014 to 2019, he was the leader of the Corrymeela Community. He holds a doctorate in Theology and Creative Practice from the University of Glasgow.

Wren Radford is a theologian engaged in developing creative and collaborative projects with community groups around experiences of inequality and justice. Based at the University of Manchester, they publish and teach on research methodologies, liberative theologies, and literature and theology.

Anthony Reddie is Professor of Black Theology in the University of Oxford, where he is also Director of the Oxford Centre for Religion and Culture. He is also Extraordinary Professor and Research Fellow in Theological Ethics at the University of South Africa.

Nicola Slee is Honorary Professorial Research Fellow at the Queen's Foundation, Birmingham and Professor Emerita at the Vrije Universiteit, Amsterdam. She has wide-ranging interests in feminist and practical theology, poetics, spirituality and faith development, and has published in these areas. A recent anthology of essays, co-edited by colleagues Ashley Cocksworth, Rachel Starr and Stephen Burns, *From the Shores of Silence: Conversations in Feminist Practical Theology* (SCM Press, 2023), explores and extends her work in these areas.

Frances Ward is a retired priest, former Dean of St Edmundsbury Cathedral in Suffolk, living in Cumbria, and continuing as licensed theologian in the Diocese of Carlisle.

Ariel Zinder is a senior lecturer in the Department of Literature at Tel Aviv University. His primary research interest is medieval Hebrew liturgical poetry. Zinder is a published poet and translator. He has published three volumes of poetry, as well as translations of Shakespeare's sonnets and Seamus Heaney's poetry into Hebrew.

1

Lingering at the crossroads: Practical theology between imagination and empiricism

Elaine Graham

Between imagination and empiricism

Practical theology is inherently multi-disciplinary and embraces disciplines as varied as biblical studies, ecclesiology, ethnography, organizational studies, psychotherapy and sociology. It draws on a range of research methodologies, including textual analysis, quantitative and qualitative investigation, autoethnography and cultural criticism. For some, the welcoming arms of scientific and social-scientific research methods, as championed by empirical theology, provide objective and respectable means of understanding the contemporary life-world. For others, approaches such as theopoetics, which harness the fruits of the creative imagination, or liberation theologies, which seek out hidden voices in the quest for transformation and empowerment, offer a more expansive canvas on which to project the complexities of lived experience.[1]

Heather Walton is well placed to comment on practical theology's versatility in this respect. During her career, she has conducted qualitative research into the experiences of Black and minority ethnic Methodists

---

[1] Heather Walton, "Seeking Wisdom in Practical Theology", *Practical Theology* 7:1 (2014), pp. 5–18.

and the everyday rituals of pub-going.[2] She has also championed the adoption of autoethnography and life writing within practical theology as imaginative representations (or reconstructions) of personal and corporate journeys of faith.[3] She would insist that all these approaches represent equally legitimate ways of knowing. As she has observed, however, there are constant pressures on practical theology to establish its disciplinary legitimacy and prove its wider economic or social significance by opting for research methods that favour measurable outcomes over reflective contemplation and critical thinking. In its anxiety to uphold its worth in an increasingly results-driven culture, Heather argues, practical theology is at risk of becoming "restrained in an empirical captivity"[4] and over-dominated by research methodologies "that focus our vision upon what can be conceptually objectified and reasonably analysed and do not encourage us to quest for traces of the 'somewhere else' of the creative arts".[5] In opting for pragmatics and application, represented by the objective security of evidence-based research, practical theological enquiry risks becoming reduced to "a dreary matter of programmed instrumental action in pursuit of clear goals".[6] Hard-wired into an emphasis on *making a difference* lies an indefatigable work ethic that obscures attention to beauty, contemplation or transcendence. Practical theology has gained a scientific credibility at the expense of its soul: the creative, imaginative dimensions of theological discourse are crowded out by a race for relevance which impoverishes and attenuates its vision.

---

[2] Heather Walton, *A Tree God Planted: Black People in British Methodism* (London: Methodist Publishing House, 1985); *An Ethnographic Study of a Moss Side Pub* (University of Manchester: Working papers in applied social research 12, 1987).

[3] Heather Walton, *Imagining Theology: Women, Writing and God* (London: T&T Clark, 2007).

[4] Heather Walton, "Poetics", in B. Miller-McLemore (ed.), *Wiley Blackwell Companion to Practical Theology* (Chichester: Wiley-Blackwell, 2012), pp. 173–82, at 175.

[5] Walton, "Poetics", p. 174.

[6] Walton, "Seeking Wisdom", p. 13.

"Practical theology does not linger idly at the crossroads. It does not surrender to the distracting loveliness of life as it flashes by."[7]

Heather is not the only practical theologian to address the tensions between imagination and empiricism, or action and reflection.[8] Even so, to "linger at the crossroads" of these two approaches is to see points of convergence as well as divergence, in which the tension between them becomes a creative dialectic. In this chapter, then, I want to explore what it means to dwell at the intersection between imagination and reason, wonder and utility, heart and head.

Some of this exploration will be prompted by the recent history of practical theology as well as reflections in the form of narrative interludes based on the story of Martha and Mary in the Gospel of Luke. This technique is an attempt to honour Heather's use of creative writing to elicit an imaginative reading of a story that has often been interpreted as an illustration of this very tension within Christianity: of action versus contemplation, body and spirit, intuition and reason. Yet I will argue that this is ultimately a false dichotomy, and holding them together constructively calls for a form of *attentiveness* that is characterized by nuanced accounts of lived experience unafraid of encounters with profound suffering, schooled in the values and virtues of sacred tradition and driven by a desire for transformation.

Good girls and bad women

As Jesus and his disciples were on their way, he came to a village where a woman named Martha opened her home to him. She had a sister called Mary, who sat at the Lord's feet listening to what he said. But Martha was distracted by all the preparations that had

---

[7] Walton, "Poetics", p. 174.

[8] Nicola Slee, *Fragments for Fractured Times: What Feminist Practical Theology Brings to the Table* (London: SCM Press, 2020), Part I; Callid L. Keefe-Perry, *Sense of the Possible: An Introduction to Theology and Imagination* (Eugene, OR: Cascade, 2023); Pavol Bargár, *Narrative, Myth, Transformation: Reflecting Theologically on Contemporary Culture* (Jihlava: Mlýn, 2016).

to be made. She came to him and asked, "Lord, don't you care that my sister has left me to do the work by myself? Tell her to help me!"

"Martha, Martha," the Lord answered, "you are worried and upset about many things, but few things are needed—or indeed only one. Mary has chosen what is better, and it will not be taken away from her" (Luke 10:38–42, New International Version).

The story of Martha and Mary is a favoured subject for preachers and is frequently presented as a choice between preoccupation with material, worldly concerns and faithful obedience to the teaching of Jesus. Theologically, the sisters have been styled in terms of the tension between action (love of neighbour) and contemplation (love of God). In early Christianity, the contrast was enshrined in the dichotomy between justification by works or by faith, between salvation in this world or the next (according to Augustine) or the choice between an active or contemplative life (according to Origen).[9]

The story in Luke's Gospel does seem to be structured around just such a binary opposition. Although Martha and Jesus converse as independent equals, the narrative chooses to applaud Mary's silent obedience. She may confound traditional domestic roles by adopting that of a disciple, but still nevertheless as a largely passive recipient of the word, with no commission to preach or teach in public.[10] And is there more than a trace of narcissism about Jesus' commendation of Mary's obedient devotion as she hangs on his every word? And yet, "If the Christian ideal is to integrate contemplation and action, why are the two cast dualistically, with one approved and the other impugned?... Why is only hearing the

---

[9] Elisabeth Schüssler Fiorenza, *But She Said: Feminist Practices of Biblical Interpretation* (Boston, MA: Beacon Press, 1992), pp. 55–75, at p. 58. See also Mary Grey, "Rescuing Martha from the Dishes: A Challenge of Retrieval and Proclamation", *Feminism and Religion* (online) 29–31 August 2013.

[10] Loveday Alexander, "Sisters in Adversity: Retelling Martha's Story", in Amy J. Levine (ed.), *A Feminist Companion to Luke* (London: Sheffield Academic Press, 2002), pp. 197–213.

word esteemed here, when the gospel as a whole insists on the importance of both hearing and doing the word?"[11]

Martha

It appears that our brother in Christ Luke is serving up hostages to fortune. Inevitably, Mary and I are set up as polar opposites: the good girl (silent, obedient, attentive) and the bad woman (argumentative, complaining). The role of active serving is discounted in favour of passive listening, with the latter being upheld as the exemplary, "better part" for us... and by implication, all women. Or else we become ciphers for other, more important, male disciples: so I am compared to the Apostle Peter: "practical, impulsive, and short-tempered to the point of rebuking the Lord himself", whereas Mary is likened to the Apostle John: "reflective, loving and calm."[12] Have people forgotten what a privilege it was to exercise diakonia? I was more than a mere housekeeper! I was host and patron, a leader of the worshipping community, bearing a considerable degree of responsibility.

Mary

People may praise me for my obedience in sitting quietly at the feet of Jesus, but they fail to see that as a woman I was assuming a new role: not as handmaid but disciple. I relish that opportunity on behalf of all my sisters in Christ, because knowledge is power!

Although some interpretations invite the reader to admire, even emulate, Mary's acquiescence and silence, the picture is altogether more complex. Martha is engaged in an important work of supporting Jesus in his itinerant ministry and should thus be considered a leader amongst those who exercised a role of *diakonia*.[13] Mary, too, demonstrates a

---

[11] Veronica Koperski, "Women and Discipleship in Luke 10.38–42 and Acts 6.1–7", in Amy J. Levine (ed.), *A Feminist Companion to Luke* (London: Sheffield Academic Press, 2002), pp. 161–96, at 182.

[12] See <https://www.learnreligions.com/martha-and-mary-bible-story-summary-700065> (accessed 8 April 2024).

[13] Turid Karlsen Seim, "The Gospel of Luke", in Elisabeth Schüssler Fiorenza (ed.), *Searching the Scriptures, Volume 2: A Feminist Commentary* (London: SCM Press, 1995), pp. 728–62, at 745–8.

courage in subverting a conventionally female role and assuming the role of disciple, reminding us that education has always been an important route to empowerment for many marginalized groups, although (as I will argue later) it can also reinforce patterns of social inequality and cultural conformity.

I will also return later to the question of whether the gospel narrative requires us to choose one sister, one mode of being, one way of knowing, over another. But now I return to discussions about practical theological method, and the tension between forms of research that are orientated towards tangible objective results versus more reflexive and imaginative methods.

The race for relevance

Mary
I love to assist Martha when we open our house to give alms to the poor. But when she says to me, "Mary, you spend too much time talking to our visitors when there's a queue building up of others waiting for food parcels!" I want to say, "But Martha. All our guests are children of God. Sometimes they just need someone to treat them with respect and love. Surely we do the Lord's work when we acknowledge the face of Christ in everyone. Is that not what it means to say they are poor in spirit as well as in body? Is that not, too, truly a work of diakonia?

It may seem odd that a discipline which places "theological reflection" at the heart of its method and epistemology should fall prey to the spectre of empiricism. But as Terry Veling argues, in dialogue with Heather in 2017, the quest for "scientific" credibility has skewed practical theology away from poetics towards utility. He asks, "Is practical theology licensed for poets, or only for pragmatics and application?"[14] The dichotomy also calls to mind C. P. Snow's characterization of the "two cultures" divided between "art" and "science", the former concerned with the subjective,

---

[14] Terry A. Veling, "Poetic Licence", *International Journal of Practical Theology* 23:1 (2019), pp. 39–48.

beauty, value, meanings and affect, the latter with objectivity, fact and proof. Even so, the value of empirical research, qualitative or quantitative, can be justified on the grounds that it is important to ground one's actions in the lived experience of others.[15] For this reason, over the past two generations, practical theology has legitimately and productively turned to the social sciences in order to understand the human and social contexts in which it works, the better to inform its own practices. There are evident benefits to this: it can demonstrate an impact on professional formation; it can furnish transferable skills; it can produce concrete results and outcomes.[16]

In fact, "empirical research" applies to any form of practical enquiry, informed by scientific methods, aimed at gathering knowledge about the life-world.[17] What Heather and Terry Veling are objecting to, however, is a form of reductionism that equates authentic knowledge exclusively with that which can be measured, and with an assumption that the results of our research efforts provide us with an objective, unbiased account of reality in order to reliably "categorize religious practices and spiritual understandings into reassuring forms of useful knowledge".[18]

Throughout higher education, this trend is a clear and present danger. With the rise of performance-related and evidence-based measures within public policy (including higher education), the arts and humanities (including theology) are tempted to measure the utility and value of their research against the criteria of hard science. Yet there is a danger that such an approach risks hollowing out less tangible aspects of

---

[15] Elizabeth Conde-Frazier, "Participatory Action Research", in B. Miller-McLemore (ed.), *Wiley Blackwell Companion to Practical Theology* (Chichester: Wiley-Blackwell, 2012), pp. 234–43, at 239.

[16] Stephen Pattison, *The Challenge of Practical Theology* (London: Jessica Kingsley Publishers, 2007), pp. 261–89, at 270–3.

[17] Hans Schilderman, "Quantitative Method", in B. Miller-McLemore (ed.), *Wiley Blackwell Companion to Practical Theology* (Chichester: Wiley-Blackwell, 2012), 123–32, at 127; Walton, "Seeking Wisdom", p. 7.

[18] Walton, "Seeking Wisdom", p. 7.

complexity, meaning, narrative and interpretation.[19] Research protocols become procedures that are "stuck with simply managing the present as a problem of technique without having the possibility of imagining something more, or something better".[20]

Pressures from the academy to prove one's value in terms of measurable outcomes and practical utility are also replicated within many parts of church organization. In this context, insofar as practical theology serves a diversity of "publics",[21] it is mindful of its accountability to religious bodies through its stake in theological education. Yet here, too, there are strident criticisms of the mindset that seeks solutions to long-term institutional decline in managerial methods in which the objectives of research are so closely circumscribed (or institutionally hide-bound) as to be incapable of questioning their own premises. Elisabeth Jay has issued a blistering critique of the lack of intellectual or political weight of the Church of England's public pronouncements during the Covid-19 pandemic. This develops into an extended remonstration against the dominance of managerialism by a Church leadership whose priorities seem increasingly at odds with the routine priorities of local clergy and congregations.[22]

It must be remembered, however, that any body of knowledge is essentially a work of representation or interpretation. Heather's own work in theopoetics as a legitimate form of theological enquiry serves to highlight this. The uses of imaginative devices such as life writing and autoethnography in practical theology are essentially one kind of construct of "lived experience". They are not factual or transparent accounts of reality but pieces of communication, mediated through conventions of writing and self-representation, as well as the social

---

[19] Henry A. Giroux, "Critical Pedagogy in the Age of Fascist Politics", *Policy and Practice: A Development Education Review*, Vol. 37 (Autumn 2023), pp. 159–75, at 163.

[20] Pattison, *The Challenge of Practical Theology*, p. 280.

[21] David Tracy, *The Analogical Imagination* (London: SCM Press, 1981).

[22] Elisabeth Jay, "The End of the Church", in Bridget Nichols and Nicholas Taylor (eds), *The End of the Church? Conversations with the Work of David Jasper* (Durham: Sacristy Press, 2022), pp. 101–14.

conditions of culture, race, gender, class and religion.[23] However, readers should not be discomforted by the proximity to fiction of such imaginative or literary forms. We are not necessarily looking to such writing (or any other kind) to unearth the authentic self that lies beneath; we are offering up the fruits of narrative labour for further edification. For example, the study of congregations within practical theology has been significantly shaped by its use of literary and creative devices. Heather herself has noted how James Hopewell's classic investigation into the life of three Protestant congregations in the small North American town he called "Corinth" was shaped by his interpretative use of Northrop Frye's four narrative genres.[24] Similarly, Mary Fulkerson's autoethnography of Good Samaritan Church forms a kind of woven narrative incorporating her own personal reactions with other sources of fieldwork observations.[25]

So, even empirical research is an exercise in constructing a social (or often congregational) imaginary: an artifice for the purposes of engendering a "thicker" description. Yet as Hans-Günter Heimbrock points out, "In the perspective of natural or quantitative social sciences, it makes sense to look for objective knowledge. However, some *objectives* are not simply to be *objectified*."[26] In other words, the practice of research can never end in certainty or closure, but should serve to fuel further exploration and enquiry. Good research is akin to *poiesis:* a form of making and doing that stimulates the creative imagination, in order to facilitate a greater apprehension of "the inbreaking of the new".[27]

---

[23] Heather Walton, *Not Eden: Spiritual Life Writing for this World* (London: SCM Press, 2015), p. 15.
[24] Walton, "Poetics", pp. 175–7; see James F. Hopewell, *Congregation: Stories and Structures* (London: SCM Press, 1987).
[25] Mary McClintock Fulkerson, *Places of Redemption: Theology for a Worldly Church* (Oxford: Oxford University Press, 2007).
[26] Hans-Günter Heimbrock, "Practical Theology as Empirical Theology", *International Journal of Practical Theology* 14 (2011), pp. 153–70, at 164, my emphasis.
[27] Heather Walton, "Foreword", in Callid L. Keefe-Perry, *Sense of the Possible: An Introduction to Theology and Imagination* (Eugene, OR: Cascade, 2023), p. 9.

Out of the ruins

Mary to Martha
In time, we will come to see that our Lord, despite being God's chosen one, made himself like a servant, embracing weakness that we may be strong. I firmly believe that his power to heal comes from his own woundedness, from which he draws a love that is stronger than death itself.

Martha to Mary
It was only after our brother Lazarus was raised from the dead that I came fully to realize this. Out of my grief and suffering came a new self-knowledge and I declared Jesus to be the true Messiah! I pray that though I am a mere woman I may be remembered as a witness to our Lord's compassionate love.

The tension between "useful knowledge" and "practical wisdom" within practical theology can also be traced in one of its favourite origin stories, namely the birth of Clinical Pastoral Education. CPE was established in 1925 at Worcester State Hospital in Massachusetts, USA by a medical practitioner and Unitarian layman, Richard Cabot. Cabot proposed that students in training for ordained ministry in the Protestant churches should undertake a programme of field education in healthcare institutions, similar to the clinical placements provided for medics. Cabot co-opted a local Presbyterian minister, Anton Boisen, to work with him, and together the two pioneered a form of practice-based or case study training. Students were required to produce transcripts or "verbatims" of their conversations with patients, which were then used as the basis of formal supervision. Cabot believed that such direct exposure to pastoral situations would foster appropriate professional and theological skills. Boisen coined the term "living human documents" to describe such encounters, believing that insights mediated through pastoral and clinical experience were as significant as canonical sources such as Scripture and tradition for developing students' theological understanding.[28]

---

[28] Daniel S. Schipani, "Case Study Method", in B. Miller-McLemore (ed,), *Wiley Blackwell Companion to Practical Theology* (Chichester: Wiley-Blackwell, 2012), pp. 89–101.

Boisen's own life experience was pivotal to this approach. Beginning in his early forties, he experienced six severe psychotic episodes, leading to his own hospitalization. He subsequently devoted himself to understanding the significance of the spiritual dimension to mental health conditions and the theological significance of the journeys and narratives of those, like him, living with various forms of psychiatric trouble. He advocated a form of "co-operative enquiry" in which patient and therapist worked side-by-side in trying to find meaning in such extreme mental states.[29]

This presents us with an intriguing tension here, between "the pastoral and clinical . . . as a tool in ministerial training" and the value of the verbatim as "primary material for theological hermeneutics".[30] Clearly, self-understanding and a degree of what contemporary practitioners would term "reflexivity"[31] is a significant element of any professional formation, and it is easy to draw too strong a contrast between the two approaches. Nevertheless, Cabot seems to have regarded the clinical placement as enhancing the trainee minister's practical competence—listening, observing and responding—in order to equip them with tangible expertise and accreditation. On the other hand, Boisen's vision of CPE appears to have emerged precisely from his own vulnerability and brokenness. For him, therefore, the adoption of the verbatim as a component of theological education was not merely (or even primarily) about honing the listening skills of trainee hospital chaplains, but a matter of generating primary qualitative data by which "the pastoral practitioner would be brought face to face with the painful search for meaning in the

---

[29] See Sean J. LaBat, *Anton Boisen: Madness, Mysticism, and the Origins of Clinical Pastoral Education* (Minneapolis, MN: Lexington Books/Fortress Academic, 2021); Robert Charles Powell, *Anton T. Boisen (1876–1965): Breaking an Opening in the Wall Between Religion and Medicine*, 2nd edn (London: CSP Press, 2021).

[30] Elaine Graham, *Transforming Practice: Pastoral Theology in an Age of Uncertainty*, 2nd edn (Eugene, OR: Wipf & Stock, 2002), p. 66.

[31] Zoë Bennett, Elaine Graham, Stephen Pattison and Heather Walton, *Invitation to Research in Practical Theology* (London: Routledge, 2018), pp. 34–56.

lives of others, and ... to a more honest confrontation with searching and disturbing questions within his or her own life".[32]

Advocates of a pure empiricism might be horrified, then, by the extent to which, once again, the autobiographical appears to intrude on what should be an exercise in value-free enquiry. Boisen's openness in the face of his own vulnerability, and the willingness to see his greatest advances emerging "out of the depths"[33] is truly counter-cultural and resists any attempt—then or now—merely to instrumentalize research in the quest for efficiency and progress. Yet the exercise of reflexivity in practical theology should entail a degree of self-awareness and transparency; and research must take account of unexpected consequences, power dynamics, risk and vulnerability to researcher and researched alike. Such factors serve as a corrective to the "interventionist/effectiveness orientation of the prevailing professional ethos" in much higher education.[34]

Such practical theological reasoning embodies an essentially tragic spirit, as Heather herself has argued. In an essay on the contemporary German artist Anselm Kiefer, she notes how at the heart of much of great creative work there lies a paradox: of the persistence of hope amidst destruction, of resistance amidst oppression—of life, even resurrection, after death.[35] This means reconciling oneself to the fractured and partial nature of the theological imagination. Out of chaos, silence and death comes life—such is the nature of *kenosis*. The fruits of such theological imagination, rooted in the Christian narrative of death and resurrection,

---

[32] Mark Sutherland, "Psychiatry and Religion in Mental Health", in S. P. Pattison and J. W. Woodward (eds), *The Blackwell Reader in Pastoral and Practical Theology* (Oxford: Blackwell, 2000), pp. 272–82, at 275.

[33] See Anton T. Boisen, *Out of the Depths: An Autobiographical Study of Mental Disorder and Religious Experience* (New York: Harper & Co., 1960).

[34] Zoë Bennett and Elaine Graham, "The Professional Doctorate in Practical Theology: Developing the Researching Professional in Practical Theology in Higher Education", *Journal of Adult Theological Education* 5:1 (2008), pp. 33–51, at 47.

[35] Heather Walton, "Rubble and Dust", in Bridget Nicols and Nicholas Taylor (eds), *The End of the Church? Conversations with the Work of David Jasper* (Durham: Sacristy Press, 2022), pp. 35–53.

resist closure or triumphalism in favour of "a deep and loving attention to what is damaged, derelict and yet possessed of piercing power".[36]

But if the Church has betrayed its prophetic and pastoral calling through its indifference or even complicity in the face of suffering, Heather has argued that renewal may actually begin at that very "moment of betrayal, of blood at the roots, as the moment of genesis. Indeed . . . the Church as a community . . . is constituted precisely at the moment of betrayal".[37] Once the Church has fully come to terms with its own failures and uncertain future, it may be able better to "contemplate the possibility of generative stirrings within the questionable chaos of our own wreckage".[38] In the face of the Church's timidity and denial of the challenges facing our world, it is those who deal in the creative imagination who are capable of summoning the courage to name the reality around them and to construct alternative narratives of hope and repair. "In other words, accept that it may be our academic vocation to be poets of the broken form in theology."[39]

Sisters under one roof

Luke the Evangelist

Martha, you have been an enigma to me, but you are not invisible. You made our Lord's ministry possible by offering hospitality to him and serving others in his name. But never forget that activism needs to be grounded in the well-springs of faith. You may welcome Christ into your home, but do not forget to receive him also in your heart and mind.

Many commentators argue that the story of Martha and Mary is best understood in the context of a number of Lukan travel narratives in which Jesus moves from house to house, accepting hospitality from

---

[36] Heather Walton, "A Theopoetics of Practice: Re-forming in Practical Theology", *International Journal of Practical Theology* 23:1 (2019), p. 15.
[37] Walton, "Rubble and Dust", p. 41.
[38] Walton, "Rubble and Dust", p. 46.
[39] Walton, "A Theopoetics of Practice", p. 18.

propertied supporters, many of whom were women.[40] Martha is no longer incidental but emerges as one who facilitates Jesus' itinerant ministry. A re-evaluation of Martha's status emerges, also, if Luke 10 is juxtaposed alongside the account of the raising of Lazarus (brother of Martha and Mary) in John 11:1-44. Here, the ambivalence of the Lukan portrayal contrasts with an unequivocal portrayal in the Johannine tradition of Martha as an exceptional, exemplary leader and evangelist.[41]

If Martha is at fault, then, it lies not in her choice of role but the manner of its conduct. She is depicted as weighed down by her responsibilities such that hospitality becomes a matter of duty rather than joy.[42] She has allowed herself to become distanced from the very source of her faith. There must be a constant and mutual interplay between action and reflection. Rather like practical theologians over the past half-century, who consciously reworked their disciplinary identity from one of "applied doctrine" and ministerial "hints and helps" into a primary theological discourse,[43] Martha needs to return to the theological wellsprings of her vocation. "The theological task of locating God's presence and activity in the world through reference to the story of Jesus Christ works best when it includes a thorough knowledge of the narratives and images within which human life is to be interpreted."[44] The two sisters represent complementary virtues of practical service and attention to the Word.

Practical theologians sometimes frame this in terms of an aspiration towards a fusion of immersion in the immediate and concrete (afforded through empirical methods or social analysis) and a more reflective attention to the voices of Scripture, culture and Christian tradition. Heather has characterized this way of knowing as "a wisdom that attends

---

[40] Koperski, "Women and Discipleship", pp. 174–7.

[41] Warren Carter, "Getting Martha out of the Kitchen: Luke 10.38–42 Again", in Amy J. Levine (ed.), *A Feminist Companion to Luke* (London: Sheffield Academic Press, 2002), pp. 214–31; Seim, "Gospel of Luke", pp. 741–3.

[42] Carter, "Getting Martha out of the Kitchen", pp. 220–1.

[43] Elaine Graham, Heather Walton and Frances Ward, *Theological Reflection: Methods*, 2nd edn (London: SCM Press, 2019), esp. pp. 2–4.

[44] Clive Marsh, *Christ in Practice: A Christology of Everyday Life* (London: Darton, Longman & Todd, 2006), p. 23.

to lived experience, which is transformative and change seeking and always interprets the lived context in the light of the values and virtues of sacred tradition".[45]

Paying attention

"ATTEND
    1. verb (BE PRESENT)
    2. verb (NOTICE)
    3. verb (PROVIDE HELP)"[46]

Martha
My desire to be useful, to prove my worth, clouded my vision: I stopped attending to the grace and wonder of God at work in the world.

Mary
Martha's tireless care and hospitality reminds me that if I wish to see the risen Christ today, I must attend to the very lost and wounded people whom she serves.

In reality, like other researchers in the humanities and social sciences, practical theologians adopt hybrid and multiple methodologies.[47] In their case, they do so for the purposes of understanding the "living human document" of personal and corporate experience in the light of Christian claims about the nature of God. But in effect, all such modes of research may be valued as a search for ways of dwelling alongside others in the world: a way of being as much as acting—and certainly never reducible to mere technique. This chapter has considered how best practice in practical theological research is born of a kind of attentiveness that comes from the places of suffering and vulnerability and refuses to substitute "useful knowledge" for "practical wisdom". Heather has consistently

---

[45] Walton, "Seeking Wisdom", p. 9.
[46] <https://dictionary.cambridge.org/dictionary/english/attend> (accessed 28 October 2024).
[47] Walton, "Seeking Wisdom", p. 10.

argued that the best kind of theological enquiry will not countenance the domestication of the presence of suffering and evil. In our haste to render the incomprehensible somehow more palatable, we risk descending into bathos and "banality".[48] Rather than imposing order and harmony on our enquiries we must learn to contemplate chaos and passion as the sites of "the supreme, restless, transformative capacity of humans to reshape their world and create meaning out of the mundane".[49] For Heather, authentic theological reflection wrestles with angels, weeps in the face of the world's suffering, startles with its strangeness and beauty as it undertakes "a journey drawing closer to the heart of God".[50] Her work constantly reminds us that the divine often dwells in unexpected, tragic and disturbing quarters.

"The researcher must take the risk of journeying out of their own safe space and entering new worlds in which they will be changed and formed. They must abandon the illusion that they can present a true mirror of an existing situation whose veracity is confirmed either by their theological framework or their methodological rigour. A dialogical process is what makes good research—a *truly attentive listening to the other*. This requires a certain self-emptying, a letting go, and a willingness to let the process change the person whose own self is the vulnerable research instrument employed. The products of this research are seldom tidy data sets; the more dialogical and transformative the process has been the less control the researcher has over the outcomes."[51]

---

[48] Walton, "Seeking Wisdom", p. 12.

[49] Walton, "Seeking Wisdom", p. 13.

[50] Heather Walton, in Judith Thompson, Stephen Pattison and Ross Thompson, *SCM Studyguide to Theological Reflection* (London: SCM Press, 2008), p. 30.

[51] Heather Walton, "Locating Ourselves", in Zoë Bennett, Elaine Graham, Stephen Pattison and Heather Walton (eds), *Invitation to Research in Practical Theology* (London: Routledge, 2018), p. 27.

2

Hello darkness, my old friend: Generating theology from loss and waste

Frances Ward

Hello Heather, my old friend. I've come to talk with you again.

It's always a delight—to anticipate time and conversation with Heather, and then to participate in the rich fullness of the reality. Glass of red wine in hand, you will travel widely—through personal stuff, gardening and allotments, food, literature, politics, even theology (although, of course, always remembering that we have never been theologians[1])—you name it; and you quickly discover that she loves to be polemical and bold; to stir you out of any perceived or real complacencies, whether political, or interior design, or the nature of reality. And good luck to you if you seek clarity or want to pin something down into a nice little definition, for Heather will remind you just how much our rationality is embedded in our imagination, and that the darkness is not far away. For things aren't clear, and meaning is elusive, and God cannot be easily contained by this or that sort of theology, particularly when it trades off the too-easy polarization between transcendence and immanence. Her ways of expression are poetic, suggestive, full of desire and anxious lest the end of desire might come too soon. Perhaps anxious, also, that the conversation might end too soon, in the clarity of agreement. For the darkness is full of possibility, the dazzling is endless. From the darkness life begins, in all its mess and confusion, for in the beginning there was the dark warmth

---

[1] H. Walton, "We have never been theologians: Postsecularism and practical theology", *Practical Theology* 11:3 (2018), pp. 218–30.

of the womb. Heather's theology begins here. Not in clear reflections or pure contemplation. But where it hurts. Where the loss makes itself felt. "What has become sacred for us was generated from the fecundity of impurity", she writes.[2] The conversation, like life, is drunk to the lees.

Heather's imagination is richly generative. But we need to be careful of such words, for this is not to write of a God who begat remembered generations through long-recorded history, nor is to be generative to focus on the fruitful outcome of purposeful activity. No. Heather's writing suggests participation in a divine who is discerned where the darkness remembers the forgotten, the wasted, the cockle shells left by the wayside. To write from here is to stand under—to understand—how theological reflection must disturb former frames of meaning by engagement with the darkness of ambiguity, the murky muddle and fragments of loss, within the partial, the flux and flow of life. Then writing becomes a creative activity that makes meaning, but which is never complete or able to say it all, for good spiritual writing takes the author and reader in directions that question superficial meanings and insights, to places and times that generate ways of understanding deep enough to cope with the experience of loss and waste, the infertile and sad. It is then, perhaps, that the theological imagination might begin to participate in the divine in new and different ways. The human experience of the complexities and confusions that the body generates, and that are generated when bodies come together, in love and affection, or in conflict and pain, enables the imagination to enter the living soil, the loam that is alive with God. And where better to experience such creativity than in the warmth of friendship that holds pain, conflict and difference, and also embraces the darkness of polarized and oppositional perspectives, such that new ways of being are generated, in writing that opens up paths towards a deeper participation in the divine.

I first met Heather when she was heavily pregnant with Maia. I was about to start as her colleague at Luther King House, as it was called then, in Manchester, UK, and one hot summer day she showed me around Hulme and Moss Side, where students would be placed to learn sociological and congregational analysis. We sat in her slate-floored

---

[2] Walton, "We have never been theologians", p. 226.

kitchen and talked, and it was then that the exploration began. It was only later that I learned of the traumatic journey of infertility that Heather and Reinier had travelled; later, too, that Heather wrote of the experience. Her paper "Passion and pain: Conceiving theology out of infertility"[3] is a vivid account of just how raw and awful it is to be turned inside out, alongside other women on a ward that brings together those who can't conceive; with those who wait with a dead baby inside; those who need a termination. Then, wrote Heather, then,

> you begin to understand when you hold your sister to you. Her baby is dead inside her. Or perhaps she is preparing to end a life that was ill conceived. Maybe, just perhaps, in the future the almost impossible birth might take place in one of us. But not yet. All of your life you have been told only to look towards the light. Now you may begin to see beyond the little lights and into the greater darkness.
>
> Here is your faith
> God is God
> Of the Living
> And the Dead.
> This is how theology is done.[4]

Writing is the way into the greater darkness. Her words are playful, contrary, ambiguous, and she encourages spiritual writing in others, by example, that they might follow the metaphors that are strong in life experience.[5] So as Heather reflects on her life, it is Not Eden where she belongs, where writing " . . . is not innocent; [for it] has lost all nostalgia for the pure representations of pure forms. A writing that lives spiritually

---

[3] H. Walton, "Passion and pain: conceiving theology out of infertility", *Contact* 130 (1999), pp. 3–9.
[4] Walton, "Passion and pain", p. 9.
[5] H. Walton, *Not Eden: Spiritual Life Writing for this World* (London: SCM Press, 2015), p. 35.

in this world—while still yearning in its travails."⁶ The writing itself bears all things, hopes all things, as, like life, words belong together (or not) in a rich web of nuance, where meaning emerges in creation. Her writing is profound, as she wrestles with infertility in word and deed, in the faith that something sacred will be revealed (though there is no guarantee). There she writes of how her (non)-generative theology not only celebrates embodiment but also allows the naming of limits, the "griefs and tragedies of the flesh",⁷ which have such a profound impact. She knows that her "own deep awareness of embodiment was stamped upon me not by sensuous enjoyment, aesthetic intensity, feminist epistemology or sublime experiences in nature. It came through infertility. The grinding, everyday pain of being unable to conceive."⁸ This is Heather Walton at her best, I'd say, where the personal, the life-lived, is the real matter of theology, where "blessed normality"⁹ is spun through with the sacred.

This sacred is entangled throughout "the earthy, commonplace material of lived experience",¹⁰ where connections are made—people, nature, divine—and the yearning is there, for something that reaches beyond. The "beyond" is not a purified realm of clarity and enlightenment, but discerned in glimpses and fragments, as frail as our bodies, as delicate as a lichen observed through a field eyeglass. No longer can we, or should we, allow a dualistic world view that distinguishes immanent and transcendent, or material and spiritual; but rather a sense of gift instils in us "a new sense of wonder that is being generated out of our recognition that we belong within the natural and material orders as embodied creatures".¹¹ To write of such a world is to be "an adaptive and pragmatic borrower from traditions, an embodied and relational self, a creative protester", who resists and remakes "in an ambiguous but

---

[6] Walton, *Not Eden*, p. 42.
[7] Walton, *Not Eden*, p. 26.
[8] Walton, *Not Eden*, p. 26.
[9] Walton, *Not Eden*, p. 72.
[10] Walton, *Not Eden*, p. 3.
[11] Walton, *Not Eden*, p. 19.

enchanted environment".[12] This is a deeply incarnational way of writing theology, with an "acute attentiveness to the world as a theatre of grace".[13] The self is likewise—always in flux, in the flow of life—to be told in story, in autobiography, which goes some way towards the coherence that is a gift realized in relation—to other people, nature and/or God. We are not solipsistic individuals, children of the Enlightenment and its shadowy Romantic era, but always embedded in rich loam, or thin soil, never quite sure what will grow, which seeds will germinate, if any; for perhaps, after all, it is a wasteland, without landmarks or signposts, that we inhabit. Or a wilderness.

But certainly Not Eden, for the gardens we live in are the ordinary gardens and allotments of life. Heather remembers her own mother, who populated the cracks and edges with the seeds of weeds (so-called), for "my mother liked plants that were not easily domesticated. She scraped among the stones with a tablespoon and planted forget-me-nots, foxgloves and poppies ... once those tiny seeds are planted in a garden they will take hold. She also planted sea pinks all the way up beside the steep garden path, because it is a lovely plant and because its common name is 'Thrift.'"[14] Heather learned as a child that growing things is "a dangerous business",[15] for growing is not a one-way process, but often we grow into our girlhood, as the familiar stories unravel, and the contradictions proliferate. Her mother taught her that things don't stay the same, herself disrupted by the death of her own mother, too early.[16]

Theological reflection becomes an enfolding in and through people, nature and the divine, discerning through metaphor the presence of a barely detected "song of the Spirit sounding out across the starry heavens and all along the darkling plain".[17] Looking through a glass darkly, back into her childhood, the reflection is on the power of the generations before and after her to shape her life, where the strength comes from

---

[12] Walton, *Not Eden*, p. 20.
[13] Walton, *Not Eden*, p. 24.
[14] Walton, *Not Eden*, p. 51.
[15] Walton, *Not Eden*, p. 52.
[16] Walton, *Not Eden*, p. 58.
[17] Walton, *Not Eden*, p. 61.

somewhere deep and hidden underground, and as she observed her father making a garden of the "half-begun, half-ended space" around, the metaphors begin to create reality:

> When he had fashioned the paths and garden walls, when the old stumps and rubble had been removed, my father felt that more was needed than my grandfather's dahlias and tea roses or my mother's semi-civilized flowers. He started to bring the woods into barren ground the builders had left us. He took his wheelbarrow and slung his spade over his shoulder and strode out to see what he could find. Whole trees staggered stiffly down the cinder road and climbed over our gate. There was a rowan tree, and my father said that this was for my mother. It was young now, but soon it would be as tall as the house and hung with berries for the birds in winter. Rowan trees were to protect the home and all who lived there. They were guardian spirits. For me he planted a silver birch, the maiden tree, slender, light and supple. Always the first to grow again when ground was cleared. When Ella was born at Christmastime, he celebrated with a shop-bought conifer. Sweet smelling and perfect it looked timid and tiny in its plant pot but soon naturalized, growing a foot a year, losing its nursery neatness and finding its place among the rest.[18]

Plants came and went from the wild to the domestic, creating a sweet disorder. Her first sexual encounters were potent and full of fear of pregnancy: "'Oh God', I prayed, 'please don't let me get pregnant', and 'please, please let me go to university.'" Hindsight, and her adult tells her child, "You should be very careful indeed what you pray for."[19] The journey of infertility reshapes her childhood and adolescence, as she contrasts her adult experience with the time when pregnancy tests taken when negative, meant freedom, when fertility and potency went hand in hand:

---

[18] Walton, *Not Eden*, p. 75.
[19] Walton, *Not Eden*, p. 78.

Then I used to smile to myself at the powerfulness of the girl. This was because I was the young girl who Simone was writing to death but could not kill. I think I must have been fertile then. I was certainly potent. Perhaps it was then I should have had my child. Then when everything was possible. But I was too busy sitting with the artists and looking out of windows with them.[20]

Many years later, Heather is again sitting with an artist—on a Friday, 15 May, between Ascension and Pentecost—when her daughter is 16, and is completing her portfolio for studies in Art and Design, with the theme "At the Window".[21] She reflects on her child, conceived through IVF, and how Maia's birth transformed her understanding of God, for

> God came to me as child. As the child I ached for. I desired God deeply and God came to me as child. Nothing was unchanged. Every cell, every charged impulse of my soul and body transformed in that birth. I was broken and I was healed and I was remade and forever transfigured in that encounter. I have known such love as cannot be contained beneath the heavens. And I have held it in my arms.[22]

This encounter is real, life-changing; bodies in embrace, that bring with them all the dirt and mess of any human encounter. As Heather contemplates the Ascension of the body of Christ into the heavens and the coming of the Holy Spirit, what does it mean, she wonders, to talk of purity, and pure relationship?

It's a good question. Purity can be understood in a number of ways. In the Anglican liturgy, the Collect for Purity asks God, "to whom all hearts are open, all desires known, to cleanse the thoughts of our hearts by the inspiration of the Holy Spirit". To make us ready to worship God

---

[20] Walton, *Not Eden*, p. 85.
[21] H. Walton, "Between Ascension and Pentecost: A Theology of Adoption", in John Swinton and Brian Brock (eds), *A Graceful Embrace: Theological Reflections on Adopting Children* (Leiden: Brill, 2017), p. 206.
[22] Walton, "Between Ascension and Pentecost", p. 211.

in spirit and in truth. This is a God, you could say, before whom we are etherized, opened up on an operating table, purified and cleansed of all sin, dirt and waste, that we might be ready and eager to serve in the pure light of love. Purity can be this hard, white, bright thing. Sterility bottled, like some pure, clear acid. For too long—and still today—religion has disciplined by purity codes, with all the power and force of exclusion, so menstruating women could not cross into the sanctuary, where only the beautiful, submissive virgin mother could go, the receptacle of male fantasy, projection and desire, against whom no human woman can ever compete. A sanctuary as clean and sterile as a theatre ready for its shaved and stripped patient.

But what of the purity that inhabits the heart of any friendship worth the name? Where the friend is enjoyed for her own sake, for the blessing she is? Is this not another sort of purity? The purity of heart of those who are blessed, where purity is freedom from that instrumentality that turns everything to some purpose, service, use and end, where nothing is done for its own sake, but motivation is determined, ultimately, by the will to power, to serve the self. And of course, I hear Heather say, just as a couple seek to adopt a child, nothing will ever be for wholly "pure" motivation; always there will be a sense of self-gratification, the need to fulfil "mixed, ambivalent, passionate longings".[23] Always there will be a complex and beautiful mixture to what it means to be a human person, full of desire. Yes—of course. But still, we do need pure and sterile operating theatres—as pure as we can render them. And purity of heart with no motivation but love is worth striving for. The love that is as powerful as the God who comes as child.

And what of this God who stirs our reflections? The God whose love, whose mercy endures for ever, prompting our yearning to reach out and touch the heavens, to call with sighs too deep for words? Yes, the goodness, kindness, tenderness, mercy of our hearts will be mixed, will never be wholly pure, but can we still long to be the "blessed [who] are pure in heart", who seek to know the God who is abundant love that gives, and gives, and asks nothing in return? To seek this God is to find that transcendence and immanence are falsely polarized—which is the great

---

[23] Walton, "Between Ascension and Pentecost", p. 208.

message of Heather Walton's work—as she writes: "For transcendence lurks in the loveliness of everyday life and our immanent desires compel us to reach out and touch the heavens."[24] Always, that love is there, within the everyday, the ordinary, and then the fullness of Easter life is found, which does not evaporate at Ascension, but is entirely fulfilled at Pentecost. Human yearning, expressed in life writing, is the impulse of the soul for the fullness of God-given life, where all is held and honoured, all waste and loss, all pain and joy.

For whatever we feel, think, imagine or care—there is always more, and there is nothing more than the fullness of God, as Paul captured, writing to the Ephesians:

> I pray that you may have the power to comprehend, with all the saints, what is the breadth and length and height and depth, and to know the love of Christ that surpasses knowledge, so that you may be filled with all the fullness of God (Ephesians 3:18–19).

To participate in that fullness of God which is all in all is to experience something of the immensity of a love that sustains all matter from galaxies, known and unknown, stretching over vast expanses of space to the tiniest nanoparticle, a quark, a neutrino—too small to be seen, but detectable all the same; through all the boundless extent of all there is. To talk of "matter" as if it is "dead matter"—empty, a thing, mere commodity—is a legacy of modernity, as Hans Jonas pointed out, and when matter is understood as inert, as dead, then "life" becomes the problem. "Our thinking today is under the ontological dominance of death",[25] he says, which makes "the existence of life within a mechanical universe which now calls for an explanation, an explanation [that] has to be in terms of the lifeless".[26] Jonas resists all dualisms, particularly that of life and death, reclaiming "life" from the biologists who render it a

---

[24] Walton, "We have never been theologians", p. 228.
[25] H. Jonas, *The Phenomenon of Life: Towards a Philosophical Biology* (New York: Northwestern University Press, [1966] 2001), p. 12.
[26] Jonas, *The Phenomenon of Life*, p. 10.

lifeless phenomenon, to be scrutinized and dissected to death. On the contrary, for him

> life means material life, i.e., organic being. In the body, the knot of being is tied which dualism does not unravel but cuts. Materialism and idealism, each from its end, try to smooth it out but get caught in it. The central position of the problem of life means not only that it must be accorded a decisive voice in judging any given ontology but also that any treatment of itself must summon the whole of ontology.[27]

To begin with Life—in a universe that is made of Life and which is in love with Life—is to contemplate the inner life of the body where the knot is tied that resists all dualisms. It is in the heights and depths of the human heart, soul, mind and body where we participate in Life, where "experience" begins and never ends, taking us towards the most sublime experience, leaving us filled with overwhelming joy as moved by some wonder of the natural world; or ecstatic at a familiar and fine piece of music; or towards the intense pain of irredeemable loss, such that our heart and guts, our bowels, are torn and ripped. Whatever our human experience, wonderful or traumatic, there is always more, for it partakes of Life in all its fullness. The fecundity and the waste of the world around—where life might be destroyed in a moment, even in utter depths of depravity and cruelty—all tells of Life, which, like Love, never ends. There is always more. Wherever we go, as human beings, we can never come to the end of the experience of Life.

Heather approaches life experience with the great apprehension that it tells the story of a dazzling darkness that can generate meaning, although it might not be the meaning we desire. When we resist the dualisms we have inherited, then something is created that is beyond our control. We may seek to control, to exert a will to power, but to dominate the matter is to lose it. This is the tentative assertion of the creative person, that there is more than the finite infinity that expresses the limit of modern humanity; there is more, beyond the utmost bounds of human thought, like the love

---

[27] Jonas, *The Phenomenon of Life*, p. 25.

that passes human understanding. Life, love ineffable, beyond, beneath, behind, before the seemingly endless reaches of human understanding and experience. Whenever I read Heather's writing, or engage in real or imagined conversations, I know there is always more; I know we are exploring the fullness of God, participating together in an endless, overflowing abundance that is behind all my common yearnings, that urges from me the desire to create, to make beautiful the wonder and awe that always escapes human control, the grasp of human reach.

This experience of amazement, wonder, enchantment, collapses the tired old dualisms of Life and death, of matter and spirit, of pure and mess, for all are entangled within a sense of fullness that in its abundance, holds all there is. That's why there's such a turn to a word like "enchantment" today with the perception of all that has been lost in the mechanistic sterilities of modernity, which strips out the sacred in a supposedly secular world, where all can be commodified and utilized; this perception particularly hits hard as the created order reaps its whirlwind with the ravages of climate catastrophe. The flourishing of so much nature writing is lament; and, too late, we hear the cry of the dispossessed who tell the Western world how to live by braiding sweetgrass, of the horrors of neo-liberal economics that terrify as the Windigo consumes, eating, in its greed, even its own lips.[28] Heather's work has a sense of lament, as she challenges the human pride and confidence that seeks transcendence, that fails to see the beauty of the ordinary sacred around. Her attention is alert with awe for a world that is always enchanted, and her writing reminds her readers of the wonder that goes hand in hand with enchantment, to be content with not-knowing, embraced by the darkness that has not evaporated in the cold light of modernity. With Heather, we are reminded that all is not lost, even as she speaks of loss and waste, for the fullness of life will always break through and surprise us.

---

[28] R. W. Kimmerer, *Braiding Sweetgrass: Indigenous Wisdom, Scientific Knowledge and the Teaching of Plants* (Minneapolis, MN: Milkweed Editions, 2020). See Chapter 26 for description of the Windigo, which is sometimes spelt "Wendigo", and originates from the folklore of the Algonquian people as a mythological evil spirit, often of human form, with a heart of ice and foul smell, that compels its victims to feel an insatiable desire to consume.

Heather Walton holds paradox before us, again and again. She writes of the experience of non-generation, and generates life in her writing. She holds up the dualism of immanence and transcendence, and her poetry takes us beyond, deep into the soil where the roots of trees take hold. She equates purity with sterility, yet cares for people and things for their own sake, even as she delights in her own desires. She reminds us that all experience holds and generates loyalty and kindness, tenderness and care, intermingled with curiosity and critique, with polemic and bold thinking. In a world that suffers the degradations of political injustice and neo-liberal economics where everything is turned and tuned to monetary value, where nothing is done for its own sake—she helps those who cry out, as they observe and lament the degradations that humanity inflicts on the natural environment. Her writing makes the personal political, as she asks, with Bruno Latour, what would it be for humanity to realize that the world has never not been enchanted? What is it to live in and love the world, to be seized by it and to seize it quite differently,[29] as Heather's creative writing does just that, with words that sing with joy and hope, with the wonder of love.

Hello Heather, my old friend. Thank you for the darkness that stirs in others a sense of fullness of Life, that overflows the boundaries of self into something delicious, exciting, unmistakeable. Where unspeakable loss and trauma happens, and words cannot find their footing. Thank you for your words that ring true, lovely, and good, in ways that can't be explained, but take your readers towards the realm where poetry comes into its own, and language opens out beyond control. Thank you for the way you engage with others, within friendships that seek, with a purity of heart, and loving curiosity, to hear the profound truths of life, lived and known, in a world where everything lives and moves and has its being in the fullness of the God who is love.

---

[29] Walton, "We have never been theologians", p. 219.

3

A writing life: On leaving nothing out

Nicola Slee

Heather Walton and I have been friends, colleagues and co-conspirators for a fair few decades. We are amongst many who have chosen a writing life, to write our lives as honestly and creatively as possible, in dialogue with a wide range of conversation partners, theological, literary, philosophical, within academia but also drawing more widely on literary discourses and conventions from the worlds of fiction, poetry, life writing and more. Writing has not been the *only* pursuit of our lives: there has also been the whole gamut of fostering and maintaining relationships which is core to most human life and has been a particular work of women, mothering of different kinds (biological and non-biological), teaching and the development of curricula, supervision of research, political engagement of various sorts (both within and beyond our own educational and church communities) and the crafting and conduct of worship, including preaching and presiding as lay women. Feminism and faith have been and are central to both our lives and have fuelled the various commitments that constitute our lives and have been the cement in our friendship—as well as writing itself, which has been a core theme of our conversations.

Heather's writing output has been richly varied and, when one surveys it as a whole, quite magnificent. It includes studies of literature and theology,[1] women's literature as it relates to feminism and faith,[2] collaborative and pioneering works on theological method, reflection and what it means to do research,[3] as well as solo work on creative writing methods in theological research and reflection,[4] specifically on theopoetics.[5] Beyond this, there are many other interests, for example in the status and vocation of practical theology as well as public theology, the nature of materiality and how it relates to spirituality and intentionality, the history and politics of feminist theology and early pieces on infertility and IVF treatment, as well as racism and race in the Methodist Church and other fascinating occasional pieces.[6] Writing, in its many, varied forms, is core to all these works: it is the medium of the works (of course) but also the focus in the vast majority of them, ranging from a concern with women's fiction to theoretical positions in feminism on women's literature, from different ways of employing writing for theological

---

[1] For example, Heather Walton (ed.), *Literature and Theology: New Interdisciplinary Spaces* (Farnham: Ashgate, 2011) and many years of editing the journal *Literature and Theology*.

[2] For example, *Imagining Theology: Women, Writing and God* (London: T&T Clark, 2007), *Literature, Theology and Feminism* (Manchester: Manchester University Press, 2007) and numerous articles.

[3] With Elaine Graham and Frances Ward, *Theological Reflection: Methods* (London: SCM Press, 2005) and *Theological Reflection: Sources* (London: SCM Press, 2007). With Zoë Bennett, Elaine Graham and Stephen Pattison, *Invitation to Research in Practical Theology* (Abingdon: Routledge, 2018).

[4] *Writing Methods in Theological Reflection* (London: SCM Press, 2014) and *Not Eden: Spiritual Life Writing for This World* (London: SCM Press, 2015).

[5] For example, "Poetics", in B. J. Miller-McLemore (ed.), *The Wiley Blackwell Companion to Practical Theology*, (Chichester: Wiley-Blackwell, 2012), pp. 173–82; "Creativity at the edge of chaos: Theopoetics in a blazing world", *Literature and Theology* 33:3 (2019), pp. 336–56; "Theopoetics as challenge, change and creative making", *Literature and Theology* 33:3 (2019), pp. 229–32; "A theopoetics in ruins", *Toronto Journal of Theology* 36:2 (2020), pp. 159–69.

[6] For a more complete list of Heather's publications, see bibliography in this volume, pp. 214-19.

reflection to Heather's own varied genres of autoethnography, journals and life writing.

It is not surprising, then, that I want, in this piece, to reflect on the writing life and on creative writing as a particular form of creative practice. Specifically, I want to consider, albeit in somewhat fluid, non-precise ways:

- the writing life of the theologian, and the feminist theologian in particular;
- the writing life of women writing from and to their own unique and ageing bodies;
- the writing life of one who dares to break various silences and speak the unsaid—writing the lives that didn't come to be, the lost bairns, lost lives, lost women's histories, the memories that never got to be made;
- the writing life of a feminist literary critic and literary creator whose writing dives down into the wreck of patriarchy in order to dredge up treasures and find the book of myths, bringing it all up for examination: sodden, dripping, drying it out, separating the pages, deciphering the script, reading the illegible;[7]
- the writer who opens up hidden scriptures, exegeting long lost lives, reading between the lines of holy writ, searching within the cracks, leaving nothing out;
- the writer who holds all life as sacred, holy, God-shaped, God-breathed, finding new ways to say God, beyond traditional doctrines and belief for:
- God saw and said; we see and say, carrying on that divine work;
- God proclaimed everything good, even knowing the fracturing and agony to come; we do the same, through our tears and unexpected laughter;

---

[7] The reference here is, of course, to Adrienne Rich's much-quoted and possibly most famous poem, "Diving into the wreck", in *Diving into the Wreck: Poems 1971-72* (New York: W. W. Norton, 1973) pp. 22-4.

- God divided: night from day, sea from land, different kinds of creatures, male from female; our writing divides, categorizes, questions, orders, classifies;
- God formed a world, a whole out of all its constituent parts; our writing connects, cherishes, cajoles into conversation, ties together the unlikely and oppositional to make of it (*poesis*) something that exists in its own right/rite/write, however fragile and temporary.

As Heather has used various writing voices including those that employ the autobiographical, autoethnographic "I", I will do the same. I will mainly use the form of journal writing, because this is something I regularly do and a way of writing that has become important to me (on which I reflect in what follows). It is also a form that is both fluid and personal and can employ many different voices and moods (incorporating the moods identified by David F. Ford[8] as the indicative, imperative, interrogative, optative and subjunctive). It is a form that can bring into its orbit anything and everything of interest to the writer, as Heather's work has done over the decades.

31 May 2024. Feast of the Visitation

I'm at Glasshampton monastery with a small group of research students, all women, doing our annual stint of house-sitting for the brothers, who are at Hilfield on their annual chapter. We keep the rhythm and spirit of the monastic framework, adjusting the timetable a little, so that we can have a large portion of the day to do our own work—reading, writing, revising drafts—as well as pray four times a day, share food in silence and gather in the evenings to relax and talk. The conversation ranges far and wide, but always includes reflections on how our own writing and research are going, and we seek to listen well to each other and support each other in the hard work of writing well.

---

[8] David F. Ford, *Christian Wisdom: Desiring God and Learning in Love* (Cambridge: Cambridge University Press, 2007).

I love the Feast of the Visitation, one of the few biblical stories and Christian festivals that focus on the meeting and relationships between women. Mary travels to see her older cousin, Elizabeth, to share with her the astounding news of her fearful and wonderful pregnancy and to discover that Elizabeth, too, is pregnant after years of barrenness. The child in each woman's womb leaps in recognition of the other, and the two women rejoice at the work of the Spirit in each other's lives, supporting and affirming that work in the other. Mary speaks the words of the *Magnificat*, the gospel in miniature, long before Jesus is born.

I have always seen this as a story emblematic of what female friendship and soul friendship, in particular, can do: inspired by the Spirit to travel beyond the self towards the other, to recognize the work of the Spirit in the life of the self and other, to rejoice at that work and to connect in solidarity and support with the other, affirming and strengthening the Spirit's work in the woman friend, soulmate, companion.

It's a good day to be beginning this piece for Heather. I think of our friendship and connection as akin to that of Mary and Elizabeth. Raised in households of faith and schooled in Methodism, with an early love of learning and of literature, we recognized each other as sisters in faith, sisters in the scholarly pursuits of research and writing, and sisters in feminism from our first meeting (a meeting Heather has described in a parallel collection of pieces written for me[9]). Although there have been long gaps in our contact with each other down the years since that early meeting, Heather has always been there as someone with whom I have shared a deep sense of vocation and an inner certainty that she understands and supports my own work, which finds particular expression in my writing, although it is not confined to that. I have always regarded Heather's work as akin to my own, although quite distinct. Her varied and skilful oeuvre, across a wide range of genres, has encouraged and inspired my own, helped me to believe in my own quirky and wide-ranging oeuvre, that it has meaning and purpose. I hope I have been

---

[9] Heather Walton, "Registering: Theology and Poetic Practice", in Ashley Cocksworth, Rachel Starr and Stephen Burns (eds), *From the Shores of Silence: Conversations in Feminist Practical Theology* (London: SCM Press, 2023), pp. 57–71.

able to support her vocation and am very glad to have this opportunity to express something of what Heather's friendship and work has meant, and does mean, to me.

1 June 2024. Ordinary time

I'm sitting in my room at the top of one of the towers in the monastery overlooking the garth, the enclosed garden with its large lawn and flowerbeds around the four sides of the quadrangle, where the founder, Father William, is buried. The roses are in full bloom, the weeds are growing apace with the herbaceous border plants and, somewhere, Sienna, the monastery cat, is sunbathing. A breeze ruffles the branches of the trees which surround three sides of the monastery. There is a profound peace, and it is a perfect environment in which to think deeply and well, and to write.

We are in so-called "ordinary time", the beginning of that long stretch of liturgical time after Pentecost and Trinity Sunday which carries us through the summer, with one or two notable feasts, right through to the beginning of a new liturgical year in November, marked by All Saints and All Souls. Ordinary time, no less than the two main liturgical seasons of Advent–Christmas–Epiphany and Lent–Passiontide–Holy Week–Easter, is time in which disciples are encouraged to seek actively for the work of God in the world and in our own lives, and to discern the signs of its presence. Perhaps in ordinary time, the focus is more on finding God precisely *in* the ordinary, rather than in the extraordinary miracles of incarnation, passion, death and resurrection. But this distinction between "ordinary" and "extraordinary" falls down almost as soon as one thinks about it. What is more extraordinary than the "ordinary", everyday miracles of breath, life, movement, food, work, sleep and so on? And what is more ordinary than the extraordinary moments of birth and death, which are happening around us in thousands and thousands of households and hospitals?

The work of the theologian, and the work of the artist, is to discern and articulate, in appropriate forms, the activity of God the Spirit in the ordinary and extraordinary events of life, in individual, communal, national, international and cosmic settings. Writing in its many diverse forms, as practised within theology, poetry, journalling, life writing and so on, has this same task, among others. Heather's writing has performed this costly work for very many of us, alerting us to incidents, issues and inquiry that we would otherwise hardly have noticed or, if noticed, probed and interrogated to the same degree. Her vivid, poignant, at times funny, always searingly honest accounts of her painful, uncertain journey towards motherhood, her involvement in politics in South Africa and elsewhere, her strong Methodist commitment and all the many doubts that go with it, her love of material things and her vulnerability to depression and anxiety (amongst many other things) unfolds beauty and pain in almost equal measure and gives these things heft, weight and substance—which is part of what writing and other creative practice does. And beyond particular issues, Heather's work has attended closely to questions of form in writing and the significance of poetics in theological work, in ways which are groundbreaking. As she says, "There are questions, actually theological questions, about form (incarnation) which very few theologians ask and which writers have to wrestle with day in day out. I think these are exciting"[10]—and so do I.

2 June 2024. Leaving nothing out

I've been thinking about Heather's expressed desire, in her/our theological work and writing, "to do it differently"—something that has been a hallmark of so much feminist writing, including feminist theology. It isn't just the "what" but also the "how" that we want to do differently, breaking the old moulds, shaping new forms and breathing new life—S/spirit—into them. I've expressed this for myself as "leaving nothing out" of my writing. Conventional academic and theological writing has left huge tracts of life out of consideration, very often the personal, domestic, relational work that women have done in the background that has allowed men to do their own "important" work, largely untroubled by the needs of childcare, cleaning and cooking which have been regarded as menial

---

[10] Walton, *Writing Methods*, p. 59.

and certainly of no theological or artistic merit; but also vast tracts of social and political life that form the broader canvas upon which personal life is lived—a canvas that functions as an assumed status quo in much malestream writing, providing a social and political stability that affords the luxury to write undisturbed by social or political upheaval. Those on the underside of history, which has included women and children and many other "others", have not been afforded that luxury and have written, when they have been able and enabled to write, with an urgency and engaged passion that disrupt and disturb the quiescent, neutral tone of much mainstream theology. They have also written in forms that have, rather dismissively, been regarded as "occasional" literature: letters, private journals, prayers and poems. Yet these very forms are capable of writing life as faithfully, perhaps more faithfully and authentically, than standard academic discourse.

"Leaving nothing out" is, of course, an impossible aspiration, since it simply is not possible to include absolutely everything in one's writing, not only because one is not aware of so much that is part and parcel of one's life and context but also because trying to put everything in an account of anything would result in verbose, shapeless, sloppy writing without focus or drive. One of the first tasks we have to learn as writers is how to edit our own work, cutting out much that is of interest or even excellence, but that does not serve the purpose for which we are writing. As I write this now, I can't be sure if this sentence or paragraph will stay in the final draft or have to be excised. I can't know yet, because I am still seeking, in my writing, to work out what it is I want and need to say, and I'll only know when it's been written and I can stand back and read the whole.

"Leaving nothing out", if an approximation of what Heather and I—and multitudes of others—have endeavoured to do, is an aspiration to bring "the whole of life" into one's writing, however selective the range and focus of any particular piece. It has taken me half my life to get to a point where I had the courage to bring the whole of life into my academic writing; because I had been schooled in Western liberal conventions in which much was left outside the door of the study, it felt a terrifying proposition to open that door wide and bring back in what had been excised: emotions, passion, desires—including, but not limited to sexual desire—dreams, instincts and intuitions, politics, memory, urgency and insistence on a right to be heard. Like many women, I had learnt to split the self and the writing voice into different rooms and compartments; there was my thinking, academic self who wrote in the third person, employing reason and calling on the authority of scholarly texts approved of by my male teachers, and then there was my private, personal self who wrote in my journal, letters and poetry, shared only with intimate other selves like me—women friends and spiritual mentors—bringing into my writing voice all that was excised from my scholarly writing voice. Actually, these were not two selves/voices but multiple selves and I only began to recognize how varied the voices were once I had finally gone deep down into the terror and learnt to speak/write with one voice conjoined of what had been, up to then, split asunder.

Looking back, it seems strange that this was such a terrifying proposition, and I realize that I was most afraid of claiming my own power, giving birth to an authentic, authoritative voice that would take on much that I had been taught and speak back to the patriarchal powers. I have written about this most extensively in *Seeking the Risen Christa*.[11] Little had prepared me to become the powerful woman scholar/poet/Christian who did not need to ask permission to speak and who could say, "This is what I believe/know", "This is not acceptable" and "I will not behave like this any more, however much you punish me." Heather writes about the same, or similar, struggles to claim her own self and power, and the temptation to give the self away—to male lovers, teachers and/or the male God. I understand that there are women who have not had to struggle with this interior battle to own the self and the writing voice, and I am glad for those who have been able to claim their power more readily than I have; yet I also think that the birthing of any creative gift or voice almost always entails some kind of death and rebirth process, the losing of a life in order to find a new one. This is the heart of the paschal process of which Jesus spoke and which he lived and died, and it is a process endlessly repeated in human life as well as in the life of the creation and other creatures.

---

[11] Nicola Slee, *Seeking the Risen Christa* (London: SPCK, 2011).

Heather has written honestly about facing this fear in some of her journalled extracts in *Writing Methods*. I know myself from supervising many doctoral projects that women, and others, often face a fear of their own voices, their own power, and doing it (whatever "it" is) in a different way from standard academic conventions. Can I do it? Do I have the skill and the right to write/speak like this? What if I am found out for the fraud I really know myself to be? It's been a key aspect of my work in supervising research students—and I think Heather would say something similar—to create a safe space where these fears can be articulated and explored, and to support the nascent scholar/writer to claim their own voice with confidence and use it to speak truth to power.

19 June 2024. Journal writing

There's been a bit of a gap in writing this, as I've been preparing for and then participating in the R. S. Thomas and M. E. Eldredge Festival at Aberdaron, on the Llyn peninsula.[12] I was giving the second Jim Cotter Memorial Lecture, celebrating his life and writing, which also sought to "leave nothing out". Jim wrote vivid liturgical texts and prayers in expansive and embodied language and addressed the Church's fear of sexuality (especially gay and lesbian sexuality) in his endeavours to forge a truthful sexual spirituality.[13] It was a marvellous occasion, with some fantastic lectures (Mark Pryce's on R. S. Thomas' spirituality was particularly fine[14]) and events (a huge women's choir singing newly translated hymns in St Hywn's Church on Saturday night, the Festival Eucharist, at which I preached, and a lovely, meditative walk up the valley led by the Festival organizer, Susan Fogerty).

---

[12] See <https://rsthomaspoetry.co.uk/> (accessed 29 October 2024).

[13] For more on Jim, see my chapter in the forthcoming collection, *The Vitality of Tradition: British Anglican Spiritual Writers of the Late Twentieth Century*, co-edited by Michael Brierley, Stephen Burns and Nicola Slee (Leiden: Brill).

[14] Mark also has a chapter in the forthcoming collection noted above, on R. S. Thomas.

I haven't been to the area for well over ten years and it has been powerful to return after such a long absence. I am deeply drawn to such edge places, especially those in these islands I call home, recognizing in the western coasts and islands of Wales, Scotland and Ireland a topography similar to that of the southwest of England where I was born and raised.

Although I wasn't actively working on this piece for a couple of weeks, I carried on thinking about it. I've been thinking, particularly, about journals and journal writing. I have loved reading the journals and letters of writers, artists and people of faith since my student days, when I discovered Thomas Merton and avidly read all his journals.[15] From there, I discovered and devoured the journals and letters of Sylvia Plath,[16] May Sarton,[17] Henri Nouwen[18] and Philip Toynbee,[19] and more recently have added to this list the writings of Ronald Blythe,[20] Michael Morpurgo's account of a year on the Devon farm where he worked in the 1970s[21] and Michèle Roberts' *Negative Capability: A Diary of Surviving*.[22]

I love reading journals and letters because they take one right into the heart of the writer's life; unedited or expurgated, as they should be,

---

[15] Published as a seven-part series by HarperOne, 2009.
[16] Karen V. Kukil (ed.), *The Unabridged Journals of Sylvia Plath* (New York: Knop Doubleday, 2000); Peter K. Steinberg & Karen V. Kukil (eds), *The Letters of Sylvia Plath*, 2 volumes (New York: Faber & Faber, 2017, 2019).
[17] *Journal of a Solitude* (London: Women's Press, 2005); *The House by the Sea* (London: Women's Press, 2002); *Recovering: A Journal* (New York: W. W. Norton, 1997), and many more.
[18] *Spiritual Journals* (New York: Continuum International, 1997).
[19] *Part of a Journey: An Autobiographical Journal 1977–1979* (London: Fount, 1982) and *End of a Journey: An Autobiographical Journal 1979–1981* (London: Bloomsbury, 1989).
[20] E.g. *Next to Nature: A Lifetime in the English Countryside* (London: John Murray, 2023); *River Diary* (Norwich: Canterbury Press, 2008); *Stour Seasons: A Wormingford Book of Days* (Norwich: Canterbury Press, 2016); and many more.
[21] *All Around the Year* (Ford: Little Toller Books, 2023).
[22] (Inverness: Sandstone Press, 2020).

they are fresh, immediate and written in the moment—not necessarily every day, but regularly, so that, over time, journal extracts amount to an account of the artist's life in time. There are no rules about what can or can't be included in a journal; everything can go in, nothing need be left out. When I first read Merton's journals, I loved the way in which he would mix what he had for breakfast with accounts of the weather, his manual work at the monastery, the spiritual reading he was doing and his thoughts about the great doctrines of the Catholic faith, which he was teaching to the novices, as well as his voluminous correspondence with theologians, politicians and artists around the world. This represented a far more embodied form of theology than the abstracted thoughts in the books I was reading for my essays and exams.

Reading women's journals—particularly those of May Sarton in my thirties—was formative of my own writing life, as I read of the ways in which Sarton and others struggled to find their own authentic voice as women; balanced the solitary life of the writer with the demands of relationships, hospitality and the making of a home and garden; and did or did not regard themselves as "women writers" or "feminist writers", along with their reasons for making those particular choices, and what those choices cost them. Even or perhaps especially when I was struggling to write, knowing that I had it in me to do so, but lacking the self-belief to bring the gift to fruition, reading writers' journals kept alive the hope in me that I would eventually become the writer I knew myself to be.

And, of course, I have kept a journal for most of my life. I have shelves and shelves of them in my little garden room down the path of our Stirchley garden; the last time I counted, there were 120 volumes, and there must be more like 150 by now. I have no idea what I am going to do with them, or what will become of them once I am no longer here. I probably first started keeping a journal when I was given a large page-a-day diary in 1976, the year of my "A" levels and the beginning of my gap year. This set a pattern: journals in the late 1970s were a bit sporadic but became fuller and entries more regular as my life in the early 1980s became unhappier and my own sense of my self more fragile (my parents' marriage fell apart, my own love life was going badly and my attempts to do a PhD even more disastrously). My journal became the confidante to whom I could pour out all my pain, agony and angst and try to believe in my life. It was largely therapy, and I didn't consider any artistic merits of the form.

But as my life has continued, and I've carried on keeping a journal, I can now see how important it has been for me as a place in which to "leave nothing out" and seek to discern the larger patterns under the surface of the ordinary, quotidian, both in my own life and in the larger life of church and world. It has also been a place in which to learn my craft as a writer. Whilst I have largely not thought of it in this way, keeping a journal has been a discipline in which I've learnt to observe my life and environment and set them down, as vividly, compactly and truthfully as possible, and to reflect on what is happening in my life and the lives of those closest to me. By and large, I have not engaged much with bigger political events, although I do record the more significant ones which have impacted on me most obviously (the results of local and national elections, the decision to leave the European Union and the USA's election of Trump, wars in Syria, Ukraine and now Gaza, any major weather events and so on; in the week that I've been revising this piece, the new Labour government's first week in power, England's defeat in the Euros and the assassination attempt on Trump have seemed too significant not to make an appearance). I have used my journal as a way of doing the Ignatian examen,[23] not necessarily every day but as and when I have material I need to ponder, identifying the consolations and desolations of the day and taking time to unpack them in order to discern the work of the Spirit in my life. In this sense, my journal is a form of theological reflection, one of the main places and ways in which I do that work of seeking theological and spiritual meaning in the everyday events of my ordinary life.

---

[23] An Ignatian method of daily meditation: see <https://www.ignatianspirituality.com/ignatian-prayer/the-examen/> (accessed 29 October 2024).

20 June 2024. In the beginning was the Word

I'm gazing at sumptuous, beatific images from illuminated Bibles in Taschen's huge coffee-table book, *In the Beginning Was the Word*.[24] I bought it this afternoon from the Oxfam bookshop in Harborne, along with a stash of poetry books. I'm supposed to be getting rid of books, slowly culling and dismantling my large library, and I *am* doing so, but as fast as I'm getting rid of old books, I'm acquiring new ones to replace them: books I sense may accompany me into older age as I transition out of a working life into retirement. I need to read poetry constantly, pretty much daily, much as I need to eat or drink. I need to gaze on visual art too, which nourishes, inspires and stimulates in a similar but different way.

I'm no biblical scholar, but I have read the scriptures more or less every day of my life for most of my life, and so am steeped in the Bible's narratives, history, poetry, teaching, wisdom literature, prophetic writings and the rest. I love the work of artists who paint or sculpt or illuminate the biblical text and this huge, sumptuous volume is a treasure chest of wonders. Amidst dozens of biblical scenes and gorgeously decorated capital letters and margins, there is a constantly repeated image of the scribe seated at his desk in the monastery (and it invariably *is* a "he"), working with great diligence and attention, copying the sacred text. This reminds me that writing, in its earliest days, was a highly skilled task and the writing of books a painstaking, elite activity which only the most learned could do; and that the copying of manuscripts by monks in monasteries was as much visual artistry as it was technical skill. Although this is no longer the case for modern writers, the image of the scribe at his or her desk is a reminder of the dedication, absorption, attention and skill required of any writer.

Although this book does not seem to include images of the woman writer, I am very fond of the image of Hildegard of Bingen dictating to her scribe Volmar one of her many books, where she is shown with Pentecostal flames sitting on her head and the scribe leaning over his

---

[24] Andreas Fingernagel & Christian Gastgeber (eds), *In the Beginning was the Word: The Power and Glory of Illuminated Bibles* (London: Taschen, 2003).

desk, writing out her dictation.[25] I also love images of Mary and the book: in scenes of the Annunciation, she is often depicted reading a book—the book of scripture—seated alone in an enclosed garden when Gabriel approaches.[26] This is a way of depicting Mary's faithful obedience to the Word that is uttered by the angel, but it is also a visual theology of Mary herself as the carrier, bearer and birth-giver to the Word. Her vocation to bear Christ the Word in her own body and then to bring him forth to the world is a sign and symbol of the vocation of all faithful people and perhaps, particularly of artists and writers, to incarnate the living word and to bring it to being in life-giving ways. Thomas Merton speaks of Mary as the "Queen of poets" in *Seven Storey Mountain*,[27] which inspired my own "Artists' litany to Mary".[28]

I would have bought the book anyway, but then I turned to the title page and, with a start, saw inscribed on it the name of my former young Queen's colleague, Lynnette Mullings, a promising Black theologian who died from cancer in 2014 when she was only in her thirties and before she was able to complete her doctorate on a Black biblical hermeneutics for the African Caribbean community in the UK. Lynnette was an energetic woman with huge talent, and I was privileged to co-teach with her and other colleagues on the MA in Applied Theological Studies (as it was then) which, for a number of years, attracted an international community of students at Queen's. One of the modules, "Contextual and intercultural readings of the Bible", brought together a wide range of hermeneutical approaches to the reading of scripture—feminist, womanist, post-colonial, LGBTQI+ and queer, to name a few—and the classroom was almost always charged with enormous energy as, student and tutor alike, we grappled with the challenges and creative openings of new perspectives on the biblical text. I remember one evening in particular, when we were looking at the story of the concubine in Judges 19, one of the "texts of terror" as identified by biblical critic Phyllis

---

[25] Very widely available on multiple websites.
[26] See my reflections on Mary and her book in *The Book of Mary* (London: SPCK, 2007), Chapter 6 and notes.
[27] (London: Sheldon Press, 1975), p. 393.
[28] In *The Book of Mary*, pp. 86–7.

Trible,[29] featuring the brutal rape and dismemberment of the woman's body; Lynnette and I both wrote pieces on this text and brought them to the class.[30] I regret that Lynnette's scholarship and writing never came to full fruition due to her untimely death, and that we have been deprived of a theological voice and vision we can ill afford to lose. Nevertheless, she made a lasting impact on the hundreds of students she taught at Queen's and in her own Wesleyan Holiness Church, an impact that lives on in their lives and ministries.

Underneath her name and the date she acquired the book in the title page of this fabulous gathering of images of readers and writers of the Bible, I have written my own name and today's date. I want to connect my name with hers, I want my writing to acknowledge and celebrate the work of young Black scholars like her, and to keep on being challenged by her work and that of many other Black and Asian colleagues at Queen's, who push me to read and write beyond my own white, European culture and context, to name and own my white privilege and to use such creative talents as I possess to undo the damage done by centuries of colonial oppression. The creative Word of God will remain shackled so long as it is only interpreted by those who speak from positions of white privilege, as I inevitably do.

24 June 2024. No conclusion

It's high time I finished this piece, but I don't know how to conclude it. Journals don't have any conclusion, at least until death or senility makes a more or less abrupt one. Some journal writers choose to stop writing, but that's not a choice that, at present, seems possible for me. Nor can I imagine Heather ceasing to write, as she, like me, comes to an end of her full-time academic career. As I have stepped down from my role as Director of Research at Queen's and anticipate full retirement

---

[29] Phyllis Trible, *Texts of Terror: Literary–Feminist Readings of Biblical Narratives* (London: SCM Press, 1984).

[30] My poem appears as "The concubine's communiqué" in *Seeking the Risen Christa*, pp. 80–1.

in the coming 12 months, one of the exciting prospects is to discover what writing I want and can do, when there are no external pressures or requirements from academia to write anything at all. I have a sense that there is still plenty of writing in me, but that the form and substance will look quite different from anything I have written up to now. I will be keen to see how the creative impulse in Heather expresses itself as she also faces into life beyond academia; I only know that it will take shape and form somehow, even if that shape and form are quite different from anything that has gone before.

4

No answers—Four poems and a midrash

Ariel Zinder

(Translated from Hebrew by Maeera Shreiber and Ariel Zinder)

The Lord of Wonders

finds no joy in me
I should be carrying His Being like an electrifying jewel
To enflame my children
Instead I carry him like a bullet still lodged in my body
No one will know Him like I do
Such is the pain
Those hewn from my blood will not know

Theology of a Broken Vessel

He lifted my chin and straightened my back
He said: stretch your head high, let your spine expand
He lifted my chin and my neck softened
He said: Let it happen, don't worry,
And added: God is with you.

He lifted, and everything swelled a bit,
As little as the distance between these days and those to come
And we two, standing in the studio, knew:
The pain has fled. God is with me.

Then he removed his hands and my spine crumpled back.
There was nothing more to say.
We knew: God is no more.
All that's left is broken idols,
Inside, outside, everywhere.

Band

A soul like a womb and within it
The soul of the soul, a prickly cube,
And surrounding both of them the body, a
    banged up jalopy: off they go.
Such a strange band of three,
Entangled in their stupor, asleep most of the time, but nevertheless:
Off they go.

I trouble them no more with questions
Such as: What's the time, how's it going, where are you headed?
Because in truth I wish to ask: Where in heavens is He?
And what does the truck know, with its womb and cube?
They're too busy with potholes, with wrong turns and discord.
They have no answers. Off they go.

Reunion

He looked at me as if I was
The key to all that is locked, a guide to all dark forests.
We hadn't seen each other for years.
Things had changed for him and now
He wished to know the ways of God.
He thought I might help him with that.

We sat there, in a café by the Tel Aviv Seashore.
He asked what to study on Shabbat. He asked how to hold on
And he looked my way as if I was
The image of all answers.

> My turn to speak came. I answered gravel, I
> answered crushed shards of seashells
> I answered books slammed angrily, one after the other,
> I answered and answered until I was myself again:
> A barricade of doubts
> Impossible to see through.
>
> I'm sorry, I said.
> I wish you hadn't asked.

I have no answers. Sometimes the questions themselves fade and evaporate. Questions were my way of moving forward, confident of arriving at answers. Now they fade away, and yet, the movement proceeds. It is a terrifying process, but it must lead somewhere. Dimly I know that this bleak path is still laden with expectation, and that though it has no end, it leads to clearings where I will be able to stand and wait for others, clearings where we will congregate for fleeting moments, those of us who have no answers yet have not given up on the journey. In these clearings we are banished and welcome, disgraced and caressed. We follow in the footsteps of Eldad and Medad:

> And Moses went out, and told the people the words of the Lord, and gathered the seventy men of the elders of the people, and set them round about the tabernacle. And the Lord came down in a cloud, and spake unto him, and took of the spirit that was upon him, and gave it unto the seventy elders: and it came to pass, that, when the spirit rested upon them, they prophesied, and did not cease. But there remained two of the men in the camp, the name of the one was Eldad, and the name of the other Medad: and the spirit rested upon them; and they were of them that were written, but went not out unto the tabernacle: and they prophesied in the camp.
>
> And there ran a young man, and told Moses, and said, "Eldad and Medad do prophesy in the camp." And Joshua the son of Nun, the servant of Moses, one of his young men, answered and said, "My lord Moses, forbid them." And Moses said unto

him, "Enviest thou for my sake? Would God that all the Lord's people were prophets, and that the Lord would put his spirit upon them!"

Numbers 11:24–29 (KJV)

According to a midrashic retelling of this story, Moses began this process with 72 elders (six from each tribe) and had to conduct a lottery to get down to 70. He took 72 notes, wrote "elder" on seventy of them, and left two blank. To those who took the "elder" note he said: "God has already sanctified you." To Eldad and Medad, who took the blank notes, Moses said: "He does not need you, and I, what can I do?"[1] That was their cue. They were free.

So the 70 elders followed Moses to the tabernacle while Eldad and Medad, the rejected ones, stayed in the camp. Rejected, they stayed insiders; insiders, they remained threatened by zealots and by official doctrine. They will have no peace on either side of the fence, and that is the wellspring of their prophecy. Indeed, the Torah tells us they prophesied, but neglects to mention the content of that prophecy. I like to think they were simply writing poetry which scripture had no name for. While the elders in the tabernacle whispered to each other, "God is with you, with us", Eldad and Medad's poetry proved that none of them are absolutely with God.

Those are my brothers and sisters, my fellow poets, those who watch over the gaps, at a heavy price, without end. And this is my letter to Heather, who has led me to believe that I might even succeed, I might go on and meet fellow travellers; that we may all find our footing within the camp and outside it, banished and welcome, disgraced and caressed.

---

[1] *Midrash Yalkut Shimoni, Ba'haaloteha 737.*

5

Theology through creative listening

Andrew W. Hass

There was a moment during the early days of my doctoral degree when I experienced, almost simultaneously, two major epiphanies. The first was in the form of a theological crisis: I had a sudden realization that the old assumptions I had held about how the text of the Christian scriptures ought to be read and interpreted were, for me, no longer tenable. This realization shook me to the core. It meant a readjustment of my entire being. The second was in response to this crisis. Within hours I had put on a piece of music in an attempt to calm my spirit. The music was not sacred or religious in any way. It happened to be from a jazz CD I was particularly fond of at the time, the song a modern take on a popular tune from a 1950s musical film. The version carried no lyrics; the music was performed by a trio of instrumental players. But while listening to this piece, a transformation took place. Something in the performance, or something in my *listening* to that recorded performance, held itself out to me. To this day I could not tell you what it was. But it was epiphanic, an epiphany to the epiphany, because although music had moved me many, many times before—I was no stranger to its power—it had never moved me *theologically*. And here I don't mean it moved me to change my intellectual position on any one point of theology. I mean it moved my very body and being as a kind of theological event, the movement itself being theological. It is this movement, as a form of listening, that I want to explore in what follows.

We do not normally conceive of theology as movement, though in more recent shifts towards theological reflection as a method, "theological discourse is now seen in terms of *process* rather than *product*", as Graham,

Walton and Ward tell us.[1] Here experience is central, as reflection is no longer principally upon abstract concepts pertaining to the nature of God, nor, in a practical sense, upon ways our understanding of God should be applied, but upon developing a creatively reflective response to what one's own subjective experience has been within the frameworks of spirituality, what Heather Walton calls "the crafted use of experience in theological reflection".[2] This shift has been immensely helpful in releasing the proprietorial grip upon theological discourse by prescribed figures of authority (clergy, theologians, academics) and allowing the full spectrum of laity, including those who traditionally had no voice and those who continue to struggle for a voice, to lay claim to theology as a life-changing practice. And Walton especially has done much in showing how writing can be transformative in this regard. But writing, and reflective writing in particular, works from that which is already given: to reflect upon one's own experience relies upon a set of events, situations, feelings and impressions that have already occurred, much as to set these down in writing requires a language system with signs and symbols predetermined with referents and meaning. The "methods" with which Walton and others carry out this task are, we might say, wholly reflexive in that they return the writer back to what has transpired, even if one is recrafting that personal experience in the process. It is in this sense that theological reflection is seen within a hermeneutical model.[3]

But music is not accessed through a reflective mode; music has a different hermeneutics. For listening to music does not present to us meaning that is previously given or established. In semiotic terms, music's sonority has no referent. A "B-flat" does not refer to anything other than to its own sound. It does not *mean* anything, or at least anything any two people could agree upon. This is not to say that music operates completely outside referentiality. Written music, for instance, presents a symbolic schema by which a musician can equate notation on a staff with certain

---

[1] Elaine Graham, Heather Walton and Frances Ward, *Theological Reflection: Methods*, 2nd edn (London: SCM Press, 2019), Introduction, p. x.

[2] Heather Walton, *Writing Methods in Theological Reflection* (London: SCM Press, 2014), p. xiii.

[3] Graham, Walton and Ward, *Theological Reflection: Methods*, p. x.

pitches on an instrument. Or "B-flat", we could say, refers scientifically to a certain frequency of waveforms. Moreover, the produced sound of a certain cluster of notes in sequence can, for the listener, conjure up many impressions and memories, as when a familiar song transports us back to a certain period of our life or to a certain experience. Popular music, we know, excels at this phenomenon. But the engagement we encounter here, even if repeated, is in most circumstances not deliberately, and much less methodically, *reflective*, insofar as we rarely set out in our listening to intentionally revisit or contemplate something that has pre-existing meaning, and then try, through interpretation, to make meaning anew for our current context.[4] We do not, in a technical sense, reflect on a piece of music at all; we encounter the music, as a listener, always as if for the first time, because music's content is "empty", and each time we hear it we must fill in that content ourselves—even the most familiar of strains. It is in this sense that the early German Romantic figure Ludwig Tieck would say that he felt music, "the ultimate mystery of faith", was "as though it were still in the process of being created".[5]

This goes even for music with lyrics. Certainly, words attached to music have referents like any other written texts. When one hears words of lost love being sung, there is a preconception both of "love" and of what it means for love to be "lost". But if we were truly to reflect on lost love as an idea or experience, we would read the lyric sheet, or think about the words in isolation from its musical rendering. Listening to the sung words in their immediacy offers something different. They might evoke a sentiment of lost love, but that sentiment is not asking to be interpreted. One is listening not for meaning; one is rather listening to a sonority

---

[4] There are exceptions, as in the conceit behind *Desert Island Discs*, the BBC radio programme that asks participants to reflect upon music that has been meaningful in relation to formative stages of their life. But that the premise is itself fanciful—guests are castaways on an island that somehow retains the conveniences of modern technology, such as stereos and speakers—shows just how rarefied, and disconnected, such listening is in relation to our real and everyday experience.

[5] As quoted by the music theorist Carl Dahlhaus in *The Idea of Absolute Music*, tr. Roger Lustig (Chicago, IL: Chicago University Press, 1989), p. 89.

that exceeds meaning in the strict sense of a correspondence between utterance and inference. The very fact the words are *sung* transposes the words—all words—into another register, where referentiality and signification give way to aurality, to the embodiment of sound vibrations in movement, and "love" is no longer what the dictionary says it is, nor "lost" a mere adjective that describes it. The lost love that is sung will not even be what we could have experienced ourselves in the past. As Carl Dahlhaus writes: "What did we understand in the text of a Palestrina mass, a Bach cantata, a Handel oratorio, as long as we did not join in the singing? Only for those who join in the singing is there vocal music: the listener confronts it as absolute music."[6] And we could go further: even vocal music brings out only the vocality, not some prior essential understanding. Music is, we say again, a space that is empty of content. As Vladimir Jankélévitch says, music becomes "the silence of words", and singing "a way of being quiet".[7] And yet when we enter into that space and its silence, we find there a resonance.

It is the nature of this resonance that moves us in listening. What then constitutes this nature? The first thing we can say is that it is immediate. It does not come to us by means of something else, but only through itself, as sound. It is, therefore, a re-sounding, but a re-sounding of itself, not of anything outside itself, like a meaning. Secondly, in this re-sounding, it moves, as vibration, as pulsation, as rhythm. It is thus always an embodied experience: it moves the body, and by doing so it *becomes* the body. Resonance is thus an immediate embodied experience of being moved through a reciprocation of sound and body, where the sound becomes greater than the acoustic phenomena by uniting with our very being as music.

Jean-Luc Nancy, in his short but dense text *Listening*, draws attention to this resonance as foundational to how we should make sense of our "self". He first suggests that resonance, in its purity, provides the opening of sense—not "sense" as meaning, but "sense" as "beyond-sense or sense

---

[6] Carl Dahlhaus, *Between Romanticism and Modernism*, tr. Mary Whittall (Berkeley, CA: University of California Press, 1980), p. 115.

[7] Vladimir Jankélévitch, *Music and the Ineffable*, tr. Carolyn Abbate (Princeton, NJ: Princeton University Press, 2003), pp. 139, 140.

that goes beyond signification". When we respond to music, our body is moved by the opening up to a sense that takes us beyond what words or language can signify. Here the body becomes "a resonant chamber or column of beyond-meaning [*l'outre-sens*]". In this space beyond, our self's being, that is, our subjectivity as "subject", thus becomes "that part, in the body, that is listening or vibrates with listening to—or with the echo of—the beyond-meaning".[8] Nancy's analysis of resonance here allows us to understand why, even when we listen to music with lyrics, we are taken beyond the sense of meaning, for what moves us is not any kind of reflection on the words and their referents but rather a syncing of ourselves, through listening, to the beyond-meaning.

Our challenge, then, becomes how we ought to understand this "beyond-meaning", or the space to which we are moved by the resonance that is music, as in any way *theological*. For at the heart of theology is "logos", which, within the long tradition of Christian orthodoxy, has functioned as the very conceptual framework for meaning. Indeed, Christ as the "Logos" has been understood by standard theological interpretations of John's Gospel as the possibility of meaning's manifestation, or the manifestation of meaning's possibility, so that all that follows the Logos, there from the beginning, is onto-theologically grounded in its coherence. Even Karl Barth, who famously understood the Logos as inextricable from incarnation, would see the task of the theologian as one "ready to submit the coherence of his concepts and formulations to the coherence of divine revelation and not conversely".[9] Would then our engagement with music,

---

[8] Jean-Luc Nancy, *Listening*, tr. Charlotte Mandell (New York: Fordham University Press, 2007), p. 31.

[9] Karl Barth, "The Gift of Freedom: Foundation of Evangelical Ethics", tr. Thomas Wieser, in *The Humanity of God* (Atlanta, GA: John Knox Press, 1960), p. 93. For Barth's reading of John's Logos as necessarily both Son of God (eternal) and Son of Man (incarnated in time and space), see for example *Church Dogmatics* IV:1 *The Doctrine of Reconciliation*, §64, eds G. W. Bromiley and T. F. Torrance, tr. G. W. Bromiley (London: T&T Clark, 2009), pp. 31–2. See also Andrew W. Hass, Laurens ten Kate and Mattias Martinson, *The Music of Theology: Language—Space—Silence* (London: Routledge, 2024), p. 19: "The history of Christian theology is thus possible

if we held to Nancy's beyond-meaning, fundamentally threaten this kind of theological endeavour, because it disrupts the coherence on both sides, and indeed the coherence between both sides? Is this why music, when it has not ostensibly submitted to the coherence of divine revelation in the form of words, has always been seen by theology as a threat, something the Augustine of the *Confessions* readily admits when listening to music without the sacred words he claims give music its life?[10]

Let me return to my own example. My theological crisis was triggered precisely when I found reliable meaning unanchored from the scriptural text. We might say, hermeneutically, I discovered in the written words an abiding existence of a beyond-meaning that, at the time, could only present itself to me as a no-meaning. And I had no capacity to resonate with any such no-meaning, nor to appreciate any beyond-meaning that might come from it. This was incoherence, and incoherence was profoundly untheological. I was thus confronted with existential peril. In immediately turning to music, I had no intention to seek existential comfort, nor any expectation to find spiritual redemption. I was simply grasping at something to fill temporarily the emptiness that had opened up. But something transpired in the listening that I could not have anticipated. I felt I was being rescued, drawn up from the depths of an abyss. I do not mean an emotional abyss, though I recall being emotionally moved. I mean a theological abyss, though I could not point to any logical coherence, and even less to any logical justification. The music simply took me over, pre-logically—intuitively, as Schleiermacher would say; "music invades us", not persuades us, said Eduard Hanslick a generation later[11]—and I felt in profound resonance not just with the sonority of the music as it emerged from my speakers, but once again with my very being, even if that being was profoundly altered. I felt, strangely, not reassured, but reconciled.

---

to view primarily as the ongoing reflection on the *practices* that are connected to the religious enactment of the event [of incarnation], practices centred around the remembrance of the divine gift of the incarnated *logos*."

[10] See *Confessions* X.33.

[11] Eduard Hanslick, *On the Musically Beautiful*, tr. Geoffrey Payzant (Indianapolis, IN: Hackett, 1986), p. 50.

In retrospect, I might now say that what I was experiencing, or what I was sensing, was a movement towards the beyond-meaning, and, in that movement, the re-emerging of myself that Nancy has called "listening to the beyond-meaning". I was listening to something that had no framework for meaning; I was listening, in effect, to the very lack of that framework. But rather than being unsettling, or threatening, or perilous, it offered a sense of renewal, because my listening was reconstituting my being. Or we might say it was constituting it for the first time, but in repetition, as in a continual rebirth, taking the form of a persistent becoming. Nancy offers the image of the womb, in all its philosophical operations of creation since Plato's *Timaeus*, as a germane description of this process of resonance:

> The womb[*matrice*]-like constitution of resonance, and the resonant constitution of the womb: What is the belly of a pregnant woman, if not the space or the antrum where a new instrument comes to resound, a new organon, which comes to fold in on itself, then to move, receiving from outside only sounds, which, when the day comes, it will begin to echo through its cry? But more generally, more womblike, it is always in the belly that we—man or woman—end up listening, or start listening. The ear opens onto the sonorous cave that we then become.[12]

The theologian Catherine Keller, in her text *Face of the Deep: A Theology of Becoming*, written around the same time as Nancy's *Listening* essay, makes much more of this matrical becoming in her many-layered reflections on the first two verses of Genesis, where creation comes into being through the depths of chaos. There has been a theological ellipsis of those womb-like depths in the second verse, she argues, and she wants us "to 'hear into its own speech' (to cite a beginning-word of feminist theology) the muted utterance of that next verse, the verse of chaos".[13] I had never confronted that ellipsis in my own prior (and male) reading of

---

[12] Nancy, *Listening*, p. 37.
[13] Catherine Keller, *Face of the Deep: A Theology of Becoming* (New York: Routledge, 2003), p. 5.

the biblical text, but now in facing it through music—the ellipsis, which is to say the ellipsis of an ellipsis—it was as if I was becoming a new instrument by which to experience the chaos as something musical. As Keller later references Deleuze, chaos is not the opposite of rhythm; there is something in the very absence of order that carries its own impetus or impulsion.[14] And Nancy suggests it is resonance that brings chaos and rhythm together. This coming together is perhaps captured in that rabbinic tradition that says Yahweh sings creation into existence. Here we could say, theologically, that from the depths of chaos emerges a new organon, and in listening to it, we listen to the echo of the sonorous cave that we ourselves, through creation, have become.

Here we should remember that in its original sense of the fourteenth century, organum was a generic name for a musical instrument. We have the vestiges of this meaning only in the specific pipe organ that we associate almost exclusively now with churches. It was only in the early seventeenth century, especially in relation to Francis Bacon's *Novum Organum* of 1620, that the term came to designate an instrument of thought or knowledge. Here in this semantic shift we have the hermeneutical problem I encountered: theologically, the biblical text was for me only an instrument of thought and knowledge. I could not in any way see it as a musical instrument, one that takes me beyond meaning. It took a new sense of listening for me to see this possibility. And this new sense required the actual, embodied listening to music. Only then could the muted utterances of chaos' rhythm, its ellipsis, become heard.[15]

To become a new organum of resonance is to attune ourselves to a different set of tones and pitches of the theological. It is not to suggest that theology, and reflective theology, should no longer act as an instrument of thought and knowledge, even self-knowledge. Theology and theological thinking will always have this role, and my thoughts here about music

---

[14] Keller, *Face of the Deep*, p. 169.

[15] Jankélévitch tells us that Francis Bacon himself says "that silence is thought being fermented" (*Music and the Ineffable*, p. 136). Fermentation is an apt image, insofar as music has always been associated, as Nietzsche reminds us in his Dionysian emphasis on dithyrambic power, with the impulsive chaos of inebriation.

confirm this: I am, with no lack of irony, reflecting theologically on a different mode of theological engagement. But if theology is to remain relevant, agile and creatively open to new possibilities, and if it is to be *practical* in a world where it has less and less cultural currency, it must move beyond the instrumentality of knowledge, of the kind that Bacon inaugurated in the name of a new science, and of the kind that logocentric theology has insisted upon ever since. It must embody itself in a world where conventional religious structures no longer resonate with the so-called enlightened masses. It must find new registers for our attention to *theos*, or, it must create these new registers as what the young Schleiermacher called music—"a special, self-contained revelation of the world".[16]

Now the question before us is how we might cultivate a kind of attentive listening that can be experienced as a creative, theological practice. What I have described from my own experience did not arise from any act of intention; epiphanies are not to be conjured. And yet, I have since tried to develop a habit of listening theologically that remains in its essence musical. This involves listening to music, yes; but it also involves transferring that listening to other forms of experience.

The first practice, by way of beginning, is to listen to music as a form of conditioning the ear theologically. Here we need to shift expectations from meaning as signification to meaning as movement. The ear is not pursuing some pregiven and reproducible sign or set of referents, by which thought can then give a rational account. We apply this even to music with words, given what we have said. John Cage, who more than any other composer has considered the nature of sound in relation to music, wrote:

> A sound does not view itself as thought, as ought, as needing another sound for its elucidation, as etc.; it has no time for

---

[16] Friedrich Schleiermacher, *On Religion: Speeches to its Cultured Despisers*, tr. John Oman (New York: Harper Torchbook, 1958), p. 51.

any consideration—it is occupied with the performance of its characteristics.[17]

The listening ear must also be occupied with this performance. And it does this by positioning itself so that the body can be moved, whether kinetically (dancing, tapping or bodily pulsing with the music's rhythm) or by some other somatic manifestation (a slower or faster heart rate, a stillness of the nervous system, an opening of the tear ducts, etc.). In this movement, the ear fully attunes itself to sound, and to sound's own internal sound. Listening to sound reflexively is like tuning the ear to hear the inner ear. Walter Benjamin once referenced Hofmannsthal's words, "to read what was never written", as the true task of the historian, and we might think the same of the listener: to hear what was never voiced.[18] To hear this, one needs full bodily attention.

To sharpen this attention, one needs to develop a discipline not merely of receptivity but of engagement, which leads to resonance. Much has been made recently of the American composer/musician Pauline Oliveros' practice of deep listening, which she describes as a form of meditation, and which involves a range of bodily positions, exercises and movements, many taken directly from Eastern meditational practice, as ways of enhancing our sensitivity and consciousness to what she calls the "sound/silence continuum", and which captures "all perceptible vibrations (sonic formations)", not just those we associate with a musical piece.[19] In developing deep listening, we are tuning our inner and outer being to a world that is pulsing with sonic activity, so that we may join in its endless resounding with an amplified awareness of the affective forces at work in that activity.

---

[17] John Cage, "Experimental Music: Doctrine", in *Silence: Lectures and Writings* (London: Marion Boyars, 1968), p. 14.

[18] Walter Benjamin, "Paralipomena to 'On the Concept of History'", in *Walter Benjamin: Selected Writings 1938–1940, Vol. 4*, tr. Edmund Jephcott et al., eds Howard Eiland and Michael W. Jennings (Cambridge, MA: Belknap Press of Harvard University Press, 2003), p. 405.

[19] Pauline Oliveros, *Deep Listening: A Composer's Sound Practice* (New York: iUniverse, 2005), p. xxiv.

As Oliveros' deep listening suggests on multiple levels, bodily attention leads to spiritual attention. We need to be highly careful of the notion of "spirit" here, lest it disembody us from the somatic attention we have just laid out. But if we consider Augustine's image of the Holy Spirit as the ear of the heart, and retain the sense of the heart's pulsation, we might see "spirit" as the true organ of our hearing. For what we hear is never that which we can concretize in permanence or representation—sound is always decaying—and yet it stays alive in its movement. "As the spirit moves", so the saying goes.

To be moved as a form of attention here is more akin to how Simone Weil understands attention, which she distinguishes from will. The will, she acknowledges, can impel certain muscles to move certain parts of our body. But moving the inner self through inspiration, truth, beauty and goodness requires not the will but a heightened form of attention, one that is "unmixed" and "extreme" in nature, whose purity becomes both the creative faculty in humans and, more radically, a form of prayer.[20] This kind of praying, which nudges us into the spheres of both Christian mysticism and Buddhism, involves giving up the self or the "I" in its desires, where the "I", through an extreme passivity, empties itself kenotically. "Attention alone—that attention that is so full the 'I' disappears—is required of me. I have to deprive all that I call 'I' of the light of my attention and turn it on that which cannot be conceived."[21] Listening to music requires this kind of heightened attention, which moves us in the same way prayer moves us—"the non-acting action of prayer".[22] This for Weil is "authentic religion", and in the same way, we could also think of musical attention as an authentic theology, since, as Weil insists, it "presupposes faith and love"—which means we are giving ourselves over to something of which we cannot conceive, and putting ourselves into intimate relation with it.[23]

---

[20] Simone Weil, "Attention and Will", in *Gravity and Grace*, tr. Emma Crawford and Mario von der Ruhr (London: Routledge, [1952], 2002), pp. 116–17.
[21] Weil, "Attention and Will", p. 118.
[22] Weil, "Attention and Will", p. 119.
[23] Weil, "Attention and Will", p. 117.

But if this move is going to be characterized as theology, and not merely meditation, or piety, then we must conceive of the *logos* (of *theology*) in new terms. For even in the sound/silence continuum of musical attention, new thoughts are being generated all the time, though they do not carry the usual sense we associate with referential language and semantics. Here we need to develop a practice of listening to the *sound* of these thoughts. This is an injunction in one of Oliveros' practical exercises: "Include the sounds of your own thoughts. Can you imagine that you are the centre of the whole?"[24] Meditation customarily focuses on our breath. What would it mean to focus instead on thoughts that have been born by the sounds that are music and, in listening, to isolate their unique sonority? Musicians play with both their body and their mind. They cannot be thoughtless or mindless to perform successfully. But as there is musical time distinct from clock time, so there is musical thought distinct from rational, cognitive thought. To hear musical thought—what Hanslick had called "mind giving shape to itself from within"[25]—we must first be attentive to it in any musical piece we engage with, listening for its movement in the composer and performer(s), and then in the musicality of the music itself (rhythm, pitch, timbre, tone, etc.). This listening must involve the body, for the body attunes itself to the thought, and without either, without absolute mutuality, there is no listening, only hearing. Deep attention then calls us to the beyond-meaning of this musical experience. Here we move to a "meta" level (*meta-* as a prefix denoting a change of place, order, condition or nature beyond a given position or state), where we are not seeking specific meaning as such, but the condition of meaning, or meaning-ability.

Benjamin's early theory of language is apposite here. There he is interested not in how language is a medium for thought, but how thought is manifested *as* language—that is, a mind expressed *in* language but not *through* language. The question becomes not the content of communication but communicability itself. So to the question of what language communicates, Benjamin answers: "All language communicates

---

[24] Oliveros, *Deep Listening*, p. 12.
[25] Hanslick, *On the Musically Beautiful*, p. 30.

itself."[26] If we modulate this musically, we listen then for a meta-music, or what Schelling once called a music within music,[27] which is to say, we listen to how music communicates itself, beyond meaning, a listening that is at once theological as it is musical, for it returns us to the very possibility of the *logos* in its embodiment.

In attuning ourselves to the sound of *logos* in this way—and here we might consider if in the beginning the Word became sound—we open ourselves up to a thought that is strictly no longer ours to possess, since we have given up the "I" that could make any proprietorial claim upon it. In this space beyond ourselves, we prepare ourselves for newness. If we take seriously Gaston Bachelard's words, that "thought is always in some respects a trying-out of or a move towards a new life, an attempt to live differently, to live more or even, as Simmel has argued, a will to go beyond life",[28] then listening to the sound of thought, to sound resounding itself as the capacity and the call to live out meaningful thought—this creative listening positions us to resonate anew. If lived thought is the thought of our everyday experience, the prosaic, commonplace thought we need to get through the mundane realities of our life, or the instrumental thought of science and commerce, then musical thought takes us outside of ourselves and our everyday experience, and forces us to reckon with something that is not yet made, not yet conceived.

This reckoning begins within our very own self. In positioning ourselves to be re-thought anew, we bring ourselves into resonance with all our fellow created beings. Here again we must stress: in listening to the sound of our thoughts we are not listening to ourselves, to our *own* thoughts, but rather to the communicability that music makes manifest, a communicability that must be commensurate with community. This

---

[26] See Walter Benjamin, "On Language as Such and the Language of Man", in *Walter Benjamin, Early Writings: 1910–1917* (Cambridge, MA: The Belknap Press of Harvard University Press, 2011), esp. p. 253.

[27] F. W. J. Schelling, *The Philosophy of Art*, tr. Douglas W. Stott (Minneapolis, MN: University of Minnesota Press, 1989), p. 109. For the young Schelling of this period, such music within music was what he called rhythm.

[28] Gaston Bachelard, *The Dialectic of Duration*, tr. Mary McAllester Jones (London: Rowman & Littlefield, 2000), p. 82.

is Hartmut Rosa's emphasis in his sociological analysis and employment of resonance as a concept: "Resonance is a kind of relation to the world ... in which subject and world are mutually affected and transformed."[29] This allows him to contend that, whereas the language of signification can thematize one particular relationship to the world, music "negotiates the quality of relation *itself*", the "'ur-relationship' from which subject and world originate".[30] Bringing then our deep listening attention to bear upon our thought, we necessarily listen *together*, and become engaged in a corporate theology, even if we listen in the solitude of our own home or in the isolation of our earbuds. As a kind of prayer, musical attention is always and already intercessory. To listen theologically is to open together a new world we would all inhabit.

This may seem like an impossible task, a practice well beyond the practical. But does not listening to music—deep listening, attentive listening, prayerful listening—always inspire the possibility of the impossible? Is not even the simplest encounter with music always an encounter with possibility whispering to us of the silence between notes, a silence that "speaks" of something that does not yet seem possible, until it is heard? As Nancy suggests, "'Silence' in fact must here be understood [*s'entendre,* heard] not as a privation but as an arrangement of resonance".[31] Might we see music then as a certain arrangement of the impossible? Keller opens her *Cloud of the Impossible* with a personal anecdote about music: as she tried to play the high C of "The Impossible Dream" on her French horn for her school musical as a young teenager, she missed or cracked the note. But did this experience presage an obsession with the impossible, she wonders? For "here I am", she says by way of introduction to writing on the impossible, "still trying to crack open the im/possible".[32] In concert with Keller's opening confession, we can say that to listen

---

[29] Hartmut Rosa, *Resonance: A Sociology of Our Relationship to the World*, tr. James C. Wagner (Cambridge: Polity Press, 2019), p. 174.

[30] Rosa, *Resonance*, pp. 94–5.

[31] Nancy, *Listening*, p. 21.

[32] Catherine Keller, *The Cloud of the Impossible: Negative Theology and Planetary Entanglement* (New York: Columbia University Press, 2015), p. 1. Keller ends this entire book—and all too intentionally, we should think—with

creatively becomes our attempt, as collective individuals, to split open the im-possible, to make the impossible possible. For is this not how we have always tried to grasp eternity?

Ever since Pythagoras, and no doubt before, music has been associated with the eternal. To contemplate the harmony of the heavens, to listen to the harmonic strains of music, was to hear eternity. The Romantic theorists, in the same spirit as Schleiermacher, made much of this: "Music dissolves our own consciousness into the perception of the eternal. Accordingly, the characteristic, essential use of music is the religious one."[33] Even today, this idea remains prevalent: Nancy finishes *Listening* with words that echo Nietzsche's understanding of the eternal, Nietzsche for whom music was the very pulse of life: "Music is the art of making the outside of time return to every time, making return to every moment the beginning that listens to itself beginning and beginning again. In resonance the inexhaustible return of eternity is played—and listened to."[34]

I began with my own epiphanic encounter, a divine encounter with music. I have returned to that encounter again and again, not to relive it, nor to recapture it, but to draw from its sound and its silence a sense of the eternal. I still cannot make rational sense of that encounter, but I have found there is a theology to be heard there, and in listening for it intently, with extreme attention, in the practical and creative manner I have tried here to lay out, I place myself into its resonance, there to be lost, and there to be remade. To begin anew, again and again, from the impossible. In listening is the return of eternity, not now as metaphysics but as the outside and beyond of what I once knew of myself and the world. In this beyond, there is a new kind of meaning, but I hear it only as a meaning on the move, as though it were still in the process of being created.

---

the lyrics of a song (p. 316). But it is the opening note she didn't reach that remains most indicative of the impossible that music inspires.

[33] Karl Wilhelm Ferdinand Solger, *Vorlesungen über Ästhetik*, ed. Karl Wilhelm Ludwig Heyse (Darmstadt: Meiner Verlag, 1969), p. 341. As quoted in Dahlhaus, *Between Romanticism and Modernism*, p. 76.

[34] Nancy, *Listening*, p. 67.

6

Theology in the making: A glossary of theopoetic practices (for relating to oneself, others, materials, traditions and the Sacred)

Wren Radford

Arranging: to select and put in order; creating a collection or gathering of things

I am arranging here a list of practices that are employed in theology through creative practice. In choosing to list verbs, I am engaging a theopoetic articulation of theology as always "in the making": the ongoing, constructive nature of theological work, as influenced by Heather Walton. Courtney Goto emphasizes this creative element in all theology, noting:

> We are *always* imagining, creating, constructing, and fashioning answers to theological questions (as well as re-forming the questions)—perhaps not with paint, marble, or music but with images, ideas, and approaches that are by definition interpretations. In other words, we have been functioning as theologians, imaginatively, all along—without recognizing what we have done as creative, aesthetic, and theological.[1]

---

[1] Courtney Goto, "Reflecting Theologically by Creating Art: Giving Form to More than We Can Say", *Reflective Practice: Formation and Supervision in*

This phrasing here of "imagining, creating, constructing, fashioning" begins to resonate with Richard Serra's *Verb List*, a compilation and enactment of "actions to relate to oneself, material, place, and process" that has been a source of inspiration for many in reflecting on creative processes.[2] In arranging my own list, I could choose an overtly "Christian theological" set of verbs; indeed, Walton has argued that the liturgical arts need to be reclaimed as creative practice, and so preaching, presiding, praying, proclaiming, prophesying could all have been included. Similarly: reading, reflecting, repenting, confessing, loving, believing, witnessing. However, my purpose here is not a complete list, nor pinning down these practices into a kind of "how-to" for theology through creative practice, but rather, as Serra suggests, to be "continually inventing new strategies so as to avoid going back to something that may have become a reflex action".[3] The list raises the question of what makes such actions theological and in what way might they be making theology? Is it as simple as expanding Serra's formulation to describe these actions also for relating to oneself, others, contexts, materials, traditions and the sacred? Is it then the context or materials assembled that would discern the divine or theological nature of such activity, or the person performing the action?

Glossaries are an accompaniment to a main body of work, and answers to these questions may be contained in that body. Yet, this list appears here without the main body of work to which it refers; perhaps because *I am writing a glossary for a field, a programme, a discipline that does not (yet) exist, that perhaps cannot fully exist*. Walton's work signals the possibilities of arranging together the practical, political, literary and creative in theology; yet she presents it to us so often in her writing as split—for example, in physically staging the divide between theology and life writing—or as a practice of working with the ruined, discarded

---

Ministry 36 (2016), pp. 84, 88.

[2] Richard Serra, *Verb List* at <https://www.moma.org/collection/works/152793> (accessed 29 October 2024).

[3] Richard Serra, "Tools and Strategies", 2000. Available at <https://art21.org/watch/extended-play/richard-serra-tools-strategies-short/> (accessed 29 October 2024).

and fragmented.[4] In writing a glossary without the main body, I seek to work in a partial way, refusing to stabilize or make whole the impossible task of doing theology. A glossary can be the telling of a story, even as the reader may discern a different story in the terms that do appear here, and those that do not.[5] In remaining provisional, ongoing, interruptible, I aim for a work that invites response, continued making.

The verbs reflect my own practices across areas of collaborative arts-based research with activist groups; scholarship in practical and liberative theologies; and queer, disabled living, which most often looks like turning to rest, to community, and to art making. I use the selected verbs to stage a conversation between contemporary artists, practical, liberative and queer theologians, and scholars exploring making and practice. By working with principles of montage, fragment and assemblage as ways of continually developing and interrupting meaning, I aim to emphasize the multiple breakings and re-makings in the work of theopoetics. Arranged alongside the entries into this glossary are images from the practising of these verbs, taken from my sketchbook or early forms of creative pieces. I am also informed by Mayra Rivera's description of theopoetics as modes of "knowing, being, and acting in the world",[6] and in presenting verbs in their progressive verbal form (-ing), I aim to invoke theological "action as ongoing, interrupted, incomplete".[7] This is not simply an aesthetic or

---

[4] Heather Walton, "Registering: Theology and Poetic Practice", in Ashley Cocksworth, Rachel Starr and Stephen Burns (eds), *From the Shores of Silence: Conversations in Feminist Practical Theology* (London: SCM Press, 2023), pp. 57–71; "A Theopoetics in Ruins", *Toronto Journal of Theology* 36:2 (2020), pp. 159–69; "A Theopoetics of Practice: Re-forming in Practical Theology", *International Journal of Practical Theology* 23:1 (2019), pp. 3–23.

[5] Eve Tuck and C. Ree, "A Glossary of a Haunting", in Stacey Holman Jones, Tony Adams and Carolyn Ellis (eds), *Handbook of Autoethnography* (New York: Routledge, 2016 (originally Left Coast Press, 2013)), pp. 639–58, at p. 640.

[6] Mayra Rivera, *Poetics of the Flesh* (Durham, NC: Duke University Press, 2015), p. 4.

[7] M. Shawn Copeland, "What is Poetics", in *Syndicate Symposium on Poetics of the Flesh*, <https://syndicate.network/symposia/theology/poetics-of-the-flesh/> (accessed 29 October 2024).

stylistic choice but rather a practising of theology, enmeshed in divine transformations in the ordinary.

Attending: an active orientation to the overlooked, denied, submerged and ignored

Attending might be thought of as a kind of noticing, a kind of seeing. It might call to mind Simone Weil's work on the redemptive yet passive nature of attention, attention as prayer, although I am more drawn to notions of Ignatian attentiveness to God in all things. In pastoral and practical theologies, attending is considered as expansive, requiring patience, care and respect, described as a "deeply theological action", invoking a search for the divine in what is "not obvious".[8] Yet this attending also traces the links between inner spiritual and psychological wellbeing and the interpersonal, relational, social, political and economic, and how such elements play out in daily life; it requires connecting different kinds of analysis. Attending to situations highlights the unity of action and reflection in practical theology, showcasing that practical theology is at once "contextual and problem-based" and also "interpretive, hermeneutical, and theological".[9] Elaine Graham notes that attending

> synthesises a pastoral role of being present and mindful of the needs and well-being of the other, with an openness to new insights that transcend functional considerations. Rather, it creates a space in which divine revelation and transformation may appear: "Attending creates temporal space for God,

---

[8] Barbara McClure, "Pastoral Theology as the Art of Paying Attention: Widening the Horizons", *International Journal of Practical Theology* 12:2 (2008), pp. 189–210, at p. 191.

[9] Elaine Graham, "Is Practical Theology a Form of 'Action Research'?", *International Journal of Practical Theology* 17:1 (2013), pp. 148–78, at pp. 176–7.

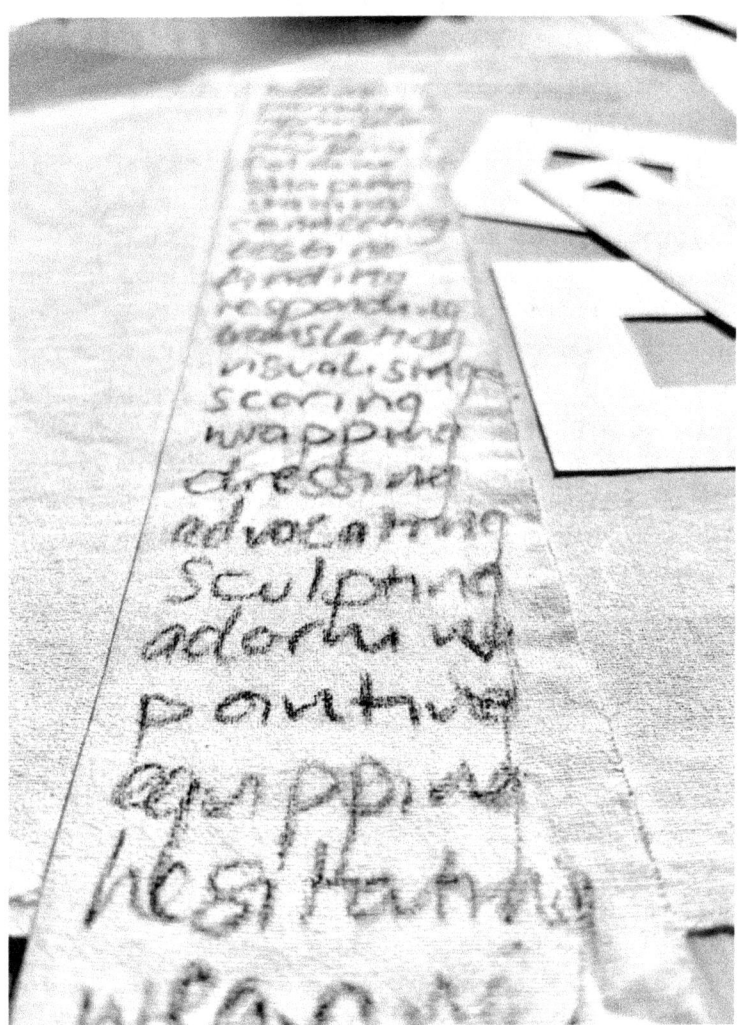

Figure 1: Arranging-Framing

truth, mystery, the sacred to present itself. It presupposes the possibilities of new realities breaking forth."[10]

---

[10] Graham, "Is Practical Theology a Form of 'Action Research'?", p. 176; quoting McClure, "Pastoral Theology as the Art of Paying Attention", p. 191.

In this light, attending is not only an orientation towards what is already there, but a making space for what is to come, an active patience for a revelatory element to emerge.

This attending is more than an exhortation to noticing "the little things in life", and I want to avoid a sense of "the power of the mind" in favour of fully embodied, world-orientated attending.[11] Attending is not neutral but is shaped by the theological and political socio-material frameworks that are performed and inhabited as we go about our daily lives. As Christina Sharpe reflects in her search for a "camera lucida of the Black maternal", the logics of coloniality structure both seeing and unseeing. She reflects that a photograph of her mother and grandmother from 1928 would have been misinterpreted by Roland Barthes through the white gaze evident in his work; for Sharpe, it is the elegance of her mother's hands, even as a child, that arrests or pierces her.[12] Womanist theologian Phillis Isabella Sheppard highlights the connection between Black women's religious interiority and various practices of art, spiritual teachings, poetry and ritual that make public and embody Black women's religious experiences. Sheppard articulates that these interlinked elements of Black women's interiority and expressive religious practices are frequently ignored in political and theological discussion because "we perceive what we have been taught noteworthy of our attention, and what is noteworthy is that which is obvious".[13] She states that "unless trained to listen for the undercurrents in narratives of religious experience or to question, and even interrogate, what we see, we are less likely to be aware of how the interior life shapes, sustains, and transforms religious experience in public domains".[14] Sheppard highlights the necessity of her approach that privileges Black women's particularity in ways that aim towards "relief

---

[11] Kotva notes the issues with Weil's priority of thought and the mind–body dualism in her work on attention. Simone Kotva, "Attention: Thomas A. Clark and Simone Weil", *Journal of British and Irish Innovative Poetry* 11:1 (2018), p. 5.

[12] Christina Sharpe, *Ordinary Notes* (London & Oxford: Daunt Books, 2023).

[13] Phillis Isabella Sheppard, *Tilling Sacred Grounds: Interiority, Black Women, and Religious Experience* (London: Lexington Books, 2022), p. xvi.

[14] Sheppard, *Tilling Sacred Grounds*, p. xvi.

from psychological, material, spiritual, and political tyranny", noting that "womanist scholars have long valued shining a light on what has previously been missed or ignored in the study of Black life and culture".[15] Sheppard reflects that what is at stake is how Black women are spoken of in a context that devalues Black life and culture, and ignores Black women's interiority: "It is in the rich ground of interiority that, when moved into the public sphere, Black women's religious life emerges and is even created over and against the practices of occlusion."[16] This highlights where attending, as a theological practice, requires *interrogating and questioning why we frame certain elements as worthy of theological attention and what we have been trained to see as "noteworthy" in colonial frames, recognizing that moving something into focus may still replicate colonizing stereotypes around race, gender, sexuality*[17] It is questioning how we might work to re-attend to the particularity of bodies and bodies of knowledge in constructing alternative framings.

Attending is perhaps the thread that runs through all elements of collaborative arts-based research: from the initial planning discussions of what will work practically and ethically for a group to facilitating sessions that register the everyday poetry and exhaustion in people's words; conducting quieter days to reflect on what has been shared; checking out with the group emerging ideas and understandings; and fashioning exhibitions or art books to share our learning in ways that does not pin down meaning, and can include blank pages and the not-knows, what cannot be said. I have written about the necessity of attending to the particularity and alterity of our own and others' embodied experiences as critical for collaborations, yet this shows up in a much more ordinary way than those words sometimes suggest. Attending is so often the work that activists and groups are already doing in their community, typically unnoticed, and collaborative arts-based projects are often finding ways to shine a light on that in ethical and respectful ways. This involves asking

---

[15] Sheppard, *Tilling Sacred Grounds*, p. xvi.

[16] Sheppard, *Tilling Sacred Grounds*, p. xviii.

[17] Phillis Isabella Sheppard, "Raced Bodies: Portraying Bodies, Reifying Racism", in Bonnie J. Miller-McLemore and Joyce Ann Mercer (eds), *Conundrums in Practical Theology* (Leiden: Brill, 2016), pp. 219–49.

whether research is the right kind of intervention, recognizing that collaborative arts projects cannot be assimilated so easily into research epistemologies, and attending "to the productive tensions between genres/epistemologies, to gather the benefits of what might be a dialogical relationship between research and art".[18]

Whilst I have been describing attending in a very active way, I do not want to make it seem as if it requires one kind of energy and embodiment; it is not a demand for uprightness and exhaustive physical presence. *Living with a long-term chronic illness, I have spent periods where life has been lived from bed, or at least long portions of each day are there. Each time a bad flare-up comes around (again), I worry (again) how long it will be, if this is the time it will be too long... another month... another year ... another seven years (again)...*

I think of this continual process of gains and losses. Movement, actions, vision returning somewhat, making it possible to reinstate activities and relationships... which may then be pulled back out with each wave of the retreating tide. Yet, the last time in bed (again) with pain causing tremors to roll across my body, and skin to bloom with the viciousness of spring, I (for the first time) feverishly half-hallucinated, half-imagined how I enact creative practice through this convulsive, blurry, aching body. I saw a crumbling easel and blank page, a moment of attending in the arrested no-time past a pain threshold. I (sometimes) put on to that easel words or images from all around me—theorists, artists, collaborators, friends— finding the feel and weight of the thing. When I cannot do that (oftentimes) the texture of absence on the page itself is a work of meticulous observation: grit behind the eyes; tiny marks and grooves on plain ceilings stared at for days; a restless attempt at rest. In my mind, each page, placed alongside each other, rolled into a moving strip, a rapidly flickering animation, a kind of zoetrope. It is the attention to the smallest of changes in each image that creates movement. These days then, suspended between an exhausted body and blank pages, are the interstices from which my attending is practised.

---

[18] Eve Tuck and K. Wayne Yang, "R-words: Refusing Research", in Django Paris and Maisha T. Winn (eds), *Humanizing Research: Decolonizing Qualitative Inquiry with Youth and Communities* (London: SAGE, 2014), p. 237.

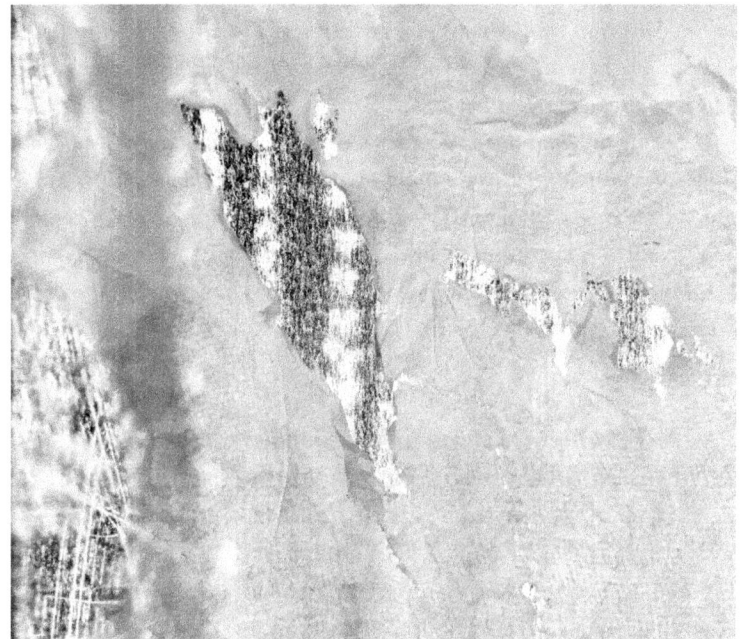

Figure 2: Grit behind the eyes/breaking

Breaking: separate into pieces through a shock, blow, or strain; interrupt

Walton writes of coming to terms with the world as a place of wonder and horror, avoiding strategies of nostalgia or simplistic calls for re-enchantment in order to "communicate in the context of broken, stone–flesh faith".[19] She argues further that "the theological edifice" is itself broken and in ruins, not simply due to "lack of imagination and communicative vitality" but through being "complicit in the abuse of power and profoundly neglectful of human suffering", and as such, "poetics in this frame represents an attentive response to brokenness and suffering".[20]

---

[19] Walton, "A Theopoetics in Ruins", p. 161.
[20] Walton, "A Theopoetics in Ruins", pp. 160, 161.

In the Christian tradition, we are perhaps used to this as the past tense. Broken, bread and body, an act of remembrance. That we come into a world of already broken forms.

To bring this into the present tense—broken to breaking—what does that do? Demand that we respond to and navigate the breakings of the present without resigning ourselves, saying "this is how it has always been"? To respond to violence and genocidal forces, to the dehumanization that is breaking people; and also, to the totalities and chains that need breaking apart?

Entangling: tying together; cause to become twisted together with or caught in; circumstances from which it is difficult to escape

Entangling is a necessary accompaniment to attending, otherwise attending becomes the work of a distant voyeur. It is a way of naming interdependences, both painful and profound. Feminist materialisms have foregrounded that making is not simply impressing a human will on inert matter but instead requires receptivity to the way we are

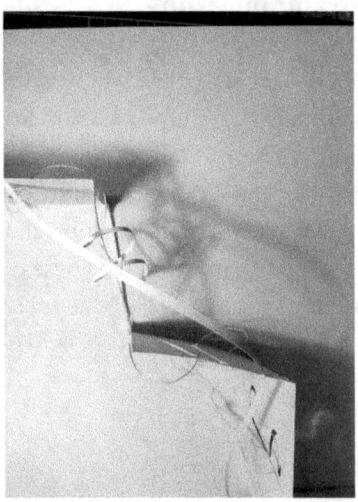 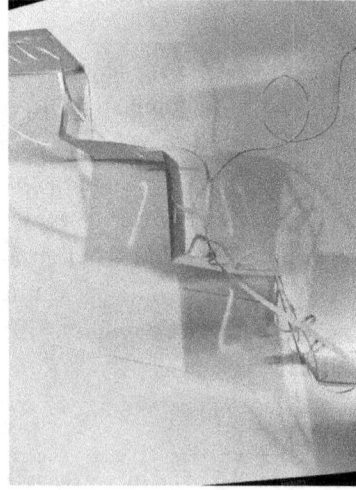

Figures 3a and 3b: Entangling/Failing.

being shaped by that same matter as we shape it. Jane Bennett offers a critique of an ecological noticing that is not truly attentive, and her writing presents attention as "the art of being receptive to the ways in which a person is not, in fact, separate from nature but entangled with and dependent on it".[21] Bennett writes: "Give up the futile attempt to disentangle the nonhuman from the human. Seek instead to engage more civilly, strategically, and subtly with the nonhuman in the assemblages in which you, too, participate."[22] Influenced by Bennett, arts-based research seeks to decentre the researcher as an individual knowing subject, suggesting instead the need for an openness to human and more-than-human entanglement, in which one is also made a subject in the process of making.[23]

When I write or say "entanglement" I think people hear too beautiful a word. I think at times I have reached after its beauty too, thinking and making it a delicate thing, as if easily snapped or lightly brushed away. But in that word is also the snagging and twisting and pulling.

The process of making, particularly making theology, is always entangled in power relations; we do not start with a blank slate or come to people, objects, materials, and ideas devoid of history. Rivera notes, "We arrive too late. The Other has already been repeatedly encountered, named, and represented, and so have we."[24] This is to acknowledge the insistence with which ongoing legacies of colonialism play out in the present, the structuring features of class, race, global location, disability, gender,

---

[21] Simone Kotva, *Effort and Grace: On the Spiritual Exercise of Philosophy* (London: Bloomsbury, 2020), p. 176.

[22] Jane Bennett, *Vibrant Matter: A Political Ecology of Things* (Durham, NC: Duke University Press, 2010), p. 116.

[23] Elizabeth Grierson, "Ways of Knowing and Being: Navigating the Conditions of Knowledge and Becoming a Creative Subject", in Elizabeth Grierson and Laura Brearley (eds), *Creative Arts Research: Narratives of Methodologies and Practices*, (Rotterdam, Boston, MA: Sense Publishers, 2009), pp. 17–32.

[24] Mayra Rivera, *The Touch of Transcendence: A Postcolonial Theology of God* (Louisville, KY: Westminster John Knox Press, 2007), p. 102.

sexuality that influence our daily encounters with one another; the multitudinous histories of the present. Rivera draws on Jorge Luis Borges' story of the unending, infinite labyrinth to name the continuous and impossible entanglements that each person comes to us with. She states, "As if looking through wide-angle lenses, I try to see each face and body in the web of relations in which persons become—a web that extends beyond our range of vision, through the world, and throughout history."[25] Whilst it is not possible to fully chart and analyse such relations, this is "no excuse for indifference", and creative practices play a role in sensing and imaging such entanglement.[26] It is also in this entangling where both the otherness-of-others and the divine are encountered. For Rivera, this is named as a relational alterity, articulating an encounter with transcendence, in which transcendence *"designates a relation with the reality* irreducibly *different from my own reality, without this difference destroying this relation and without the relation destroying this difference".*[27]

Sitting in a hospital room, I hear us all trying to describe bodily sensations, the impact of pain and painkillers. Something in the words catches in me, and I see a weaving, an entangling, not where pain has distorted the cloth that was previously smooth, but where the cloth is made from the distortions. I try to improvise a loom to test out this vision, with sketchbook pages, thread and needle from my bag. Inevitably, trying to weave distortion looks both too controlled and too clumsy in my hands, until the thread catches, pulling the weaving away from warping page; the light over the wide southern sea shifts, and the making comes alive in shadow. Not all makings make sense.

---

[25] Rivera, *The Touch of Transcendence*, p. 100.
[26] Rivera, *Poetics of the Flesh*, p. 4.
[27] Rivera, *The Touch of Transcendence*, p. 82, emphasis in original. Rivera discusses Levinas' "face of the other" and his use of "alterity" as referring possibly to the "Other" or the "Holy Other", and Rivera chooses to embrace this ambiguity in her argument, p. 60.

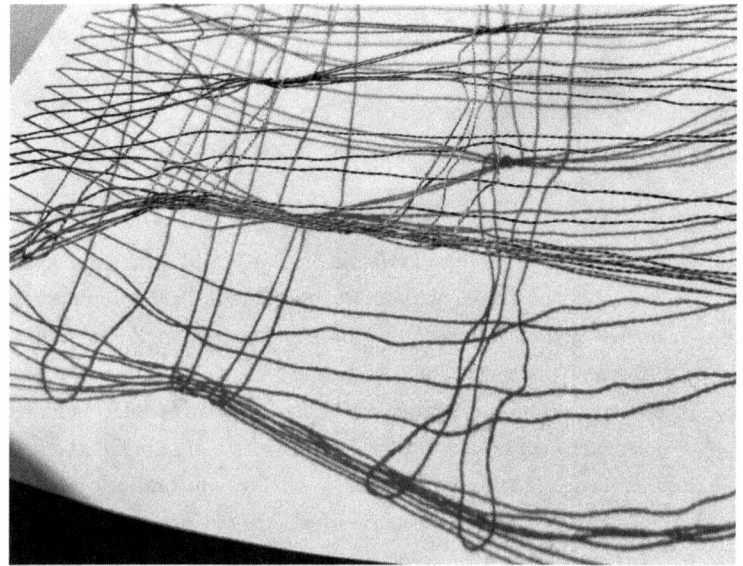

Figure 4: Not all makings make sense

Experimenting: trying out ideas or methods to discover or find out what works. See also: playing

Experimenting is "prising an opening and following where it leads. You try things out and you see what happens."[28]

The chance openings I am following here, the threads I am pulling on:

- *verbs;*
- *performing;*
- *imagery in theological works: "rich rag bags", "an image stamped on pliable wax";*
- *practices;*
- *listing; lists within lists; listlessness;*
- *physical threads;*

---

[28] Tim Ingold, *Making: Anthropology, Archaeology, Art and Architecture* (London: Routledge, 2013), p. 7.

- *incompleteness;*
- *instructions in art, craft and DIY guides;*
- *writers and artists who use lists, notes, instructions and definitions;*
- *scraps of notes I have written over the past year, gathered into an old tea-box;*
- *gestures to something/somewhere else;*
- *a desk littered with multiple medications, cold coffees, stacks of books (fiction, theology, disability and queer theory), embroideries, unsent handwritten letters, power of attorney for living family members, paperwork, paints, brushes, keys, ink, hand sanitizer, exhibition leaflets, aluminium printing plates, old bedsheets painted over, sketchbooks, a funeral order of service that I am not ready to tidy away yet and so the whole assemblage must stay, or perhaps each can be tidied away as I find a place for it in this writing, a place for theory, pain, creativity and grief.*

Experimenting in theology may need to lose a sense of the scientific experimentation, exhaustive and rigorous in its positivist values, instead embracing experimenting as a "feeling a way toward something" that "we don't already know in advance".[29] Do we make our choices on what will best lead us to the answers we already have; or are our choices putting us in a place of chance, mystery, accident, for making theology? How might we showcase the experimenting that may not lead to anything but the pulling on threads and chance openings?

---

[29] Ben Highmore, "The Arts of Noticing (Toward an Experimental Archive of Everyday Life)", in François Penz and Janina Schupp (eds), *The Everyday in Visual Culture: Slices of Lives* (London: Routledge, 2022), pp. 64, 67.

Failing: ceasing to work properly, breaking down; being unsuccessful

It is only right that experimenting should be followed by failing. Failure is often seen as a critical part of creative practice, related to risk taking and the ability to push or bend boundaries. However, Fremantle and Kearney note the scientific or positivist view of failure as one in which failure is merely an error that can be eliminated through refinement, something that provides more data; the popular idea that failure can be recuperated into a learning process that leads toward success.[30] Questioning this view and the implicit notions of progress it contains, they argue instead that creative processes that welcome failure also enable a learning from chance and accident, and the ability to sit with uncertainty and the unknown. Fremantle looks to artistic works that can incorporate failure,[31] such as Jeremy Deller's "Rejected Tube Map Cover Illustration", a work that used the different London Underground Lines to form the shape of a bike that ultimately "failed" because "word came back that it was a confusing message and unsuitable as you can't take your bike on certain lines, which was kind of the point in the first place".[32] Similarly, "Freda bringing Ann & me a cup of tea" (1983) is one of David Hockney's multiple photographic spreads, which incorporates the failure of the photo processing lab, including the half-processed photos as well as the note reading, "Sorry Mr Hockney we messed up the processing". This finds a way for the work to exist with the failure rather than throwing it all away. Clarifying that failure here does not refer to personal and professional failures that can

---

[30] Chris Fremantle and Gemma Kearney, "Owning Failure: Insights into the Perceptions and Understandings of Art Educators", *International Journal of Art and Design Education* 34/3 (2015), pp. 309–18.

[31] Chris Fremantle and Elizabeth Reeder presented a research workshop "The Art(s) of Failure". During the pandemic Fremantle uploaded the content of some of this workshop, <chris.fremantle.org/tag/sgsah/> (accessed 30 October 2024).

[32] Deller has a section of his website dedicated to his failures, which were also part of the show, Joy in People: <https://www.jeremydeller.org/MyFailures/MyFailures.php> (accessed 30 October 2024).

be a cause of great pain and loss, Fremantle advocates for creative risks and failures that take us closer to the boundaries of what is possible.

If failing is a central part of a creative process, what would it mean or look like to make theological works that can find a way to exist with the failure? Where does this failing take us deeper into the unknowns and unknowable at the heart of theological work?

What does it mean to fail at theology, to fail at being theologian? It is often something that those working across historically marginalized areas of theology (particularly global majority, queer, working class, and disabled scholars) are accused of when attending to living dynamics of oppression and injustice in our work. We have failed at theology, at the demands of rigour, certainty and purity. We have transgressed some kind of boundary, found ourselves on the outsides of the theological project, drifting.

Yet we might start to suggest that failing at the demands of white, colonial, cisheteronormative, ableist norms in theology is the beginning of liberative praxis. Failing to constrain a divine, restless, revisionary movement.

Walton's work perhaps suggests an embrace of "failing" at theology. Noting that practical theologians may be anxious about whether their work is considered really "theology", she draws on Bruno Latour's argument that the separations and divisions, the, as Walton would say, "purifications" of the modern world, such as immanence/transcendence, have never truly held and that we should embrace the impure world of hybridity, the "proliferation of transcendences".[33] Echoing the title and argument of Latour's book, *We have Never Been Modern*, Walton proclaims in her polemic mode that "we have never been theologians".[34] Such a stance enables assumed divisions, separations and boundaries to be challenged, getting beyond the "pure façade" of theology into an embrace of the

---

[33] Heather Walton, "We Have Never Been Theologians: Postsecularism and Practical Theology", *Practical Theology* 11:3 (2018), pp. 218-30, at p. 223, quoting Bruno Latour, *We Have Never Been Modern*, tr. Catherine Porter (Cambridge, MA: Harvard University Press, 1993), p. 129.

[34] Walton, "We Have Never Been Theologians", p. 223.

"heterogenous, wildly weird, and rich rag-bag of sources from which it is constructed".³⁵ By embracing this failure to contain and separate out . . .

Wait.

I am too quickly recuperating this failing at theology into a form of success, into a privileging of sites of failure as a "truer" place of theological doing . . . naming something that is no longer really failure but a kind of inscrutable sanctuary in acknowledging the limitations of our present words and images to represent the otherness of the divine and the otherness of others.

I want you to stay with the strangeness of what it is we do.

Gathering and re-using: selecting existing materials and repurposing them; a process in bricolage, collage, assemblage

Turner Prize winner Lubaina Himid's practice of gathering and re-using incorporates paint, newspaper and magazine, found objects such as playing cards, text, pins, fabric and wool, or repurposed furniture and drawers, for example in her early works of mixed media cut-out figures in *A Fashionable Marriage* (1986). Himid articulates that whilst this process of gathering and re-using has many forms used by most artists, her own definition is "more specific", as "an essential part of Black creativity, it does not mimic and it is inextricably linked to economic circumstance. Each piece within the piece has its own history, its own past and its own contribution to the whole: the new function".³⁶ Himid writes:

> Gathering and re-using is like poetry, a gathering of words, sounds, rhythms and a re-using of them in order to highlight, to pinpoint and precisely express. A real poem does not decorate a page, it changes a world.

---

35   Walton, "We Have Never Been Theologians", p. 226.
36   Lubaina Himid, "Fragments: An Exploration of Everyday Black Creativity and its Relationship to Political Change", *Art History* 44 (2021), p. 596.

> Mosaic made from broken and discarded pottery.
> Masks made from seeds shells coins crops talismans.
> Patchwork quilts made from worn clothes curtains covers and old quilts.
> Collages made from magazine and newspaper images.[37]

In this, Himid notes the relationship to time: not only in the time it takes to gather, but the histories of these objects that are re-purposed, the sense of having survived, and a "knowledge of survival" for the future.[38]

Walton draws often in her work on the activity of gathering and re-using, or bricolage, to name a theopoetics that works with ordinary, even broken and discarded things. Bricoleurs lack the wherewithal to make new, so must improvise, "retrieving odd and apparently ill-fitting fragments of things that have been used already and using them again working with what is at hand".[39] Gathering and re-using is thus the creative practice inherent in engaging with the Christian tradition as this "wildly weird rich rag bag"; Goto notes that such activity "calls upon our capacity to think with metaphors and images to reclaim, reinterpret, and create with the stuff of tradition as it relates to our lives".[40] Yet there are ethical questions raised in this practice of gathering and re-using, being a(n) (inter)disciplinary scavenger. Does a rigorous citational practice that moves away from reproducing works central to the theological canon do enough here to acknowledge original source material, labour and full argument in incorporating multiple works across disciplines and contexts? Does gathering and re-using enable us to address the harms of the theological tradition, where scholars and sources may have been re-included all too quickly? What should we refuse to re-incorporate, even in its breaking open and re-using?

---

[37] Himid, "Fragments", p. 595.
[38] Himid, "Fragments", p. 595.
[39] Walton, "A Theopoetics in Ruins", p. 161. Walton draws on Claude Lévi-Strauss, Walter Benjamin and Michel de Certeau in their discussions and practice of bricolage.
[40] Goto, "Reflecting Theologically by Creating Art", p. 88.

Figure 5: Gathering and Re-using/Tea box of scraps of notes

Like Himid, Walton links this sense of gathering and re-using with a kind of poetry, detailing Eduardo Paolozzi's lists, both of "as found" objects that were cast and re-used in his metal sculptures, and of the headings for his address to the Institute of Contemporary Art in 1958. Gathering and re-using Paolozzi's words, Walton creates a description of theopoetics as a "mud language written in broken things that weeps and cries out, supplying maps for creativity. A new language of signs and shadows."[41] Similarly, Himid and Walton see the transformative and political nature of gathering and re-using, even in the sense that it might not be enough to tackle brokenness and oppression, as Himid asks, "How much does the power to create anew from what is discarded, or

---

[41] Walton, "A Theopoetics in Ruins", p. 167.

what exists as something else, equip the maker with the power to make political change?"[42]

Grieving: [...]

I tried to outrun grief because I had to. She comes back in dreams, and I beg her to tell me where she has been, how it is she can be here. When I wake, my face is stained with this absent presence.
　Is love more powerful than death?
　Is love stronger than how we were taught to name it?

Improvising: to create something at a needed time without planning, working with available resources, figure out as you go

Improvising, as a practice in music and drama, is a popular metaphor for the work of Christian life and ethics, as it suggests riffing off a central theme or tradition. Anthony Reddie incorporates drama as a key medium for liberative theological reflection, particularly in creating pieces that "invite marginalized and oppressed peoples to improvise and play with reality in order that they might be inspired by the Spirit of God to imagine a new future—a future that exists beyond the constricted and limited world in which they presently live".[43] He notes:

> The art of improvisation is the challenge to find new meaning and phrases to transform an existing melody, without departing from the original to such an extent that the previous incarnation is obliterated. In effect, it is the delicate synthesis of bringing the

---

[42] Himid, "Fragments", p. 596.
[43] Anthony Reddie, "Dramatic Improvisation: A Jazz Inspired Approach to Undertaking Theology with the Marginalised", in Dawn Llewellyn and Deborah F. Sawyer (eds), *Reading Spiritualities: Constructing and Representing the Sacred* (London: Routledge, 2008), p. 52.

new from the old—bearing witness to what has gone before, but not being limited or constrained by it.[44]

In this, Reddie draws together jazz, drama, worship and preaching to articulate improvisation as a creative practice of Black churches, particularly around the central biblical theme of "God's revelation in human history, exemplified in Christ, in order to liberate from oppression all those who have been *denied a voice*".[45]

Improvisation is also a practice of opening up and subverting restrictive and harmful norms surrounding embodiment. In Judith Butler's account, it is the repetition of embodied norms, such as those surrounding gender, that stabilize and reinforce those norms: it is the repeated *performing* of gender norms *with others* that gives the illusion of their certainty, yet also the possibility of interrupting, improvising and deviating. Whilst agreeing with the social and performative nature of this repetition, Rivera critiques Butler's description, arguing that this image of inscribing social norms as if "an image stamped on pliable wax" gives a sense of passive matter and bodies, arguing instead that "corporeal materiality is dynamically constituted in relation to social forces".[46] We learn these improvisatory, affirmative, intervening practices through communities to which we lend our bodies "in order that it may be shaped by those visions—through words, ceremony, ritual, and practices".[47]

Improvising is articulated as a central practice in queer ethics by Laurel Schneider and Thelathia Nikki Young. They note: "We have had to improvise our lives and loves, to invent codes, modes, gestures, and shimmys that, even in death, resist the forces of annihilation. We have had to build and wield humour like a shield, or a home, or a spinning wheel, or a surgeon's scalpel".[48] Schneider and Young see improvisation as deeply linked to scandal: the idea that queer people are seen as "scandalous" in

---

[44] Reddie, "Dramatic Improvisation", p. 62.
[45] Reddie, "Dramatic Improvisation", pp. 61–2. Italics original.
[46] Rivera, *Poetics of the Flesh*, p. 142.
[47] Rivera, *Poetics of the Flesh*, p. 148.
[48] Laurel C. Schneider and Thelathia Nikki Young, *Queer Soul and Queer Theology: Ethics and Redemption in Real Life* (New York: Routledge, 2021), p. 87.

refusing and exposing harmful norms surrounding embodiment and sexuality embedded in Euro-patriarchal codes of public decency. Yet, they articulate scandal as central to Christian virtue by drawing on Paul's description of Christ crucified as scandalous, as it exposed the "lie" of a "divinity separated from embodiment".[49] They state: "A revelation that God would not stay obediently segregated or immutable—because that is not what bodies do—opens all kinds of possible reworkings, not only of the many rules that govern and police bodies in Christian societies, but of the rules governing divine aseity."[50]

For Schneider and Young, creativity is also a central virtue in the development of queer ethics, although they note that they do not wish to rush to defining the "good" in queer terms, "precisely because the term queer itself is constantly in motion".[51] They articulate the creative practices of "the fibres of testimony, moral adventure, and constantly new choreographies of affirmation, protest, celebration and mourning woven together", paying particular attention to creativity as surviving and creating chosen families.[52] I am drawn to their description of queer creativity that resonates with this sense of making at the heart of this work:

> Fueled in part by vigilance, humility, and attention, the virtuous element of queer creativity energetically rushes toward the production of what is good, holy, and righteous. It does not merely try to acclimate to what others have projected and normalized as "good". It *makes* the good [...] The virtue of creativity is not exclusive to queer communities, but it has a particular resonance in the tasks of living before us.[53]

Articulating theology and theological ethics through creative practice then needs to go beyond acknowledging the work of scholar-artists or

---

[49] Schneider and Young, *Queer Soul and Queer Theology*, p. 84.
[50] Schneider and Young, *Queer Soul and Queer Theology*, pp. 84–5.
[51] Schneider and Young, *Queer Soul and Queer Theology*, pp. 42–3.
[52] Schneider and Young, *Queer Soul and Queer Theology*, p. 47.
[53] Schneider and Young, *Queer Soul and Queer Theology*, p. 47. Emphases in the original.

celebrating what happens in studios, studies and classrooms to produce texts, images and performances. It is a being and living in the world, the work of communities, lovers and friends in the creative practices of making life, making the good.

Patterning (or repeating): composition or configuration according to a pattern; a repetition of a form, shape, or action

I have been facilitating creative arts-based projects with activists experiencing poverty to explore their everyday embodied experiences of injustice, linking their inner lives with their practices of surviving, speaking out, creating change. In recent group sessions, I have incorporated a mark-making practice to free us from feeling that "neat images" or "useable information" is more important than our play. I invite people to make a line every time they breathe out, connecting breath to hand to pen to paper. I notice my own breath-lines create a series of regular if wobbly parallel lines; others create beautiful meshwork, or even fluffy clouds. I then suggest people find a mark that feels comfortable for their hand to make; trying out quick lines, a smudge of a paint stick or a circular movement; and then repeating that mark over and over for a few minutes. Not intentionally trying to make a neat series, but focusing on each movement, each mark, and seeing the pattern build up. There are sometimes a few giggles at the start: people either feel that this is a childish, silly exercise or experience a sense of freedom in this playing; but often an immersed hush settles. We try the same mark in a different colour, medium or size; or just keep going. Finally, we reflect on the patterns of mundane life, the things done each day that are often overlooked but are part of surviving and creating change. I am often still surprised at the depth that people share through this repeating pattern. Naming the repetition of feelings in their body in living with chronic pain; the desire to care perfectly for their family but being limited by the constraints of being in the asylum system; the rigid "bleak boxes" creating an oppressive grid that they spring out of through drop-ins, book groups, food justice movements. One person names how overwhelming it is in their mind having created an abundance of bright, bouncing circles: "My mind is a busy place to be: it is hard, but I try to keep it all in its place."[54]

The everyday creativity of marginalized groups is often named in a romantic way, uncritically celebrating the creativity in improvisation, re-inventing, protesting and making do, rather than asking why such practices of survival are needed in the first place. Yet there is also a demand that marginalized groups speak "authentically" about their experiences in ways that deny their creative, interpretive activity in choosing and fashioning what to present of their lives in contexts of activism and art. Focusing on creative practices does not absolve these tensions, but I think it offers a way of staying with these problems of power and representation in generative ways, keeping us alert to the shifting relations that break apart and re-form in different settings.

---

[54] Images from these sessions can be viewed in "Filled to the Brim", the creative output from the research: <http://lincolntheologicalinstitute.com/filled-to-the-brim/> (accessed 30 October 2024).

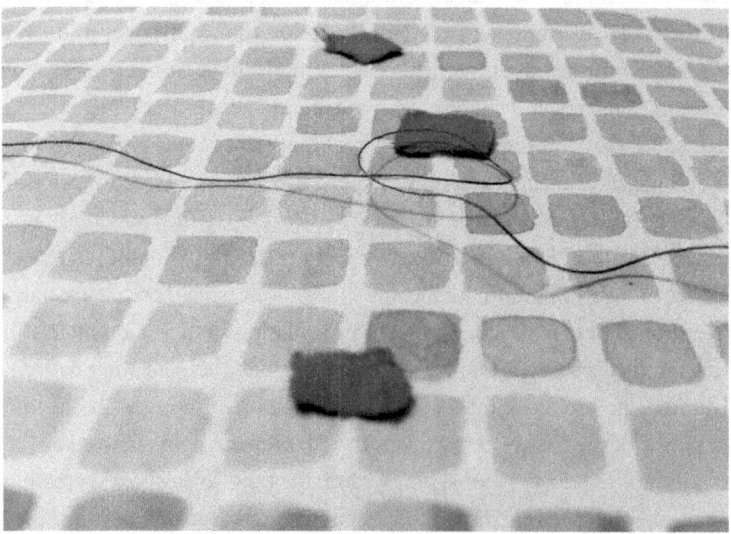

Figure 6: Improvising/Patterning

Playing: "To experience losing and finding oneself in engaging reality and one another 'as if', exploring freely a world of possibilities bounded by structure that facilitates relationship"[55]

Playing is a bit like grieving. It takes your whole body. In the moment, it can feel world-defining; but description of it feels hollow in my hands.

Serra states: "The ambiguity of play and its transitional character provides a suspension of belief whereby a shift in direction is possible when faced with a complexity that you don't understand. Free from skepticism, play relinquishes control. However, even in play the task must be carried out with conviction."[56] He makes play sound very lofty here, but he offers something about working with a complexity beyond understanding.

I write down the rules of playing as I discover them, through thread, paint, ink and rest.
 Stay in touch with the materials.
 Distortion is a matter of scale.
 Nothing comes to nothing.

Re-making: form something again, or differently

Have I made you wait too long from the entry on breaking? Were you tempted to skip along the letters? Did you want to see these actions only held together, a single entry?
 Tell me, what is it that comes after surviving?

---

[55] Courtney Goto, *The Grace of Playing: Pedagogies for Leaning into God's New Creation*, Horizons in Religious Education (Eugene, OR: Pickwick Publications, 2016), p. 15.

[56] Richard Serra, "Serra at Yale", *Yale University Art Gallery Bulletin*, 2003, pp. 31–2.

Re-making does not come through the "fair, broad highways of academic knowledge" for Walton, but "along the faultlines, cracks, and fissures in our disciplinary endeavours in which these grand designs fragment and begin to creatively re-form".[57] Re-making includes the refusal to incorporate everything into a total theory. This creative re-making does not make whole or new, nor guarantee security or even a particularly "useable" form. It is a method that "creates the opposite of a seamless whole", one of "deep and loving attention to what is damaged, derelict and yet possessed of piercing power".[58]

---

[57] Walton, "A Theopoetics of Practice", p. 18.
[58] Walton, "A Theopoetics of Practice", pp. 16, 20.

Figure 7: Sketching with both hands at once

Sketching: Make a rough drawing of; give a brief or general outline

Sketching suggests providing a brief, non-detailed overview, an initial way of laying out ideas before a fuller attempt. Ingold suggests that whilst painting aims for the totality of an image by fully covering a surface, sketching or drawing "does not seek overall coverage" and as such drawing is seen as "inherently anti-totalizing", a work that is never completed.[59] Practical theologians, influenced by anthropology and ethnography, may have been trained to prioritize "thick description", yet sketching perhaps helps to recognize the partial, provisional and even messy nature of our work, even when it involves careful attending. Sketching is "a haptic exercise", a touching and feeling of the surface; sketching is not the projection of an internal idea but something far more responsive in which "the thinking process turns into an act of waiting, listening, collaboration and dialogue [in which] one gradually learns the skill of co-operating with one's own work".[60] Social scientific and arts-based research practices have recently emerged around observational sketching,[61] although there is space for a fuller conversation, particularly in theology, about whether creative practices simply generate a different kind of "data" for social scientific paradigms, or whether they can break open existing assumptions about the nature of research. What I want to emphasize here is the value placed by practitioners on the responsiveness of sketching rather than "what may finally be encrypted in the drawing": "Drawing, like dancing, is an exploratory, sense-making process where

---

[59] Tim Ingold, *Making*, p. 127.

[60] Ingold, *Making*, p. 128, quoting Juhani Pallasmaa, *The Thinking Hand: Existential and Embodied Wisdom in Architecture* (Chichester: Wiley, 2009), p. 111.

[61] Sue Heath, Lynne Chapman and The Morgan Centre Sketchers, "Observational Sketching as Method", *International Journal of Social Research Methodology* 21:6 (2018), pp. 713–28.

the observer and the thing or idea observed, are inextricably bound together in a physical, material space/time relationship."[62]

---

[62] Maarit Mäkelä, Nithikul Nimkulrat and Tero Heikkinen, "Drawing as a Research Tool: Making and Understanding in Art and Design Practice", *Studies in Material Thinking* 10 (2014), p. 4.

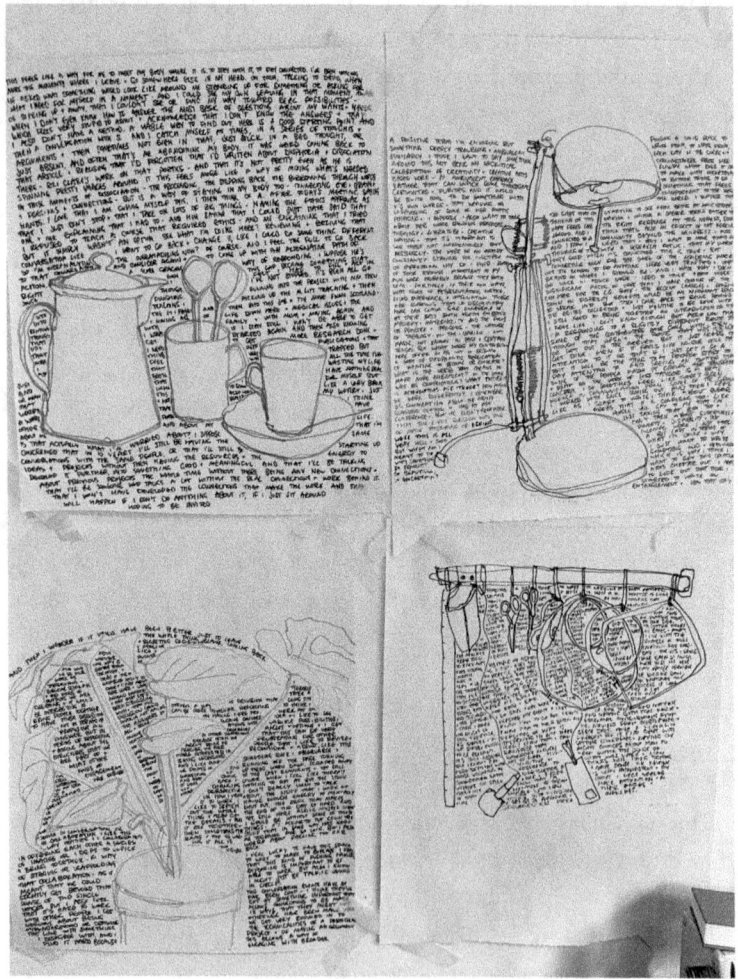

Figure 8: Sketching with both hands at once/writing as texture

Sketching everyday objects around me with both hands at the same time has become a regular practice in the past year, a way of giving up control. As pain in my joints and skin has previously precluded gripping pens, brushes and craft knives firmly enough to be making, sketching with both hands has become a way of loosening: both in the sense of working with a looser, different way of holding these tools, and in the sense of loosening the requirements that creativity produce something "good". This enabled a testing out, rather than trying to project or preserve an image. Experimenting with free writing text around the object has become a way of paying attention to my internal world as it moves over, around and through these everyday objects. Often, the writing starts with an evaluation of the drawing, but soon the physical act of writing, the movement across the page, takes over, prising open a sense of meeting my body where it is and addressing the collected detritus of academic readings and daily events. On a day of processing Ingold's work, I wrote: "Text as texture, as line, as mark, as rhythm. Finding a way across a page, as a different method each day, as difficult a journey as if never done before." It is not necessarily there to be read and viewed so much as made. Some are made on large sheets torn from a paper roll with markers that can be placed together in a book or on a wall; others with pencils in sketchbooks, paying attention to surroundings and internal landscapes in different settings.

Writing: composing texts, a symbolic system of marks and signs representing language

Writing is never just "writing up"; it is a place of composition. Writing can itself be a method of inquiry: "Writing is thinking, writing is analysis, writing is indeed a selective and tangled method of discovery."[63] Genres of fragmentation, list, glossary or assemblage enable a way of composing and quoting, a space for questions, affects, bodies and disagreements. A way of connecting the already entangled political, ethical, creative,

---

[63] Laurel Richardson and Elizabeth Adams St Pierre, "Writing: A Method of Inquiry", in Norman K. Denzin and Yvonna S. Lincoln (eds), *Handbook of Qualitative Research Third Edition* (London: SAGE, 2005), pp. 959–78.

theological, embodied, social and sacred without producing overall coverage, a theory of everything.

I am writing a glossary for a field, a programme, a discipline that does not (yet) exist, that perhaps cannot fully exist. I am struck by the descriptions of practices that work through analogy to other practices and produce transformation: sketching as dancing, or conversing; bricolage as improvisation; gathering and re-using as poetry that does not decorate a page but changes a world. I am also struck by the missing words. *But perhaps you would like to break, gather, and re-use this writing in a list or composition of your own making?*

Figure 9: Sketching with both hands, made whilst being with my mum in hospital when the chemo treatment had failed

7

"Thank the Goddess there is a book"[1]: Reading Alice Walker's *The Color Purple* as a gift of return

Fiona Darroch

In the 10th Anniversary edition of *The Color Purple*, Alice Walker describes her acclaimed novel as a "theological work examining the journey from the religious back to the spiritual that I spent much of my adult life, prior to writing it, seeking to avoid".[2] In the 2017 edition, Walker reminds the reader they are witnessing a "Spiritual Liberation" where God is reconfigured.[3] This chapter will expand on Walker's own positioning of her novel by recognizing how acts of creative practice, specifically writing fiction, are central to the practice of theology. This framework has an added pertinence and urgency in the context of womanist (and other postcolonial) fiction as creative writers work through the implications of challenging standardized racist, colonial and patriarchal representations of God and religiosity in provocative and far-reaching ways. Walker's theology locates the female sexual and labouring "everyday" body within a natural landscape, as central to its discourse, and her work was pivotal to more contemporary research within Literature and Theology. This chapter will build on previous work about Alice Walker by reading her fiction as theopoetics, alongside the influential work of contemporary

---

[1] Alice Walker, *The Color Purple* (London: Weidenfeld & Nicolson, 2017; first published: London: The Women's Press, 1983), p. xv.
[2] Kindle edition, Orion, 2011: loc 31.
[3] Walker, *The Color Purple*, p. xv.

theologians Heather Walton, Catherine Keller and Mayra Rivera, for whom theology will always take place within, not beyond, the body and its everyday creations.

Alice Walker's re-imagining of the divine, alongside the re-imagining of black female agency, has been celebrated for decades. Her work, particularly the publication of *The Color Purple*, alongside works by Toni Morrison, Maya Angelou and Zora Neale Hurston, marked a key trajectory for the literary and, as will be argued here, the theological world. Following on from Heather Walton's situating of *The Color Purple* in *Imagining Theology*,[4] this chapter will explore that point of trajectory, in the academic context of Literature and Theology, in more detail alongside more contemporary work by feminist, womanist, liberation theologians such as Melanie Harris, Mayra Rivera and Catherine Keller. The theopoetic movement, as articulated by Rivera, Keller and Walton, can be read in many ways, as owing its theoretical existence to the literary genius of writers such as Walker who are so adept at creating a *theopoiesis*, and whose works, coming from the site of trauma and fissure, allow shards of light to pour into dark spaces, bouncing off any surface they meet. And yet, a troubling reality is that women of colour are largely absent from the collective theopoetic (academic and community) network.[5] It is through such documented acts of what I would like to call "*theopoiesis*" within the late twentieth century, that writers such as Walker articulated those unspoken and often unspeakable moments of intersection between race, class, gender, sexuality and divinity with grace and authority. These profound acts of writing are a gift to us all, and particularly to the field of Literature and Theology. They paved the way for countless others to be seen and heard and are part of a move toward recognizing theology as creative practice. This gift of creativity has enabled more contemporary theologians to work towards a twenty-first-century articulation of God as

---

[4] Heather Walton, *Imagining Theology: Women, Writing and God* (London: T&T Clark, 2007).

[5] At the time of writing, however, I am encouraged to see details of the forthcoming title, Oluwatomisin Olayinka Oredein and Lakisha R. Lockhart-Rusch (eds), *Theopoetics in Color: Embodied Approaches in Theological Discourse* (Grand Rapids, MI: Eerdmans, 2024).

the mirror of (all) human and non-human bodily experience. What story does our own body tell? What history does it carry and articulate before it even speaks? What power do I have, do I negotiate with and/or am I denied in this place that my body stands? It is also through theoretical explorations of what *theopoiesis* is and does (note particularly, in this context, work by L. Callid Keefe-Perry,[6] Heather Walton,[7] Mayra Rivera[8] and Catherine Keller[9]) as well as my own work in the field of critical religion (that aims to decolonize our methodologies), and postcolonial theory,[10] that I have been guided to the genius of Walker's creative practice.

---

[6] L. Callid Keefe-Perry, *Way to Water: A Theopoetics Primer* (Eugene, OR: Wipf and Stock, 2014).

[7] In particular, see Heather Walton (ed.), *Literature and Theology: An International Journal of Religion, Theory and Culture. Special Issue: Theopoetics* 33:3 (2019). This special issue includes essays by Walton, Keefe-Perry, Rivera and Keller.

[8] In particular, see Mayra Rivera, *Poetics of the Flesh* (Durham, NC and London: Duke University Press, 2015).

[9] Catherine Keller, "Theopoiesis and the Pluriverse: Notes on a Process", in Roland Faber (ed.), *Theopoetic Folds: Philosophizing Multifariousness* (New York: Fordham University Press, 2013, pp, 179–94; *Intercarnations: Exercises in Theological Possibility* (New York: Fordham, 2017). In particular, see Chapter 6, "The Becoming of Theopoetics: A Brief, Incongruent History", pp. 105–18.

[10] Work in "Critical Religion" is inspired by a network of scholars interested in challenging the implications of the classification "religion", thinking critically about the history of the term and the potentially problematic use of the term as a descriptor. See <https://criticalreligion.org/> (accessed 30 October 2024) and The Centre for Critical Research on Religion <https://criticaltheoryofreligion.org/crr/> (accessed 30 October 2024). For examples of my own engagement with these issues in the context of Literature and Theology, see Fiona Darroch, "Journeys of Becoming: Hair, the Blogosphere and Theopoetics in Chimamanda Ngozi Adichie's Americanah", *Text Matters* 10 (2020), pp. 135–50, <https://doi.org/10.18778/2083-2931.10.08> (accessed 30 October 2024); Fiona Darroch and Alison Jasper (eds), Special Issue *Literature and Theology: Postcolonial Women's Writing and Material*

This chapter offers reflections on the challenge and beauty that dwells in these points of intersection between womanist, theopoetic, postcolonial literary criticism and a critical religion inspired framework.

As documented by Thyreen,[11] in 1992, Walker herself reminded readers that *The Color Purple* is a theological work, a factor that was, and still is, overlooked in the huge worldwide reception of this seminal novel. She wrote: "Whatever else *The Color Purple* has been taken for during the swift ten years since its publication, it remains for me a theological work examining the journey from the religious back to the spiritual that I spent much of my adult life, prior to writing it, seeking to avoid."[12] The resistance to naming God, or labelling theology or worse, 'religion', as a central concern, and character (the book is after all a series of letters addressed "Dear God" written by Celie) puzzled Walker but is still a recurring feature in much postcolonial literary criticism more generally. The nature of this absence speaks to the avoidance of "religion" that Walker herself experienced prior to writing *The Color Purple*. Under this polite resistance/avoidance lingers an unspoken fear that identifying religion/God/theology as a central concern for the writer will take this work from a *serious* work of (secular/political) literature (for *The Color Purple* is also a seminal work of political activism for Black rights in twentieth-century North America) to the separate *irrational* realm of domesticity and belief. In our still Modernist Enlightened world, this signals backwardness and irrationality. Here dwells a complex entanglement with a colonial rhetoric of civility[13] that haunts readings and academic literary responses

---

Religion 35.4 (2021); and Fiona Darroch, *Memory and Myth: Postcolonial Religion in Contemporary Guyanese Fiction and Poetry* (Amsterdam: Rodopi, 2009).

[11] Jeannine Thyreen, "Alice Walker's 'The Color Purple': Redefining God and (Re)Claiming the Spirit Within", *Christianity and Literature* 49:1 (1999), pp. 49–66. In particular, see pp. 49–50.

[12] Alice Walker, *The Color Purple* (Kindle edition, Orion 2011), loc 31.

[13] For pioneering discussions on the relationship between colonialism, ideals of civility and Christianity, see Kwok Pui-Lan, *Postcolonial Imagination and Feminist Theology* (London: SCM Press, 2005). For more recent work on the history and implications of the secularization thesis, particularly in relation to

to texts such as *The Color Purple*, as well as the creative practitioner herself. Maybe God alongside political activism signals danger within this rhetoric? I have written elsewhere about the resistance to the "religious" in postcolonial literary criticism,[14] potentially as a result of some inherited fear—both in the academic and wider publishing/literary world—that the work will be sectioned off as irrational or belonging to a different sphere of activity. These considerations are informed by a critical religion methodological framework that encourages us to decolonize our classificatory system of religious vs secular, which primarily serves to uphold powerful Euro-American and Western systems of governance.[15] I would propose that this is a significant reason for why relatively little has been written about representations of God in relation to *The Color Purple* outside of theological circles, a book which is in its fifth decade of reprints, appears on high school and university curriculums, and is established as a seminal twentieth-century literary text. If we say this novel is a work of theology and is about God, will it risk that accolade?

Womanist theologians, born out of Walker's coining of the term "womanist/womanism",[16] work tirelessly to advocate for the inseparable nature, as well as the power, of these intersections (the body, gender, spirit, God, activism, economics, nature, politics, everyday injustice and

---

gender and race, see Joan Wallach Scott, *Sex and Secularization* (Princeton, NJ and Oxford: Princeton University Press, 2018).

[14] Darroch, *Memory and Myth*, and more recently Fiona Darroch and Alison Jasper, "Introduction" to Special Issue on Postcolonial Women's Writing and Material Religion: New Directions, *Literature and Theology* 35:4 (2021), pp 379–82.

[15] As explored by theorists such as Tim Fitzgerald, Trevor Stack and Naomi Goldenberg (eds) in *Religion as a Category of Governance and Sovereignty* (Leiden: Brill, 2015).

[16] See Alice Walker, *In Search of Our Mothers' Gardens: Womanist Prose* (London: Pheonix, 2005, first published Orlando, FL: Harcourt Brace Jovanovich, 1983), p. xi for Walker's full definition, including the much-quoted sentence: "Womanist is to feminist as purple is to lavender". For an interesting exploration on the origins and use of the term "womanism", see Layli Maparyan, *The Womanist Idea* (New York: Routledge, 2012).

violence). Interestingly, however, early womanist theologians experienced a different challenge in relation to responses to Alice Walker's work: her creative works (fiction and non-fiction) have been described as too "secular" within womanist theological circles, as her "theology" is not closely enough aligned with more accepted notions of Christian morality. Walker's vision of "God" ironically resulted in her exclusion from some womanist methodologies.[17] Melanie Harris explores this tension in detail. The purpose of her book *Gifts of Virtue: Alice Walker, and Womanist Ethics* is to recover Walker's non-fiction as "worthy of womanist ethical study:

> If womanist theological methodologies have been influenced by these traditional Christian assumptions, then one reason Walker's pagan and nonfiction ethical voice may be neglected in womanist thought is the belief that paganism as devoted to the earth, is somehow anti-Christian. Although Walker holds a place for the figure of Jesus in her theology, Christian womanist methodologies may inherently limit conversation with Walker's voice... because of the perceived threat that paganism poses to established Christian theology.[18]

Harris reminds readers that whilst Walker coined the term, she rightly does not hold authority over its future iterations and direction, nor would she want to: "Beyond her contribution of the definition, Walker's voice doesn't seem to be important to the development of womanist theological

---

[17] See the controversial roundtable discussion where Cheryl Sanders critiques the theological use of a term coined by a "secular" literary writer. Cheryl J. Sanders, Katie G. Cannon, Emilie M. Townes, M. Shawn Copeland, bell hooks and Cheryl Townsend Gilkes (eds), "Roundtable Discussion: Christian Ethics and Theology in Womanist Perspective", *Journal of Feminist Studies in Religion* 5:2 (1989), pp. 83–112. See Melanie Harris's careful engagement with this controversy in Melanie Harris, *Gifts of Virtue: Alice Walker, and Womanist Ethics* (New York: Palgrave Macmillan, 2010), p. 9.

[18] Harris, *Gifts of Virtue*, p. 8.

debate."[19] But neither should Walker be "cut out of her own definition nor banished from womanist religious thought. Rather, her identity as a Black woman, a writer, and a practitioner of fluid spirituality should make a path for her to plant flowers in her own garden."[20]

In 1988, Katie Cannon, in *Black Womanist Ethics*,[21] captured the theological significance of Black women writers, because of their ability to articulate a new Christian ethics and spiritual awakening that takes into account wider and different dimensions of extreme suffering and control—although what Harris recognizes is that their bravery also carries a risk of rejection from their immediate networks of devout Christian women. Heather Walton prioritizes Walker's novel and Cannon's thesis as marking a critical conjuncture for women, writing and theology more generally: "Literature is an invaluable resource for Cannon because it bears testimony to the spiritual depth and resilience of black people. Cannon thus argued that the work of Hurston, and the contemporary women writers who claim her inheritance, should be acknowledged as a theological resource within the black community ... Cannon herself reads this literature as a form of 'theopoiesis.'"[22] In *Intercarnations*, Catherine Keller starts the first chapter, "Returning God: Gift of Feminist Theology", with reference to Walker and Shug's proposal for an un-gendering of God as "It": "All of this intensity about the naming of God was cannily cultural, practical, liturgical, political. But it was at the same time altogether theological. It surely counts as evidence for an unexpected return. Among one subset of progressive thinkers, it energized with its argumentative passions a return not just of a vague religiosity but of an engagement with the old thematic and disputatious questions of theology."[23] But the evident influence of Walker's theology feels like it runs even deeper in the pages that follow. The metaphor of return when trying to commune with the non-male/white God was

---

[19] Harris, *Gifts of Virtue*, p. 8.
[20] Harris, *Gifts of Virtue*, p. 9.
[21] Katie Cannon, *Black Womanist Ethics* (Atlanta, GA: Scholars Press, 1988).
[22] Walton, "Imagining Theology", p. 9.
[23] Keller, *Intercarnations*, p. 18.

Celie's too: "Every time I conjure up a rock, I throw it."[24] In an essay written in 1986 (published in 1988), Walker writes:

> I get a power from this name that Sojourner Truth and I share. And when I walk into a room of strangers who are hostile to the words of women, I do so with her cloak of authority... she smiles within my smile... Every experience that roused her passion against injustice in her lifetime shines from my eyes. This feeling of being loved and supported by the universe in general and by certain recognizable spirits in particular is bliss... And perhaps that is what Jesus tried so hard to teach: that the transformation required of us is not simply to be 'like' Christ, but to be Christ. The spirit of our helpers incarnates in us, making us more ourselves by extending us far beyond. And to the spirit there is no "beginning" as we know it... and no end. Always a hello, from the concerned spiritual ancestor you may not even have known you had —but this could strike at any time. Never a good-bye.[25]

Keller's thesis of *intercarnation* channels exactly Walker's own vision of continual becoming; what Keller calls the "gift of possibility":

> But the difference made, in surprise, enjoyment, and use, *is* the return. This love that shines or rains on just or unjust alike— across, in other words, the most radical difference—would not signify *in*difference to whether the unjust remain unjust. It continues to shine, no matter how dense the cloud.[26]

She continues, as she edges closer to her term *intercarnation* (also a gift to us all):

---

[24] Walker, *The Color Purple*, p. 178.
[25] Alice Walker, "A Name is Sometimes an Ancestor Saying Hi, I'm With You", in *Living by the Word: Selected Writings* (London: Weidenfeld & Nicolson, 2005, first published London: The Women's Press, 1988), p. 98.
[26] Keller, *Intercarnations*, pp. 28–31.

This boundless multiplicity of interdependent socialities offers a theological supplement to the singular event of the incarnation. We may call this supplement... The *intercarnation*. It might be narrated as the becoming body of God—but only if the God-metaphor does not defeat the multiplicity.[27]

I cannot help but be struck by the similarity of these words and Walker's channelling of Sojourner Truth's power, shining through her smile, to her model of Christ and the incarnation: "The spirit of our helpers incarnates in us, making us more ourselves by extending us far beyond". I propose that the multiplicity of being, which is also a "deconstruct[ion of] omnipotence"[28] and a perpetual state of becoming (no beginning or no end), was Walker's gift, returned again in contemporary theopoetic discourse.

Interestingly, the distinct tensions laid out at the start of this article (postcolonial literary criticism's tendency to ignore God/religion and then womanist exclusion of Walker's more divergent, pagan, non-traditional vision of God) arguably arise from a similar struggle with inherent colonial tropes of civility and control. We validate our lived experiences on the idealized model of white, Christian, colonial civility and individualized rationality, as actualized in the white (male, able, heteronormative, neurotypical) body. This model of successful "being in the world" is so entrenched that it inherently informs the work, and methodologies, of not only contemporary academia but also postcolonial theorists and is implicated in the early womanist theologians' resistance to Walker's model of Christianity and even in Walker's own reluctance to talk about "religion". In 2006, Cannon writes about the "intellectual colonization"[29] that has prevented Black women, and Black female experience, from being *heard* in the academy:

---

[27] Keller, *Intercarnations*, p. 32.
[28] Keller, *Intercarnations*, p. 31.
[29] Katie Cannon, "Structured Academic Amnesia: *As If This Womanist Story Never Happened*", in Stacey M. Floyd-Thomas (ed.), *Deeper Shades of Purple: Womanism in Religion and Society* (New York: New York University Press, 2006), pp. 19–28, at p. 25.

What does it mean that academia is so structured that Black women are severely ostracized when we re-member and re-present in our authentic interest? What does one do when told that our refusal to split, to dichotomize from God's presence in the daily fabric of our communal lives makes us a liability to civilization? What is the role of Womanist intellectuals in institutions of higher learning, where our pedagogical styles and scholarly lexicons are derailed on a daily basis? The point that I am arguing is that anecdotal evidence does a lot to reveal the truth as to how oppressed people live with integrity, especially when we are repeatedly unheard but not unvoiced, unseen but not invisible.[30]

Central to my analysis is an attempt to destabilize the colonial myths of religiosity and theology, and mind/body dualism, that haunt and limit academic scholarship at divergent ends of the spectrum (from both so-called "theological" and "secular" disciplinary locations) with Alice Walker's creative practice as my guide. I offer a contemporary (re)reading of *The Color Purple* specifically, but also her writing more generally, in order to argue that her work should be read as theology that leads the way as creative practice, as *theopoiesis*, following from insights and interconnections with Cannon, Walton, Rivera and Keller. I will channel the definitions and practices of more contemporary theopoetics to elucidate this genius.

Alice Walker epitomizes the creative writer's ability to say the unsayable through the written word. In the most recent 2017 edition of *The Color Purple*, Walker again signals the repositioning of God from the restrictions of the church building (and white, Christian institutions of civility more generally) to the natural and bodily world, as a central theme. In response to the 1985 Spielberg film, *The Color Purple* (which she recently rewatched in a special re-screening in a theatre), she writes:

> But the unseating of the Christian "white" God, in Celie's consciousness and in Shug Avery's understanding, is not handled

---

[30] Cannon, "Structured Academic Amnesia", p. 21.

in such a way that the average person understands we are witnessing Spiritual Liberation. And that Nature, and a bearded, long haired white man in the sky, have changed places."[31]

Walker identifies that the core theme of *The Color Purple*—Celie's reconceptualization of the white God as a God who feels and loves, weeps over and is mirrored by Celie's body, and its place in the world around her—is not central enough to the cinematic production of the story. To dilute this for a "secular"/mainstream, audience, is, in many ways, to miss the point of the story and speaks to the inherent colonial bias and methodologies that linger everywhere and are described above. As the introduction continues, and in response, Walker gives thanks for the *The Color Purple* as a written piece of creative work: "Thank the Goddess there is a book." The first words written on the page of *The Color Purple*, "Dear God", establish that Celie's recovery from childhood trauma of rape, ancestral slavery, institutional racism and misogyny to a model of Black female, sexually liberated, agency starts with a re-imagining of God. Her re-imagining of God is not a side show; it is central to Celie's (and to all women's) becoming, and to Walker's model of Black female agency, that is "womanism".[32]

In a 2012 interview, Walker is asked by Valerie Reiss: "*Do you have prayers that you say on a regular basis?*" Her reply is: "'Thank you' is the best prayer that anyone could say. I say that one a lot. 'Thank you' expresses extreme gratitude, humility, understanding."[33] Thanking the Goddess for the book, in response to the film, is her prayer. And I add my

---

[31] Walker, *The Color Purple*, p. xv.

[32] See Thyreen, "Alice Walker's 'The Color Purple'", p. 50. Also, Margaret D. Kamitsuka, "Reading the Raced and Sexed Body in The Color Purple: Repatterning White Feminist and Womanist Theological Hermeneutics", *Journal of Feminist Studies in Religion* 19:2 (2003), pp 45–66, at p. 51.

[33] Valerie Reiss, "Alice Walker calls God 'Mama': An Interview with Alice Walker", in W. Reed, J. Horne, M. Karr, D. Moffitt, S. Cushman, B. A. Fennelly, M. Awiakta et al. (eds), *Circling Faith: Southern Women on Spirituality* (Tuscaloosa, AL: University of Alabama Press, 2012), pp. 184–91, at p. 188.

own thanks.[34] I remember the profound impact of *The Color Purple* and *Beloved* as a first-year undergraduate studying in Scotland. These novels changed the course of my life. They stopped me in my tracks because they articulated something equally divine and horrific that I didn't think could be evoked through the written word. It was around the same time that I read Arundhati Roy's *The God of Small Things*.[35] I remember where I was when I read these novels. My career has since been committed to reading and writing about the importance of such literary works; teaching undergraduates about the impact of colonial systems of control on individuals, cultures and religions around the world; and developing the methodologies we employ as academics to talk about *others*, as well as celebrating the poetics of resistance that continue to emerge in response. I spent two years living in Saudi Arabia as a young adolescent. I was made aware of my racialized and gendered (white, female) body in a distinct way. I remember my mother encouraged me to cut my hair short when we lived in Riyadh. I hated it. Everyone thought I was a boy. She admitted much later that she was pleased by this as she thought I was safer. I also remember thinking, back in the UK, that it was normal to be whistled at and name-called in a sexually explicit way by grown men in the street as a teenage girl walking home in school uniform. My only form of resistance was stony silence. I have puzzled over the layers of racialized and gendered implications of these exchanges, and others (as many of us have in our own contexts), which occurred in my formative years, and were played out on and in response to my (gendered) body. A maternal, white, female fear of non-white male bodies, a history of orientalism, as well as the impact of distinct patriarchies and female oppression and

---

[34] With these words I sit in the discomfort of (rather than delete or edit out) the potentially patronizing voyeurism of white readers giving easy thanks for work brought to life because of generations of inherent racist violence and horror. I use Walker as my guide on what "thanks" is: as prayer and as "extreme gratitude, humility, understanding".

[35] See Jasper and Darroch, interview with Mayra Rivera (*Literature and Theology* 35:4 (2021), pp. 385–88 in particular) about the impact of works such as Roy's *The God of Small Things* on our theoretical and theological imaginings and work.

violence, informed these encounters and my understanding of my own female becoming. I give thanks to Alice Walker for widening my lens and helping me to *know* and *see* in response to these, often silenced, frames of reference:

> I write all of the things *I should have been able to read*. Consulting, as belatedly discovered models, those writers—most of whom, not surprisingly are women—who understood that their experience as ordinary human beings was also valuable, and in danger of being misrepresented, distorted or lost ... it is in the end, the saving of lives that we writers are about. Whether we are "minority" or "majority". It is simply in our power to do this. We do it because we care ... We care because we know this: *the life we save is our own.*[36]

In the context of theology, the liberating of "God" from its reductive patriarchal, heteronormative and racist template has continued to be captured by liberation and feminist/womanist theologians such as Marcella Althaus Reid,[37] Katie Cannon and more recently, particularly in relation to the field of literature and theology, Mayra Rivera and, as already captured, Catherine Keller. Such challenges to standardized and inherited concepts of "God" share intersections with the work of apophasis and atheology,[38] which posits that the mystery of God is that he/she/they/it dwells in the unspeakable and unspoken space between language and experience. The ability to capture this space through words, as well as creative practice and the arts, is the art of *poesis* celebrated

---

[36] Alice Walker, "Saving the Life that is Your Own" (1976), in *In Search of Our Mothers' Gardens*, pp. 13–14.

[37] Marcella Althaus Reid, *Indecent Theology: Theological Perversions in Sex, Gender and Politics* (Abingdon: Routledge, 2000).

[38] See Keefe-Perry's history of theopoetics, *Way to Water*, particularly Part One: "Early Articulations which includes reference to the influential work of Stanley Hopper, Thomas Altizer and the Death of God movement", pp. 17–30. See also Chapter 6 of Keller, *Intercarnations*: "The Becoming of Theopoetics: A Brief, Incongruent History", pp. 105–18.

by aforementioned theologians. In the same interview detailed above, Walker is asked about the role of silence. Silence is also that space beyond language. In atheological terms, God's existence is marked by the palpable space between language and silence:

> In our struggle with and within the theos–logos, possibilities keep opening where there were none before—in an indeterminate space, between sex and gender, between theism and atheism, between language and silence, between too much and too little. In this space nothing we say of God, including the presumption of his/her/its existence, can be said to be just true. But God might remain a gifted metaphor for the space itself, the opening in which truth can be told.[39]

In the interview, Walker replies: "Everything does come out of silence. And once you get that, it's wonderful to be able to go there and live in silence until you're ready to leave it. I've written and published seven novels and many, many, many stories and essays. And each and every one came out of basically nothing—that's how we think of silence, is not having anything. But I have experienced silence as being incredibly rich."[40] It is also Celie who deconstructs the language of "G-o-d" whilst denying her own feelings and voice. Following her last moment with Nettie before she leaves to work with Samuel and Corinne she writes: "It's worse than that, I think. If I was buried, I wouldn't have to work. But I just say, Never mine, never mine, long as I can spell G-o-d I got somebody along."[41] The letter on the following page starts with "G-o-d . . . " instead of "Dear God". Deconstructing the language of G-o-d is a significant articulation of her oscillation between trauma, self-denial and then transition to healing, finding her own voice, and to what Walker herself describes as "Spiritual Liberation". (Yet this very public deconstruction of God, and Walker's ongoing theological writings, were not in any serious way picked up by the white, male, Euro-American theologians of the

---

[39] Keller, *Intercarnations*, p. 28.
[40] Reiss, "Alice Walker Calls God 'Mama'", p. 189.
[41] Walker, *The Color Purple*, p. 19.

early apophatic/death of God/theopoetic movement although we see her importance to theologians such as Walton and Keller). What is vital to these theological works, and particularly to Walker's own theology, is lived, fleshy, bodily experience. It is Mayra Rivera who describes such instances as the *"poetics of the flesh"* inspired in particular by Edouard Glissant's Caribbean poetics of relation, alongside Fanon's epidermal schema, writings of Aimé Césaire, Judith Butler and the gospels of John and Paul: "*Poetics of the Flesh* elaborates a view of corporeality woven by its carnal relations to the world—spiritual, organic, social—describing the folds of the body and flesh, flesh and world, body and word".[42] "G-o-d" is born out of, not transcendent to, bodily experiences (both joyful and traumatic); bodies bear witness to histories, that are then transcribed in flesh and poesis. My own reading of Walker's work is therefore closely inspired by Rivera's analysis and Keller's elucidation of *intercarnation*. In her 2019 article and in a 2021 interview with myself and Alison Jasper, Rivera speaks about the importance and profound influence of work by Caribbean women writers such as Sylvia Wynter, Mayra Santos Febres and Edwidge Danticat. It is in the work of such writers that creative acts of God-making are arguably intercalated most profoundly with the silence described above—that unspoken and unspeakable weight of language and divinity.[43]

---

[42] Rivera, *Poetics of the Flesh*, p. 10.

[43] Fiona Darroch, Alison Jasper and Mayra Rivera, "An Interview with Mayra Rivera", *Literature and Theology* 33:3 (2021), pp. 383–95, at pp. 385–8 particularly. Interestingly, this influence (of Black women writers/theologians) is not explored by Rivera in *Poetics of the Flesh*, a text which speaks so closely to the socio-material realities for gendered and racialized bodies—theory utilized is predominantly by Black men (Fanon, Cesaire, Glissant) and white gender theorists (Butler); is this an example of how the accepted academic discourse and history of theopoetics (and theology more broadly) has imposed a resistance to these explorations, as described by Cannon above? It is this type of detail that compounds the feeling of exclusion from the theological and theopoetic movement felt by womanist theologians. This sense of exclusion, and celebration of exceptional creative practice, are currently being addressed in, amongst other contexts, "Black

In the 1974 essay "In Search of Our Mothers' Gardens", Walker describes the weight that is carried by those who are denied any creative outlet for their genius, and specifically the intensity of this burden for Black women from the South. It is worth quoting at length:

> When the poet Jean Toomer walked through the South in the early twenties, he discovered a curious thing: black women whose spirituality was so intense, so deep, so *unconscious*, that they were themselves unaware of the richness they held. They stumbled blindly through their lives: creatures so abused and mutilated in body, so dimmed and confused by pain, that they considered themselves unworthy even of hope. In the selfless abstractions their bodies became to the men who used them, they became more than "sexual objects", more even than mere women: they became "Saints". Instead of being perceived as whole persons, their bodies became shrines: what was thought to be their minds became temples suitable for worship. These crazy Saints stared out at the world, wildly, like lunatics—or quietly, like suicides; and the "God" that was in their gaze was as mute as a great stone ... They wandered or sat about the countryside crooning lullabies to ghosts, and drawing the mother of Christ in charcoal on courthouse walls. They forced their minds to desert their bodies and their striving spirits sought to rise, like frail whirlwinds from the hard red clay ... men lit candles to celebrate the emptiness that remained, as people do who enter a beautiful but vacant space to resurrect a God. Our mothers and grandmothers, some of them: moving to music not yet written. And they waited.[44]

Theopoetics: A New Theological Visioning!" <https://www.tomioredein.com/black-theopoetics-a-new-theological-visioning> (accessed 30 October 2024) and the forthcoming title, Oluwatomisin Olayinka Oredein and Lakisha R. Lockhart (eds), *Theopoetics in Color*.

[44] Walker, "In Search of Our Mothers' Gardens", p. 232.

As the essay continues, Walker talks about these women as being artists who were denied their craft: "These grandmothers and mothers of ours were not Saints, but Artists; driven to a numb and bleeding madness by the springs of creativity in them for which there was no release. They were Creators, who lived in spiritual waste."[45] Walker's provocative description of female genius[46] locates spiritual engagement with the world as vital for realizing one's creative potential. She recognizes the catastrophic damage caused by trying to detach your mind from your body, your (spiritual) becoming from the work of your hands, yet often, this was (and still is for many people) the only option to ensure survival. The only God they had to gaze upon was as "mute as stone" to their suffering—but it is from the silence of God that female genius can be found: "a vacant space to resurrect a God".

Walker's fictional heroines often find their voice through an intimate journey which sees their spiritual awakening alongside the fine-tuning of their craft: Celie learns to love her body, and her G-o-d in the natural world, whilst becoming a successful seamstress of trousers; Shug's journey as Celie's spiritual and bodily, sexual guide is alongside her music and singing; Nettie (with a steely determination to learn, read and write, having watched her sister's suffering and silencing at the hands of Pa and Mr____) writes beautifully crafted theological prose to Celie, working through the pan-Africanism and Ethiopianism she hears whilst working with the missionary family (and adoptive parents of Celie's stolen children) stationed in "Olinka", Africa. She writes:

> Over the pulpit there is a saying: *Ethiopia Shall Stretch Forth Her Hands to God*. Think what it means that Ethiopia is Africa! All the Ethiopians in the bible were colored. It had never occurred to me, though when you read the bible it is perfectly plain if you pay attention only to the words. It is the pictures in the bible

---

[45] Walker, "In Search of Our Mothers' Gardens", p. 233.

[46] My reflections on female genius owe a debt of gratitude to the work of Alison Jasper, shared through many enriching conversations and the reading of her text *Because of Beauvoir: Christianity and the Cultivation of Female Genius* (Waco, TX: Baylor University Press, 2012).

that fool you. The pictures that illustrate the words. All of the people are white too. But really *white* people lived somewhere else during those times. That's why the bible says that Jesus Christ had hair like lamb's wool. Lamb's wool is not straight Celie. It isn't even curly.[47]

Nettie's theological awakening, realized through her own act of *poesis* (reading, writing and working in an African community, raising her nieces) eventually makes its way back to Celie once she finds Nettie's letters, which had been hidden from her by Mr_____. In one of the letters, Nettie refers to meeting "a Harvard scholar named Edward. DuBoyce was his last name I think," who chastised an aunt for celebrating King Leopold: "You should regard it as a symbol of your unwitting complicity with this despot who worked to death and brutalized and eventually exterminated thousands and thousands of African people."[48] This connection with pan-African scholars and activists in 1900s North America, and hearing firsthand about DuBois's theory of double consciousness,[49] guides Nettie to a complex appreciation of the painful rift which will always exist as a result of the transatlantic slave trade between those within Africa and those in the African diaspora.[50] Nettie builds her quite radical (theopoetic?) theology in response to such exchanges, and alongside her own lived experience, which she then works through by writing to Celie:

---

[47] Walker, *The Color Purple*, p. 120.

[48] Walker, *The Color Purple*, p. 214.

[49] Although not explicitly stated, Samuel and Nettie appear to work through the sense of split identity, a double consciousness articulated by DuBois that emerges as a result of being descended from African slaves in a North American context: "We love them. We try every way we can to show that love. But they reject us. They never listen to how we've suffered. And if they listen they say stupid things. Why don't you speak our language? they ask. Why can't you remember the old ways? Why aren't you happy in America, if everyone drives motorcars" (Walker, *The Color Purple*, p. 214).

[50] See W. E. B. DuBois, *The Souls of Black Folk* (New York: Dover Publications, 1994 [1903]).

> God is different to us now, after all these years in Africa. More spirit than ever before, and more internal. Most people think he has to look like something or someone—a roofleaf or Christ—but we don't. And not being tied to what God looks like frees us. When we return to America we must have long talks about this, Celie. And perhaps Samuel and I will found a new church in our community that has no idols in it whatsoever, in which each person's spirit is encouraged to seek God directly, his belief that this is possible strengthened by us as people who also believe.[51]

Nettie has formulated a theology that prioritizes her community's experience of the world; she advocates the importance of listening to this experience and knowing that the key to freedom (or what Walker calls Spiritual Liberation) is through liberating the image of God from its racist patriarchal chains. But this can only be realized through community practice and collaboration. The *Imago Dei* must be rebuilt from the site of collective trauma.

It is this theological guidance, alongside her sexual relationship and liberation with Shug, that guides Celie toward her own God, which is also her own body and her own genius. In a much-quoted dialogue, Celie and Shug have already worked through some of what Nettie says:

> "Nettie say somewhere in the bible it say Jesus' hair was like lamb's wool, I say . . . Ain't no way to read the bible and not think God white, [Shug] say. Then she sigh. When I found out I thought God was white and a man, I lost interest . . . [Shug] say, My first step from the old white man was trees. Then air. Then birds. Then other people. But one day when I was sitting and feeling like a motherless child, which I was, it come to me: that feeling of being part of everything, not separate at all. I knew that if I cut a tree, my arm would bleed, and I laughed and cried and I run all around the house. I knew just what it was. In fact, when it happen, you can't miss it. It sort of like you know what, she say, grinning and rubbing up on my thigh.

---

[51] Walker, *The Color Purple*, p. 233.

> *Shug!* I say.
>
> Oh, she say. God love all them feelings. That some of the best stuff God did....
>
> Whenever you trying to pray and man plop himself on the other end of it, tell him to git lost, say Shug. Conjure up flowers, wind, water, a big rock.
>
> But this hard work, let me tell you. He been there so long, he don't want to budge. He threaten lightning, floods and earthquakes. Us fight. I hardly pray at all. Every time I conjure up a rock, I throw it. Amen.[52]

This famous piece of literature (presented as a prayer) is worth quoting at length again. Contemporary discussions of theopoetics that I have referred to help us to see the genius of what Walker has built, but it is also important to sit (in silence?) with the discomfort caused by the knowledge that Walker formulated a discourse which is now academically fashionable but at the time, as Cannon testifies, experiences like Celie's were excluded (or overlooked) from considerations of valid lived/embodied practice: "The plausibility of our claim of a valid Black woman-centred religious discourse must first be proven within and around the sacred halls of academe. Seminaries and university departments of religion possess power in defining when, where, and for whom God-talk will be extended."[53] Nettie's, Celie's and Shug's "God-talk" speaks to the

---

[52] Walker, *The Color Purple*, p. 178.

[53] Cannon, "Structured Academic Amnesia", p. 24. L. Callid Keefe-Perry's book on theopoetics, *Way to Water: A Theopoetics Primer*, provides vital definitions of theopoetics that speak closely to the God-talk presented by Walker and other Black women writers. But their work is not part of his research, which is built primarily from white male scholars. Keefe-Perry is critiqued for this in a review by Patrick Reyes, who reflects on the need to build a "decolonial theopoetics". Keefe-Perry himself responds ("Alvesian Theopoetics", *Literature and Theology* 2019) and believes that "theopoetics can decentre coloniality" (325). But he also defends his use of white male scholars to build his monograph as "those are the things of my life" whilst also acknowledging the urgent need to "remember the weight" of "coloniality":

heart of the theopoetic movement, but 50 years ago, the academy wasn't listening. It is from this point in the story that Celie starts addressing her letters to Nettie, rather than God. This is not a denial of God but a symbol of the moment that Walker describes as her Spiritual Liberation, which continues to then be reinforced by her poetic and bodily communion with Nettie, Shug and herself. The connection with her own sexual body, and the joy it can bring, the intimate spiritual connection and theological enquiry with other women, and with the natural world around her, enables her to see and be seen in G-o-d.

This chapter has celebrated the gift of continuing return of Alice Walker's theology; her creative practices are ground-breaking acts of *theopoiesis*. I have argued that resistance to the language of God and religion both within theological academic circles and social discourses of secularity have contributed to this genius being "unheard but not unvoiced, unseen but not invisible".[54] Her influence is palpable to the exceptional works of theology by contemporary theologians, particularly Walton, Rivera and Keller (which are also treasured gifts); Walker's work was a crucial turning point towards carving a space in the academy and social imagination for understanding theology as creative practice.

"For some it is an annoyance and concern, for others it hangs heavily on the neck and scrapes the shoulders raw" (209: 326). Keefe-Perry is clearly keen to address the importance of decolonizing our methodologies. I would add that it is important to acknowledge that those "things of his life" have been validated as replicating *all* lived experience by a system of power whereas Shug's and Nettie's have not; they are refused entry not just in relation to their difference to his own (white male) lived experience but *their own and all* lived experience as Cannon so aptly articulates.

[54] Cannon, "Structured Academic Amnesia", p. 21.

8

The making and unmaking of methodological habits

Tone Stangeland Kaufman and Simon Hallonsten

Multiple beginnings

"But you need to demonstrate that this is indeed research and not just your opinion." We have been at it for what feels like hours. My coffee has gone cold, and my back aches. I contemplate getting another cup but decide against it. Nearly time to wrap up.

I hatch my answer. Then I reply, "But it is only my opinion." I feel obtuse. I don't mean to be difficult, but I am not going to play that game either. If it is opinions they want, opinions they shall have. I mean, what is research if not informed opinions?

Here we go again. Some students are easy. They get it and try to incorporate feedback the best they can. This one isn't. Everything turns into an argument. "Okay, and do you think that is in any way problematic?"

Which way to go? It feels like running the gauntlet. I go all in. "No."

He isn't stupid. He knows as well as I do that his answer is highly disputable. He has picked up the ballpoint pen that lay on top of his open notebook, a notebook he has not made a single entry in as long as we have been sitting here. He twirls the pen. He does that when he gets nervous.

I wonder what I am doing. Why am I arguing, and why am I being so stubborn? A good part is probably the feeling of being misunderstood, the indignation of the tragic hero, poor me. But it's not just that. This is important. It is important to me, and I think it is important more generally. What counts as research and what we relegate to an opinion has consequences for how we understand ourselves as researchers and scholars, and it has consequences for which possibilities we have to contribute to any form of public discourse.

The funny thing is that he could actually make an interesting contribution if he wasn't so absorbed in making everything so difficult, and I really want to see him succeed. I mean, we are all part of communities and networks; practical theology is a guild, which means we need to show respect and deference to the work of our colleagues, whether we like it or not. No one is an island unto herself and part of doing a PhD is understanding that, being able to orient yourself in a landscape of different positions and approaches, and demonstrating how you relate to that landscape both critically and constructively.

I clear my throat. She still hasn't said a word. I need to turn this around.

"No, of course, I see a difference between research and opinion. I just get upset when someone suggests that this is just an opinion. I mean, I have done all the work. How can someone think it's just an opinion?"

An opening. Tread carefully now. "Okay, what about this? If someone asks you at your defence what it is in your dissertation you didn't already know before you did your project, what would you say then?"

"I would say ... I would ... " *What would I say? The fact is, all this has become so jumbled up in my brain that it is difficult to know what I learned when, where and how. As with all knowledge, it is difficult to imagine a situation in which I wouldn't know what I know now, and the way I did my ethnographic fieldwork means that it is sometimes difficult to pinpoint exactly when I came to an insight or an idea. But does that make it any less a valid instance of knowledge creation?*

"Look, I think it's great that you want to think all these things through. But people will look at your dissertation and they will ask: has this person demonstrated that he is capable of conducting independent research? And that is what you need to show: how you did your research, which includes demonstrating what you learned in the process and how that is knowledge and not just your personal opinion."

—

Heather Walton is a divisive character—or at least she was when giving a lecture at the Third Meeting of the Nordic Network for Theology and Practice at Uppsala University in December 2021.[1] Heather read from her journal recounting her experiences of being an activist-practical theologian during the COP26 meeting in Glasgow earlier that year, and she spoke about research methods, calling for an openness to other ways of doing research (autoethnographic, performative, collaborative, creative, artistic, indigenous and many others) and noting how research done through creative methods is particularly able to translate into forms of theological reflection appropriate for our times. She concluded by sharing with us recorded presentations from three of her colleagues and friends who employ creative research methods.

Some of the people we talked to after Heather's presentation simply loved it—this was what practical theology should be all about. Her approach was seen as timely, creative and full of potential. This was cutting-edge stuff, at least in our context. Others were more reluctant, not to say outright critical, asking whether her approach should be classified as *research* or as arts-and-crafts. In which way could the personal reflections in her diary ever live up to the rigour required for the production of public knowledge? Wasn't there an obvious danger of conflating personal opinion and considered scholarship?

Equally divided were participants on Kati Tervo-Niemelä's presentation. Professor of Practical Theology at the University of Eastern Finland, Kati presented the Finnish contribution to a large-scale multinational mixed-methods study on intergenerational faith transmission. A cooperation between Finnish, Canadian, German, Hungarian and Italian researchers, the international comparative study aimed at a comprehensive mapping and understanding of the dynamics of (non)religious worldview transmission between generations, looking both at factors that strengthen or inhibit successful intergenerational

---

[1] Part of this chapter, such as the following sections and the theoretical resources drawing on John Law (see below), partly builds on a keynote lecture given by Tone at the Fourth Meeting of the Nordic Network for Theology and Practice in Helsinki, March 2023.

transmission and the way in which religiosity changes in the transmission process.

Of the people we discussed this with, no one questioned whether that was research. On the contrary, participants were excited by the methodological rigour, and the cutting-edge mixed-methods design, combining survey and interview data. However, some participants asked whether Kati's work should be considered religious studies or sociology of religion rather than practical theology. Put differently, people asked what was *theological* about her study. Perhaps not surprisingly, it was often those who loved Heather who were critical about Kati and vice versa.

—

And here it is time to declare our own standpoints, to situate ourselves in this conversation.

Tone: I was very excited about—and deeply challenged by—Heather's talk. Yet, I was equally enthusiastic and inspired by Kati's presentation. My default mode is the traditional research methods in which I was trained, yet I am also slowly trying out some of the "new" methods, and I have good friends and colleagues who are far more "cutting edge" in this regard than I am myself. I have previously argued for distinguishing between different forms of normativity, and for not jumping to the prescriptive too early.[2] Yet, in my heart and soul I am also someone who believes in transformation and activism. So, in many ways I follow the Pauline principle in the practical theological landscape: I am a North American to the North Americans, a German to the Germans, a Brit to the British, and a Nordic scholar to Nordic colleagues, but I do admit that

---

[2] Tone Stangeland Kaufman, "From the Outside, Within, or In Between? Normativity at Work in Empirical Practical Theological Research", in Bonnie J. Miller-McLemore and Joyce Ann Mercer (eds), *Conundrums in Practical Theology* (Leiden: Brill, 2016), pp. 134–62; "The Researcher as Gamemaker: Teaching Normative Dimensions in Various Phases of Empirical Practical Theological Research", in Mary Clark Moschella and Susan Willhauck (eds), *Qualitative Research in Theological Education: Pedagogy in Practice* (London: SCM Press, 2018), pp. 169–84.

this can be confusing. At best, I feel like a bridge builder, but sometimes I feel more like a chameleon, like someone who is being continuously stretched in all kinds of different directions.

Simon: I actually missed Heather's lecture that day, though from reading it later I am sure I would have loved it. Indeed, even though I had missed the lecture, I walked up to Heather when I arrived later and was immediately fascinated. I had struggled for some time with questions of method and representation and sensed that there was an opening here that would allow me a different take on what it means to develop knowledge. I took one of Heather's writing classes, and she later agreed to co-supervise my dissertation. Using research methods that were regarded as non-standard meant a lot of negotiations, not only with Tone as my main supervisor, but especially with other Nordic practical theologians, who responded to different parts of the dissertation during the process and were often less than enthusiastic.

Indeed, there is an ongoing debate and tension regarding approaches, research designs, methods, methodologies and theology in Nordic practical theology. Part of this discussion is an appraisal of "new" research methods, such as action research, narrative, arts-based approaches, and autoethnography. Are these "new" methods "the real deal"? And how different are they from "traditional research methods"? And perhaps even more importantly, what is at stake in choosing and refusing specific methods and methodologies? How should practical theology relate to spirituality and activism? And what is the vocation of the academic practical theologian in this time and place? Do we make it our pride to stay "methodologically pure" in terms of separating academy and church, academy and activism, and academy and art?

Heather Walton has kept questioning partitions, arguing for "a theopoetics of practice"—a practical theology that embraces the theological, the transformative, the creative and the spiritual.[3] Drawing

---

[3] H. Walton, "A Theopoetics of Practice: Re-forming in Practical Theology", *International Journal of Practical Theology* 23:1 (2019), pp. 3–23.

on John Law's work on "making a mess with methods",[4] this paper discusses the reception of such "new" research methods as foregrounded by Walton, in Nordic practical theology, highlighting some of the tensions that exist between various ways of pursuing practical theology today. Taking seriously Heather's point of departure about our situatedness in a broken and breaking world, we conclude with some suggestions as to how these different practical theological trajectories might mutually enrich one another.

Presence, manifest absence, and Otherness

In discussing method, John Law distinguishes between what he terms *presence, manifest absence* and *Otherness*.[5] Describing the so-called "metaphysics of presence", he draws on post-structuralist thought to argue that presence necessarily implies absences—whenever something is made manifest, something else is lost from view.[6] As certain things are made present, other things are made absent. This also applies to research methods—methods that cast light on one thing simultaneously cloud other aspects in darkness. In this way, methods not only describe social realities but also help to create them as the reality we see and accept. Research methods are not normatively neutral. Methods are political yet, according to Law, this is not a problem as long as we do not pretend or imagine it to be otherwise.

For Law, "the problem is not so much the standard research methods themselves, but the normativities that are attached to them in discourses about method".[7] As Law and other scholars note, the methodological

---

[4] John Law, "Making a Mess with Method", Centre for Science Studies, Lancaster University, UK, 2003, at < https://www.lancaster.ac.uk/fass/resources/sociology-online-papers/papers/law-making-a-mess-with-method.pdf> (accessed 6 March 2025); *After Method: Mess in Social Science Research* (London: Routledge, 2004).

[5] Law, *After Method*.

[6] Law, *After Method*, p. 83.

[7] Law, *After Method*, p. 4.

"rules imposed on us carry, we need to note, a set of contingent and historically specific Euro-American assumptions".[8] To challenge these normativities, Law calls us to "subvert method" and "to unmake many of our methodological habits".[9]

A part of the unmaking of our habits is to recognize and acknowledge not only what methods bring into focus, but also the absences they contribute to. To help us disclose what is absent, Law further distinguishes between "manifest absence" and "Otherness". The former is "that which is absent but recognized as relevant to, or represented in, presence",[10] in other words, "what presence acknowledges". Manifest absence thus refers to the known unknown or an absence made explicit or manifest.

In contrast, Otherness denotes "absence that is *not* acknowledged",[11] either because of its slippery nature, or, and more significant for our discussion, because of its inherent threat to presence. In Law's

---

[8] Law, *After Method*, p. 9. Post- and decolonial writers pose a similar critique of a Eurocentric epistemological and methodological "taken-for-grantedness". See for example: Courtney T. Goto, "Asian American Practical Theologies", in Kathleen A. Cahalan and Gordon S. Mikoski (eds), *Opening the Field of Practical Theology: An Introduction* (Lanham, MD: Rowman & Littlefield, 2014), pp. 31–44; "Writing in Compliance with the Racialized 'Zoo' of Practical Theology", in Bonnie J. Miller-McLemore and Joyce Ann Mercer (eds), *Conundrums in Practical Theology* (Leiden and Boston, MA: Brill, 2016), pp. 110–33; *Taking on Practical Theology: The Idolization of Context and the Hope of Community* (Leiden and Boston, MA: Brill, 2018); "The Ubiquity of Ignorance: A Practical Theological Challenge of Our Time", *Practical Theology* 13:2 (2020), pp. 138–49; Tom Beaudoin and Katherine Turpin, "White Practical Theology", in Kathleen A. Cahalan and Gordon S. Mikoski (eds), *Opening the Field of Practical Theology: An Introduction* (Lanham, MD: Rowman & Littlefield, 2014), pp. 251–69; Anthony G. Reddie, "Transformative Pedagogy, Black Theology and Participative Forms of Praxis", *Religions* 9:10 (2018), p. 317; HyeRan Kim-Cragg, *Postcolonial Preaching: Creating a Ripple Effect* (London: Rowman & Littlefield, 2021).

[9] Law, *After Method*, p. 9.

[10] Law, *After Method*, p. 157.

[11] Law, *After Method*, p. 8.

terminology, the difference is one of Otherness as *routine, insignificance or repression*.[12] Whilst Otherness cannot fully be brought to presence and listed, Law suggests some styles of Othering. Examples are the uninteresting or insignificant, the obvious, the invisible work, the impossible and everything that is being repressed. Otherness thus implies a state of non-belonging and irrelevance.[13]

Law argues that presence, manifest absence and Otherness are mutually co-dependent, which entails that one cannot exist without the others.[14] Nevertheless, there remains a significant difference between manifest absence and Otherness in the way they relate to and shape presence. As acknowledged, or manifest, absence ensures that there is a tacit understanding surrounding presence on which presence builds. On the contrary, Otherness potentially threatens presence, by challenging both presence and manifest absence. Otherness thus needs to be excluded, repressed and placed outside the realm of relevance and normalcy precisely for presence to establish its claim.

While both manifest absence and Otherness are valuable lenses through which to understand and analyse forms of making present and absent, it is Otherness that bears the greater risk and potential for unsettling our methodological habits. In the following, we therefore use Otherness as a theoretical lens to look at ways in which Walton's work currently troubles some of the methodological assumptions in Nordic practical theology. As we don't assume readers to be acquainted with this tradition, we begin by foregrounding what research in this context makes present.

---

[12] Law, *After Method*, p. 85.
[13] There are some similarities between Otherness and Courtney Goto's understanding of *ignorance*. She argues that ignorance should also be understood as a verb, and that we produce and reproduce ignorance by habitually ignoring what we tend to ignore (Goto, "The Ubiquity of Ignorance").
[14] Law, *After Method*, pp. 84–5.

Nordic practical theology

To get a feel for this practical theological "trajectory", we consider the Nordic contributions to two recent international collections, the *Wiley Blackwell Companion to Theology and Qualitative Research*[15] and the *International Handbook of Practical Theology*.[16] Additionally, we refer to two recent publications on practice theory authored by Nordic scholars.

The complexities of the lived
Nordic Practical Theology is characterized, first, by a focus on the complexities of lived religion, lived theology and lived ecclesial life, including an awareness of nonhuman actors, as evidenced by the salience of practice and practice theory as well as sociocultural learning theories and a sociomaterial sensibility. Most of the Nordic entries in the *Companion*[17] addressed and drew on practice theories, and one of the three Nordic contributions to the *Handbook*[18] was a chapter entirely devoted to practice theory.[19] Nordic practical theologians meet at the biennial *Nordic Network for Theology and Practice*, and two publications on practice theory have recently appeared from the hands of Nordic scholars: the edited volume *Practice, Practice Theory, and Theology*[20] and a special issue on practice theory in the Nordic journal *Studia Theologica*.[21]

---

[15] Pete Ward and Knut Tveitereid (eds), *The Wiley Blackwell Companion to Theology and Qualitative Research* (Hoboken, NJ: Wiley-Blackwell, 2022).

[16] Birgit Weyel, Wilhelm Gräb, Emmanuel Lartey and Cas Wepener (eds), *International Handbook of Practical Theology* (Berlin: De Gruyter, 2022).

[17] *The Wiley Blackwell Companion to Theology and Qualitative Research.*

[18] *International Handbook of Practical Theology.*

[19] Geir Afdal, "Practice Theory", in Birgit Weyel, Wilhelm Gräb, Emmanuel Lartey and Cas Wepener (eds), *International Handbook of Practical Theology* (Berlin: De Gruyter, 2022), pp. 677–89.

[20] Ulla Schmidt and Kirstine Helboe Johansen, *Practice, Practice Theory and Theology: Scandinavian and German Perspectives* (Berlin: De Gruyter, 2022).

[21] *Studia Theologica* 75:1 (2021) <https://www.tandfonline.com/toc/sthe20/75/1/> (accessed 30 October 2024).

Practice theories are a family of often sociological theories premised on the notion that lived life appears as a network of interrelated and interpenetrating activities.[22] These activities are understood to follow certain patterns which establish the durability of social life. As practices, activities are not completely spontaneous happenings, but expressions of social and historical processes that in themselves afford specific subject positions to people participating in these practices. Put simply, practice theories propose that significant analysis does not take place, either at the level of the individual, nor in respect to society at large, but that what are important, are activities in themselves and the way in which these activities structure social life. And this focus on practices and the lived complexities that make up religious and ecclesial life is typical for Nordic practical theology.

Theology through qualitative methods
The focus on the complexities of the lived leads directly to the second prominent feature of Nordic practical theology: the salient use of empirical and qualitative methods rather than textual, historical or merely theoretical approaches. Examples from the *Companion* are Christian youth ministry and being church in a multi-cultural and multi-religious landscape;[23] folk church pastors and migrants in Danish folk churches;[24]

---

[22] Andreas Reckwitz, "Toward a Theory of Social Practices: A Development in Culturalist Theorizing", *European Journal of Social Theory* 5:2 (2002), pp. 243–63; Davide Nicolini, *Practice Theory, Work, and Organization: An Introduction* (Oxford: Oxford University Press, 2013); Afdal, "Practice Theory".

[23] Knut Tveitereid, "Lived Theology and Theology in the Lived", in Pete Ward and Knut Tveitereid (eds), *The Wiley Blackwell Companion to Theology and Qualitative Research* (Hoboken, NJ: Wiley-Blackwell, 2022), pp. 67–77.

[24] Kirsten Donskov Felter, "Fieldwork and the Person of the Theologian", in Pete Ward and Knut Tveitereid (eds), *The Wiley Blackwell Companion to Theology and Qualitative Research* (Hoboken, NJ: Wiley-Blackwell, 2022), pp. 373–81.

pre-marital counselling;[25] how listeners listen to sermons;[26] research projects on migration, confirmation and youth work, and church and digital media;[27] the role of the Church of Sweden as a welfare agent and the diaconal work of the Church City Mission in Trondheim;[28] death-related practices in the Danish Folkekirke;[29] and Christian education in Church of Norway congregations.[30] The same holds true for Auli Vähäkangas and Kirstine Helboe Johansen's chapter in the *Handbook*.[31] Nordic practical theology is deeply influenced by the empirical turn, which predisposes it to the study of contemporary and current phenomena and developments, rather than to historical processes. According to this empirical trajectory, it is through the detailed study of what people do and say and how they do and say these things, and

---

[25] Kristine Helboe Johansen, "Analytical Strategies", in Pete Ward and Knut Tveitereid (eds), *The Wiley Blackwell Companion to Theology and Qualitative Research* (Hoboken, NJ: Wiley-Blackwell, 2022), pp. 393–402.

[26] Marianne Gaarden, "Preaching", in Pete Ward and Knut Tveitereid (eds), *The Wiley Blackwell Companion to Theology and Qualitative Research* (Hoboken, NJ: Wiley-Blackwell, 2022), pp. 309–18.

[27] Jonas Ideström, "Action Research and Theology", in Pete Ward and Knut Tveitereid (eds), *The Wiley Blackwell Companion to Theology and Qualitative Research* (Hoboken, NJ: Wiley-Blackwell, 2022), pp. 425–34.

[28] Ninna Edgardh, "Queer Theology", in Pete Ward and Knut Tveitereid (eds), *The Wiley Blackwell Companion to Theology and Qualitative Research* (Hoboken, NJ: Wiley-Blackwell, 2022), pp. 243–51.

[29] Ulla Schmidt, "Continental Practical Theology", in Pete Ward and Knut Tveitereid (eds), *The Wiley Blackwell Companion to Theology and Qualitative Research* (Hoboken, NJ: Wiley-Blackwell, 2022), pp. 298–308.

[30] Elisabeth Tveito Johnsen, "Christian Education as a Community of Strangers", in Pete Ward and Knut Tveitereid (eds), *The Wiley Blackwell Companion to Theology and Qualitative Research* (Hoboken, NJ: Wiley-Blackwell, 2022), pp. 340–50.

[31] Auli Vähäkangas and Kirstine Helboe Johansen, "Wedding Ceremonies / Blessings / Partnership", in Birgit Weyel, Wilhelm Gräb, Emmanuel Lartey and Cas Wepener (eds), *International Handbook of Practical Theology* (Berlin: De Gruyter, 2022), pp. 587–97.

by following certain methodological rules, that an understanding of religious and theological life becomes possible. Often inspired by the social sciences, and sociology of religion in particular, these rules detail how research is to be designed and documented so that data collection procedures, strategies for data analysis and integration with previous literature establish reliable and verifiable knowledge, a point to which we return below.

Unveiling and articulating "reality"

A third feature of Nordic practical theology, directly related to the two above, is a focus on analysis and theory. In our experience, few Nordic scholars would embrace a positivistic claim to be representing "reality". On the contrary, they would rather adhere to constructivism, an Actor-Network-Theory flat ontology, or critical realism. Nevertheless, we also find that Law's pointed analysis of how a "common-sense realism" continues to be part of our ontological and epistemological backbone also reflects the style of research and writing in Nordic practical theology, which is strongly influenced by the sociology and psychology of religion.[32] Hence, despite insisting that we cannot capture "Reality" as it *really* is, we can still give realistic accounts of "what is out there" and thus produce reliable knowledge. The focus on reliability translates, in turn, into an emphasis on methods, methodology, orderliness and research design, seeking to unveil and articulate what Law terms "out-thereness".[33]

Further, in addition to valuing qualitative methods, Nordic practical theology has a high regard for theory as a means of providing analytical tools for understanding social realities.[34] Hence, rather than drawing on various forms of personal experience, such as journal entries, autoethnography or narrative, theoretical perspectives are often used as

---

[32] Law, "Making a Mess with Method", p. 6. According to Law, there are various forms of "out-thereness", from the primitive or naïve sense that there is "something out there", to the more specific sense that this "something" is independent, prior, definite and singular.

[33] Law, *After Method*, pp. 24–32.

[34] Tveitereid, "Making Data Speak"; Helboe Johansen, "Analytical Strategies"; Schmidt and Helboe Johansen, "Practice, Practice Theory and Theology".

lenses to create the "necessary" analytical distance.[35] Underlying such a strategy is an implicit belief that analytical distance will contribute to a more "objective", "reliable" and "truthful" rendering of what is "out there", even if we say that our empirical data are established or created and are not nuggets to be "picked up" as by miners in a gold mine.[36] Nordic practical theology thus appears as a research trajectory that works to unveil the complexities of lived religious, theological and ecclesial life by careful inductive, abductive or theory-driven analysis of empirical data, established with qualitative methods. Theory and method are then more than the tools of the trade: they function as basic guarantors for the value of the practical theological enterprise as a whole.

Negotiating theology through creative practices

The practice of making something present in and through research, Law argues, requires boundaries between presence, manifest absence and Otherness—boundaries that are in need of constant reinforcement, if they are not to collapse.[37] And here we suggest that it is this practice of policing the border that turned Heather's presentation into "something of a talking point" at the third meeting of the *Nordic Network for Theology and Practice* in Uppsala in 2021. Heather's talk brought into presence an understanding of practical theology that is usually Othered in our context, relegated to the realm of arts and activism, prevented from passing the border to the land of the academy and of scientific and scholarly work. Her presentation spurred debate and dispute because Heather invited us to consider art, activism and narrative as integral ways of establishing presence in *research*. Hence, she demonstrated and argued

---

[35] Mats Alvesson, "Methodology for Close Up Studies: Struggling with Closeness and Closure", *Higher Education* 46:2 (2003), pp. 167–93; Elisabeth Tveito Johnsen, "Teologi som ulike biter og deler: Ti år med trosopplæring i Den norske kirke", *Prismet* 66 (3) (2015), pp. 125–44, at 128.

[36] Svend Brinkmann and Steinar Kvale, *Doing Interviews*, 2nd edn (London: Sage, 2018), p. 19.

[37] Law, *After Method*, pp. 84–5.

for the crossing and even blending of borders and, thus, for the unmaking of methodological habits. Yet, included in this unmaking is also a making. Heather also pointed out that much ethnographic and empirical research takes place within what Amitav Ghosh calls the "colonial-carbon-culture grid".[38] She asked whether traditional research methodologies confine us to binaries like researcher and researched, primitive and cultured, known and unknown, thereby promoting a sense of separation and purity that might establish a false sense of control. Heather moreover foregrounded that these so-called "new" research methods are not really new, and, as she put it powerfully,

> they emerged out of the recognition that some voices had not been heard (those of indigenous people, queer people, ill people, people in trauma, women) that some issues had not been tackled, that some questions had not been asked, could not be asked within the grid. They emerged in the noisy darkness outside the fence.[39]

Furthermore, Heather argued that prevailing power structures are deeply embedded in these methodological norms, with those in authority often maintaining traditional research methods that inhibit exploration beyond established boundaries. She referenced the works of Anna Tsing to highlight how, unlike mainstream practical theological approaches, her award-winning text, *The Mushroom at the End of the World*, ventures into less conventional territories of inquiry within the field.[40]

However, in the Nordic context of practical theology, creative practice is seen to lack the necessary analytical distance, autoethnography is demoted to personal anecdote and narrative is understood as fiction, thereby being othered, as they are perceived to fail the test of a

---

[38] Heather Walton, "The Troubles", Keynote Lecture, Third Conference of the Nordic Network for Theology and Practice: Sources of Life in Times of Crises: Theological and Religious Practices of a New Normality, 2 December 2021, Uppsala, pp. 4–5.
[39] Walton, "The Troubles", p. 7.
[40] Walton, "The Troubles", p. 8.

rigorous methodological approach. Such methods, then, are seen to sit uneasily with the ways in which Nordic practical theologians usually go about establishing presence—the qualitative methods, the rigorous methodology, the strict research designs, the complex theories, and analytical strategies.

Arguably, part of the tension is a real difference in how we understand the goal of scholarly activity. Above we have claimed that Nordic practical theology aims to produce knowledge and understanding, unveiling something of the truth about the ways in which religion and theology are lived in our context today. In contrast, Heather and many theologians doing theology through creative practices are looking to provide resources for reflection and consideration, offering works that invite introspection, mirroring, exploration, spirituality and action.[41] Of course, many creative practitioners would not renounce a claim to truth, goodness or beauty, but truth is here understood quite differently from the way it is usually framed in practical theology influenced by sociological methods and theories. And it might be these competing claims to truth that have created the tension we experienced among colleagues and conference participants that winter afternoon in Uppsala.

However, borders are not only policed but also negotiated and sometimes crossed, as exemplified in our introductory dialogue. These negotiations are never easy, not least because they warp around concrete people, perceived social norms and power structures in the academy simultaneously, forcing not only some of the manifest absences, but also a good deal of Otherness into light.

---

[41] Heather Walton, "A Theopoetics of Practice: Re-forming in Practical Theology", *International Journal of Practical Theology* 23:1 (2019), pp. 3–23; Walton, "The Troubles"; "Life Writing and Religion", in Birgit Weyel, Wilhelm Gräb, Emmanuel Lartey and Cas Wepener (eds), *International Handbook of Practical Theology* (Berlin: De Gruyter, 2022), pp. 47–9; "Registering: Theology and Poetic Practice", in Ashley Cocksworth, Rachel Starr and Stephen Burns (eds), *From the Shores of Silence: Conversations in Feminist Practical Theology* (London: SCM Press, 2023), pp. 57–71.

The making and unmaking of methodological habits

Law's reasoning shares many similarities with Bruno Latour's work on the way in which modernity comprises the simultaneous moves of purification and intermingling.[42] Here we agree with Heather Walton[43] that these same processes have shaped practical theology. Yet in the Nordic region, the great separation might rather be one between knowledge and opinion than between transcendence and immanence, though these binaries are related in many ways. Our methodological habits have thus predisposed us to strive towards purity, separating research from opinion, fact from fiction, and the academy from the atelier. And in the same way Latour claims the success of the "moderns", we would claim that this strategy has been and continues to be the dominant means of producing informed accounts of religious, theological and ecclesial life in our region, especially since what we distinguish as presence continues to be intertwined with absences both acknowledged and ignored.

However, as Law, Latour and Walton have pointed out, the simultaneous acceptance of purification and intermingling establishes both a hybridity that is eternally fluid and also processes of continuous negotiation.[44] There might be periods of relative stability, but by and large research practices are disputed and disputable. One of the present challenges to uniformity in the Nordic region stems from the Theology through Creative Practice trajectory exemplified in the work of Heather Walton and similar approaches such as that of Nicola Slee.[45] Such contributions not only challenge us to rethink our methodology but more fundamentally to question the nature of the claims we make about reality and our vocation as practical theologians.

---

[42] Law, *After Method*, pp. 81–2; Bruno Latour, *We Have Never Been Modern* (Cambridge, MA: Harvard University Press, 1993), pp. 10–12.

[43] Walton, "We Have Never Been Theologians".

[44] Law, *After Method*; Latour, *We Have Never Been Modern*; Walton, "We Have Never Been Theologians".

[45] Nicola Slee, *Fragments for Fractured Times: What Feminist Practical Theology Brings to the Table* (London: SCM Press, 2020).

And here we see great potential in bringing a sensibility for creativity, activism and the "new" research methods into dialogue with Nordic practical theology, which, in the end, focuses on empirical and qualitative methods out of a deep desire to disclose and understand something about the ways in which religious life unfolds in the Nordic region. Indeed, it is through its very focus on establishing a better and fuller understanding of current phenomena and practices (helping us "see the more" of them), that Nordic practical theology has been able to make a significant contribution to the work of practitioners and the life of churches. Nordic practical theology has never been about knowledge for the sake of knowledge but has always aimed to establish informed accounts that facilitate a process of self-examination and learning for practitioners and scholars alike, as the chapters in the *Companion*[46] and *Handbook*[47] demonstrate.

Nordic practical theology thus builds on a desire to contribute to the way in which faith is lived and practised, and it is through close attention to the complexities of the lived that Nordic scholars try to achieve this. Furthermore, we believe that this rootedness in the complexities of the lived will continue to be as important—no matter which research methods we use—as the desire to speak meaningfully to present situations. We agree with Heather and the Theology through Creative Practice trajectory that the "new" research methods are "the real deal" and that practical theology can be enriched by allowing some of the practices which we routinely "other" to trouble our research processes, especially if we keep them anchored in relation to complexities of the lived.[48] In the end, we want to follow Heather in keeping the practical theological space open for different approaches, also in combination: "Practical theologians are urged to draw upon the traditional strengths of their discipline and combine creative new thinking with a recovery of insights from the arts of ministry."[49] Yet, for this to happen, we must engage in the making as well as in the unmaking of methodological habits.

---

[46] *The Wiley Blackwell Companion to Theology and Qualitative Research.*
[47] *International Handbook of Practical Theology.*
[48] Stangeland Kaufman 2023, pp. 670–1.
[49] Walton, "We Have Never Been Theologians", p. 218.

I swallow my pride and my need to be right. After all, I know she only wants to help, even if I sometimes get the feeling that there is a lot of devil in this devil's advocate. "Okay, I just find it difficult to know how much wiggle room there actually is. I understand that I need to demonstrate how I come to my conclusions and thus how this is indeed research and not just an opinion." *I use air quotes when saying "personal opinion" to indicate that I still do not fully agree with the separation.*

There. Now we are getting somewhere. "I understand. Just keep in mind that a dissertation is special in that sense. Hardly ever will your work be scrutinized in this manner and if you want to stay in the academy, you need to jump this hurdle, and that includes showing that you can live up to the expectations people have for your dissertation."

He opens his mouth, trying to argue. We have been here before; better to pre-empt this: "I know that there are different ways of doing research. But you are neither defending your thesis in the UK nor in the US, you are defending it here, in Sweden, and that means you need to accept and show that you understand that there is a particular way of doing practical theology in the Nordic countries." *He closes his mouth, looking bedraggled. Sometimes I wonder how he can go from full-fledged fight mode to apparent resignation so quickly with barely any middle ground.*

I know she is right, and I hate it. Not the fact that she is right as much as the fact that I will have to comply with expectations if I hope to have my dissertation accepted. It just feels unfair. Welcome to my pity party. I swallow again: "So, what are you saying? Do you think I need to give up on the creative non-fiction part?"

"No, you don't. I think that will be a great part, and just having that part in there will somewhat shift the boundary of what is allowed in a dissertation. You can do the whole thing differently; you just need to include sufficient traditional sections to demonstrate that you know the craft.

On 24 May 2024, to the delight of his supervisor, Tone Stangeland Kaufman, Simon Hallonsten successfully defended his PhD dissertation containing a combination of creative and more traditional elements.

9

Tiresias

Pádraig Ó Tuama

Our Lady of Tiresias

What happens when you write it? she asked,
When you place a word after another? Crossing
spaces between letters? Not knowing what comes next?
What happens when you cede control to space between
the hand and page, when language leads, not plans?
When you abandon what you thought you never could
— maps, beliefs, conclusions — what then?
When the plain stretches out in lines that follow lines,
when all you do is give what truth you have to the shape
of sound on paper, and the weather of the questions?
Then, she said, we might arrive at something like
a start. All that's needed, she continued, is your
sustained attention. Patient. Terrified. Impure.

Faithless, unadorned, and sure. Heather Walton was the main supervisor for my PhD, and her guidance was one of attention. What happens when you write this down, she asked often, when you follow the question, and witness what unfolds? She was never impressed with clever repetition. She wanted critique, originality of thought, synthesis of other writers, yes, but much more so, the presence of the person wrestling with their process on the page. I quoted psychoanalysis once, and Heather looked at it, sighed, said it was interesting, yes yes yes, of course, but wasn't it also just a new theory of everything? She wasn't looking for a bigger theory of anything, perhaps just a small exploration of a story of something through the particular body, the particular hand, the particular mind, the particular reading, the particular thought of the one she was guiding. Hélène Cixous, of course, looms large in the style of Heather Walton, but not as mimicry, more as permission. Once, because I wasn't sure if what I'd submitted for a supervision session was enough, I included some new drafts of experimental pieces: poems of eros and yearning. "I like these", Heather said, when we met. I often forget that she had an academic job: her work as a supervisor was like an artist, as in the dark as I was, but more confident in it, trusting of it, and writing her way forward through it and to it.

10

Creative Black theological writing: Explorations in being yourself

Anthony Reddie

Long before I accidentally drifted into this strange identity as an academic theologian, my most ardent ambition was to be a comedy scriptwriter. Most of my twenties, after my undergraduate studies at the University of Birmingham, were spent sending scripts to the BBC. The nearest the world of theology and creative writing came together arose during the considerable amounts of time I spent in the University of Birmingham chaplaincy centre, St Francis Hall. My time in St Francis was largely spent engaging with fellow Methodist students who were a part of the Birmingham University Methodist Society (B.U. Meth. Soc.).

It was while undertaking evangelistic mission activities as a part of the Methodist Society that I began to write "Christian Drama", this being the first tentative attempt to combine creative writing with basic theological utterances. These initial fledgling efforts marked the first forays into bringing theological imagination alongside comedy script writing. These were the formative steps in the journey towards the publication of my books *Acting in Solidarity* (2005) and *Dramatizing Theologies* (2006). The emergence of these two books has its genesis in my student activities. My drama writing first emerged in the summer of 1986. I was a member of the "Birmingham University Methodist Society", which was guided by the Revd Dr Stuart Burgess, the Methodist chaplain assigned to look after the material and spiritual welfare of we Methodist students.¹ While in the B.U. Meth. Soc, the students engaged in a variety of activities and explorations that were to shape the religious consciousness of a whole generation of us. It was a life-changing process for me and for others. It was during my time as an undergraduate in Medieval and Modern History (1984-7) that seeds for the later development of my creative, dramatic theological writing were first planted.

Prior to attending university, I had secretly penned the odd sentence of poetic doggerel or some hopelessly politically and theologically incorrect piece of rhetoric. It was whilst at university, in a wonderfully eclectic and self-consciously clever Meth. Soc., that I discovered my talent for writing, particularly within a dramatic idiom. For someone who had suffered from a debilitating stutter for most of his teenage years, the discovery of another language of communication that did not depend upon oral fluency was, without wishing to sound overly grandiose, most definitely a "God-send".

I still remember the first "dramatic" comedic piece I wrote. It was a short comedy skit entitled *The Calling*.² It was written for an evening service in a local Methodist church in Dudley, in the West Midlands. The service was led by Stephen Plant, the then President of the Meth. Soc. In an interesting, ironic twist, some 30 or so years later from this embryonic event, Stephen and I conceived a major international conference on Karl Barth and James Cone,³ whilst sat in the gardens of his Cambridge college, both of us reflecting on our initial encounter as gauche students in the University of Birmingham in the middle to late 1980s.⁴ Neither us of imagined at that juncture in our lives that we would both go on to become academic theologians. The theme for the service

---

[1] The Revd Dr Stuart Burgess was later to become President of the Methodist Conference, serving for the year 1999-2000.

[2] See Anthony G. Reddie, *Dramatizing Theologies: A Participative Approach to Black God-Talk* (London: Equinox, 2006), pp. 181-90.

[3] For the special issue co-edited by Stephen J. Plant and myself, see *Black Theology: An International Journal* 21:2 (2023).

[4] Stephen J. Plant is currently Dean of Chapel and Runcie Fellow at Trinity Hall, University of Cambridge.

that evening was "being called". I volunteered to write a short comedic sketch that could be used to augment the sermon that would be preached by Stephen Plant (the only one in the group who at the time was an authorized preacher). The event occurred at the start of my second year at the University of Birmingham.

By the time we had reached the summer of 1986, I was ready to attempt something much more ambitious. It was the time of the annual summer term retreat. On occasions such as this one, the group of students belonging to the Meth. Soc. would decamp from our usual surroundings of Selly Oak Methodist Church in Birmingham and descend upon a Methodist church in the surrounding area. We would sleep in sleeping bags on church floors and spend time in reflection and worship. It was on one such occasion that I discovered through heated debate that the whole world did not share my formative conservative evangelical theology. In fact, there were numerous ways in which one could understand the person of Jesus, interpret the Bible, make sense of the resurrection or work out one's notion of what it meant to be saved. Names such as Schleiermacher and Tillich became a part of my vocabulary. At that time, the attempts of my peers who were studying theology at the university to help me understand the claims of these two theologians did not bear much fruit. I remained wedded to the quasi-biblical literalism that carried all the answers to every perceived question one could imagine.

I do not remember the theme for the retreat. In fact, I remember very little of that weekend, save for one artefact that has stood the test of time, and that is the short piece of drama I wrote for that event. The comedic sketch I wrote for the retreat was my first and perhaps the most enduring piece of theological dramatic writing I have ever written. The piece I wrote was entitled *My God?!* I will reflect on this pivotal theological piece shortly, because in many ways, it has been emblematic of this phase of my scholarly career, as I sought to combine my youthful passion for comedy writing with an emerging love for academic theological reflection.

At the time in which I was beginning to cut my teeth as a writer of Christian drama, I was not aware of the long hinterland of practice and thought that had determined this form of practical theological engagement in the church and wider society in Britain. I was soon to learn that my own tentative forays into Christian dramatic writing were neither new nor necessarily original.

My historic development in Christian dramatic writing

As Burbridge and Watts rightly note, one of the most significant developments in the role and the utility of drama within Christian liturgical and pedagogical practices arose within the context of the traditional mass during the Middle Ages. O. B. Hardison Jr. feels that the inherent embodied re-enactment of Christ's presence at the mass provided a natural setting for the development of drama within the context of the liturgical life of the church.[5] Hardison believed that a number of significant developments regarding the relationship between the role of the priest within the mass and the ecclesial dramatic intent inherent within this sacred rite arose in France around 850 CE.[6] Reflecting upon this period, and the role of the mass as a repository for the development of drama within the church, Hardison writes that

> without exception they present the mass as an elaborate drama with a definite role assigned to the participants and a plot whose ultimate significance is nothing less than a renewal of the whole plan of redemption through the re-creation of the life, death and resurrection of Christ.[7]

It is interesting to note that Hardison does not make any clear distinction between the utility of drama within the context of worship and the role of drama as a pedagogical device. In more recent times, there has been an ongoing discussion of the relationship between worship and learning. Frequently it has appeared that there is a fundamental divide between Christian educators, whose primary concerns are those associated with

---

[5] O. B. Hardison Jr., *Christian Rite and Christian Drama in the Middle Ages* (Baltimore, MD: Johns Hopkins University Press, 1865), pp. 35–79.

[6] Hardison Jr., *Christian Rite and Christian Drama in the Middle Ages*, p. 39.

[7] Hardison Jr., *Christian Rite and Christian Drama in the Middle Ages*, p. 39.

the process of teaching and learning, and the liturgists, who would want to detach any educational function from the role of worship in the life of the church.[8]

This dichotomy has been challenged by a number of North American scholars who have argued that we need to see worship and education as being more intimately linked. Debra Dean Murphy, for example, argues that the unhelpful dualisms between heart and head, intellect and emotions propounded by the Greeks have led us to separate educational function (*didache*) from the process of worship (*leitourgia*). This dichotomy often serves as one of the intellectual bases for the separation of learning from worship. It can be overcome, she argues, if we see these differing facets of the church's life as being more intimately linked.[9] Robert K. Martin's perspective on the relationship between worship and education is, in many respects, even more radical than Murphy's, for he argues that not only should these differing aspects of the church's mission be brought together, but we should conceive them as an inter-related and inter-penetrating dance.[10]

The medieval mystery play

Whilst the role of drama within the sacred mass was often implicit and incidental to the overall rationale and purpose of this liturgical re-enactment, its primacy and educational importance become visible and intentional within the mystery plays of the later Middle Ages. It is beyond the scope of this chapter to mount an exhaustive investigation into the development, role and importance of the medieval mystery play

---

[8] For a brief discussion of this, see Anthony Reddie, "Bearing Witness to the Light", *Roots Worship: Worship and Learning for the Whole Church* 5 (May/June 2003), pp. 2–3.

[9] Debra Dean Murphy, "Worship as Catechesis: Knowledge, Desire and Christian Formation", *Theology Today* 58:3 (2001), pp. 321–32.

[10] Robert K. Martin, "Education and the Liturgical Life of the Church", *Religious Education* 98:1 (2003), pp. 43–64.

and its influence on the role of drama in the church, but some brief comments are necessary.

Rosemary Woolf, a scholar of medieval literature, argues that there is a complex relationship between liturgical drama and the medieval mystery plays. She cautions against the assumption that there is an axiomatic link between the former and the latter.[11] According to Woolf, the origins of the medieval mystery play, which can be dated to around the fourteenth century, were multifarious in form and were conceived partly as an expression of liturgical embellishment and as a "propagandist concern to instruct the laity".[12]

Woolf charts the development of the mystery play from a loose set of liturgical fragments (of the tenth century) to a more stylized and systematized structure whose collective elements might be seen as resembling a play.[13] Woolf describes some of the key features of the medieval mystery play, such as the difference between these models of Christian drama and the more recognizable passion or nativity plays. The latter two forms share a common focus upon one central, consistent, narrative theme, rather than the more disparate and eclectic structure of the mystery play.[14] The medieval mystery plays address major theological themes such as the incarnation, Christ's ministry, the passion and eschatology.[15]

Many scholars have understood the mystery play as a top-down controlling device to ensure doctrinal compliance and to provide harmless, non-licentious entertainment for the hard-working and ill-educated laity. Woolf, again, states that mystery plays offered some escape for the poor and were viewed by religious authorities as more efficacious "than the frivolous pastimes with which they would otherwise occupy themselves".[16]

---

[11] Rosemary Woolf, *The English Mystery Plays* (London: Routledge and Kegan Paul, 1972), p. 3.
[12] Woolf, *The English Mystery Plays*, p. 4.
[13] Woolf, *The English Mystery Plays*, pp. 25–54.
[14] Woolf, *The English Mystery Plays*, p. 55.
[15] Woolf, *The English Mystery Plays*, pp. 105–269.
[16] Woolf, *The English Mystery Plays*, p. 55.

A counterargument concerning the role and the relationship of mystery plays and religious drama with the poor has been propounded by Claire Sponsler.[17] Sponsler argues that through elaborate ritual of dress, roleplay and covert action within the overarching framework of the religious drama, poor people were able often to subvert the conventional quasi-authoritarian constraints of the medieval church.[18]

The historic developments in Christian drama were largely beyond my burgeoning consciousness as a comedic writer, notwithstanding my studies in Church History. It was later, when undertaking research to support the development of both books, I realized that my interest in bringing practical or what one might term "performative" theology and drama together in the guise of Christian drama was indeed a long and generative tradition. Realizing that my youthful literary escapades were part of a longer tradition was hugely significant to my emotional and psychological development as a writer.

A way of becoming a theologian?

The significance of Christian drama in my intellectual development lies in the link it established between my existing self, a young, conservative evangelical Christian, and my later exposure to Black and other theologies of liberation. As I sat alongside my Meth. Soc. friends studying academic theology at undergraduate level, I was privy to some of the existential challenges facing several of them as they came face to face with modern academic theology. I found their comments and reflections fascinating but had no access to them as a history undergraduate. In conversations on modern theology, doctrine and biblical hermeneutics that occurred during many Meth. Soc. and Student Christian Movement (SCM) meetings and retreats, I began to construct my own tentative and

---

[17] Claire Sponsler, *Drama and Resistance: Bodies, Goods and Theatricality in Late Medieval England* (Minneapolis, MN: University of Minneapolis Press, 1977).

[18] Sponsler, *Drama and Resistance*, pp. 75–103.

developing faith through my Christian drama, which began to help shape the new perspectives I held on God.

I have never studied theology in the conventional sense. I take it as some pride to be able to assert that I have never been a conventional theologian—whatever or whoever that might be. My first degree was in history and my subsequent Ph.D. was in education. The latter was concerned with critical and theological reflection on Christian formation and the discipleship of Black children and young people by means of a practical and practised approach to Black liberation theology. My training, so to speak, came from within a church-sponsored research project. My early scholarly work was very much located within the area of Christian education as an expression of practical theology. This development into practical theology by means of creative writing is an essential connection that links Heather Walton and our shared commitment to autoethnographic and reflexive forms of theological reflection. Exploring my creative outlets as a writer of comedic Christian drama has enabled me to develop my own specific identity as a Black liberation theologian. Given that I have not been trained in the traditional mode of a theologian and that I was never going to cut it as a "proper" systematic theologian, creative comedy writing became an entrée into the enticing world of academic theology. It became the means by which I became and found myself, essentially finding my unique way of becoming an academic Black theologian.

Developing a participative form of Black theology

The God that underpins Black theology is the one who is largely understood in terms of God's revelation in "Jesus Christ" in light of the historical and contemporary reality of being "Black". Black theology is a theology of liberation. Its existence is solely focused on applying the freeing power of the gospel to the existential struggles of Black people to find their freedom in the stultifying world of white supremacy.

Participative Black theology is the creative nexus between "traditional" Black theology and Christian education. This approach to critical pedagogy has been refined over the years and has developed into an interdisciplinary mode of practical, Black theological reflection. At the heart of my participative Black theology is the use of exercises and games that seek to enable participants to reflect critically on self, and through the enaction of a central activity, enable them to explore aspects of the theory and practice of Black theology in dialogue with others.

Talking with and learning from ordinary people is an important dimension of participative Black theology because it seeks to enable this discipline to have greater synergy with the lived religious experience of those at the grassroots of society. Whilst this synergy has been developed by the likes of Ernesto Cardenal, who pioneered ways of undertaking Latin American liberation theology via poetry, and in the work of the feminist theologian Nicola Slee, whose poetic work provides an alternative means by which feminist theology is expressed in the UK, Black theology has had very little that is comparable.

James Cone's final memoir, written whilst he was dying and published posthumously,[19] outlines the reasons why his foundational version of Black theology was so wedded to white Euro-American systematic theology, as a means of ensuring the legitimacy of the discipline. While I understand the reasons for this intellectual move, it does mean that Black theology, although committed to those on the margins who are oppressed, has not been able to engage in a more intentional and formative way with ordinary people. My work has been a committed attempt to engage directly with ordinary people. In order to establish a means of creating a more participative model of Black theology, it was necessary to find an underlying epistemological framework that would support this work. Paulo Freire's groundbreaking work in critical pedagogy became the means by which I was able to theorize underlying developments in participative Black theology.

Freire's work in devising appropriate pedagogies for teaching marginalized and oppressed peoples is legendary.[20] He developed a philosophy of education that challenged poor and oppressed people to

---

[19] James H. Cone, *Said I Wasn't Gonna Tell Nobody* (Maryknoll, NY: Orbis, 2018).

[20] See, Paulo Freire, *Pedagogy of the Oppressed* (New York: Herder & Herder, 1970). Also, *Education for Critical Consciousness* (New York: Continuum,

reflect upon their individual and corporate experiences and begin to ask critical questions about the nature of their existence. The radical nature of this critical approach to the task of teaching and learning brought Freire to the attention of the military government in Brazil in 1964. He was subsequently imprisoned and then exiled. In exile, he began to refine further his educational philosophy and method.

He came to international attention with the publication of his first book *Pedagogy of the Oppressed*,[21] which laid the foundations for a seismic shift in the whole conception of how poor, oppressed and marginalized people might be educated. The importance of Paulo Freire cannot be overstated. In developing a rigorous and critical approach to the task of educating those who are poor and oppressed, Freire created an essential template by means of which religious educators and practical theologians could re-conceptualize their task. One of Freire's central concepts was that of "conscientization". This is a process where poor and oppressed people become politically aware of the circumstances in which they live and the ways in which their humanity is infringed upon and blighted by the often dehumanizing contexts that surround them.[22] Allen J. Moore, commenting on this aspect of Freire's work, says:

> Conscientization in Freire's work is apparently both an individual experience and a shared experience of a people who are acting together in history. A way of life is not determined from thinking about the world but is formed from the shared praxis. In this critical approach to the world, basic attitudes, values, and beliefs are formed and a people are humanized or liberated. Conscientization, therefore, leads to a life lived with consciousness of history, a life lived that denounces and

---

1990), and *A Pedagogy of Hope: Reliving Pedagogy of the Oppressed* (New York: Continuum, 1992).

[21] Written in Portuguese in 1967/8, it was published in Spanish in 1968, English in 1970, and Portuguese in 1972.

[22] Freire, *Education for Critical Consciousness*, pp. 18–20.

transforms this history in order to form a new way of life for those who are oppressed.[23]

Freire's approach to education has opened up new vistas for religious educators, along with pastoral and practical theologians. Freire's work, with its emphasis on human transformation and self-actualization, has become a template by which various models of critical pedagogy, be they liberation theologies, liberative models of psychology or transformative education, have sought to develop differing perspectives on the task of socio-cultural and political development. In my scholarship, I have attempted to combine the radical intent of transformative education arising from the Freirean tradition with Black liberation theology in order to develop a more participative and interactive mode of theo-pedagogical engagement that moves intellectual discourse beyond mere theorizing into more praxis-based forms.

Reflections on the two books

Acting in Solidarity (2005)

Having discovered drama and dialogue as an important means of enabling Black and other marginalized people to reflect upon matters of faith, I wrote *Acting in Solidarity* as an attempt to catalogue some of the more successful and effective pieces of dramatic Christian writing I had created over the previous few years.[24] The aim was to present these pieces in a form that would assist in enabling individuals to reflect critically upon their experiences and faith, in order to become more autonomous believers, less inclined to be swayed by the blandishment of those considered their social betters.

---

[23] Allen J. Moore, "A Social Theory of Religious Education", in Allen J. Moore (ed.) *Religious Education as Social Transformation* (Birmingham, AL: Religious Education Press, 1989).

[24] Anthony G. Reddie, *Acting in Solidarity: Reflections in Critical Christianity* (London: Darton, Longman & Todd, 2005).

My aim was not to create some abstract theory that did not relate to the concrete needs of marginalized and oppressed peoples. Rather than by beginning with theory, I wanted to develop a more reciprocal relationship between practice and theory, in order to develop practical resources for critical, radical thinking so that Black theology could come to life and speak authentically to the experiences of those whose inalienable, God-given right to be free is always under threat from oppressive forces. This method for undertaking Black theology, by means of interactive dramatic Christian sketches, which involves action and reflection, arose as I attempted to combine my love for comedic script writing and Black theology. The book was largely unsuccessful in commercial terms because it failed to find a market. It was considered too transgressive and challenging for many ordinary readers, perceived as non-trained theologians. Rather than offering neatly sewn-up solutions to what can be, and often are, seemingly insoluble theological problems, the book provided critical questions and resources for further thinking. Conversely, the book failed to find a place within many academic theological library shelves because it was perceived as being too popular or not theoretically rigorous enough to warrant acceptance in the theological canon of academic theology. This non-acceptance was particularly galling given that the book had been written in order to assist ministers and lay leaders to find creative ways of doing theological reflection with ordinary people in churches.

One of the aims at the time was to find a means of tapping into the emerging field of "Ordinary Theology" as developed by Jeff Astley at Durham University.[25] Like the developments in "Ordinary Theology", the work in *Acting in Solidarity* sought to enable ordinary people to reflect on their everyday lived experiences, finding space in which to tell stories and to express important formative narratives that connote meaning and identity, using my written drama as a means of doing so. The dramatic pieces I had created were written over several years and were chosen as examples that might more practically relate to the lived experiences of

---

[25] See Jeff Astley, *Ordinary Theology: Looking, Listening and Learning in Theology* (London: Routledge, 2002).

ordinary people in churches across the UK, but especially, more multi-ethnic locations in inner city conurbations in England.

The book is divided into four sections: "Biblical Retelling", "Pastoral Care and Ministry", "Racial, Justice/Black Theology", and "Ethics/Action". *Acting in Solidarity* was intended as a humorous and interactive exercise in critical Christianity. The various pieces were small, unresolved case studies in aspects of Christian theology and practice that might be seen as problematic or challenging for many people, particularly those who might describe themselves as marginalized, whether on the grounds of "race", gender, poverty, sexuality or geography. They are, in effect, discussion or conversation starters, and not densely thought through theological treatises. The various pieces in *Acting in Solidarity* are an interactive means of "kick-starting" a process of theological exploration for individuals and groups of all ages, cultures, communities and contexts.

Dramatizing Theologies (2006)
Dramatizing Theologies was the follow up to *Acting in Solidarity*.[26] This text represented a more theoretical and scholarly exploration of the role of drama as a means of undertaking participative Black theology. Its moderately greater success than its predecessor may be due to two linked factors. First, the book did find a market. For a number of years, I am informed that a number of institutions that teach the Professional Doctorate used this text as a means of exploring methodological issues in practical theology. Second, the book contains more recently written, better quality comedic writing than that found in the previous text. Admittedly, this is subjective judgement, but sketches like *My God?!* have endured far longer than the material found in *Acting in Solidarity*. The premise of the book was to create a more explicit rendering of the ideas and rationale for creating a participative model of Black theology. This text was the first detailed, worked example of participative Black theology in action. Whereas *Acting in Solidarity* contained 15 dramatic pieces and was essentially, a practical book, with "some theory", *Dramatizing Theologies* had only five sketches, but these were accompanied by a great

---

[26] Anthony G. Reddie, *Dramatizing Theologies: A Participative Approach to Black God-Talk* (London: Equinox, 2006).

deal more theoretical reflection on the nature of drama as a means of undertaking theological reflection in general, and Black theology in particular.

At the heart of the book is a short comedic sketch entitled *My God?!* This drama, unlike much that was written in those early days, has endured.[27] I have used this piece, for example, when seeking to introduce the idea of Black theology to theological students new to the subject. The sketch is used in order to demonstrate the ways in which white hegemony has long constructed a notion of God that is synonymous with their own pretensions to power, through the prism of slavery and colonialism: namely, a God who is like the people who claim to worship God. In other words, this is a God who is white and male and becomes the template for the justification of white supremacy across the world, especially when that theo-ethical power is juxtaposed with Black subjugation and suffering.[28] The premise of *My God?!* is the relationship between who God is in Godself and the ways in which human beings project their underlying ideologies and perspectives of truth onto this generative figure we call "God".

The central conceit of *My God?!* is the interaction between four men, all of whom are broadly conceived as archetypes (a cis white male, possibly evangelical; a cis white man who is possibly a High Church Catholic; a Black Muslim; and a young agnostic/atheistic student). Each character is confronted by the God whom they have not conceived of in their imaginations, namely a Black woman. The drama that unfolds over some five pages draws the four male characters into direct conflict with what is to their minds an illegitimate and erroneous conception of God. In one telling encounter, the God character says to one of the men,

---

[27] Reddie, *Dramatizing Theologies*, pp. 65–70.
[28] This hermeneutical framework is the overarching one that has dictated the very rationale for the existence of Black Theology and Womanist Theology. Arguably the greatest single book that details this form of existential foreclosure on the relationship between white ideological reframing and the nature of God as it relates to Black subservience is James H. Cone's magisterial *God of the Oppressed* (Maryknoll, NY: Orbis, 1997).

"And where does it say that God is a man?" The man replies, "Well, it is severely implied and that is good enough for me."

Clearly, given Heather Walton's prominence as one of our leading feminist practical theologians, I am in no doubt that the dynamics of this encounter is one she will have encountered and commented upon in her own scholarship and teaching. Although the claims of *Dramatizing Theologies* extend well beyond this one sketch, the importance of this text lies in the fact that it was written when I was 21 years old. *My God?!* is in some respects a microcosm not only of the book, but also of the notion of a participative approach to Black theology. It is certainly the most used of all the dramatic pieces that I wrote in that period—approximately 1985-2005.[29] In conceptualizing God as a Black woman, the sketch has been used on many occasions as an introduction to "Womanist Theology" and the significance of reflecting on God and God's nature and agency in light of Black existential experience of hardship and struggle, especially as it applies to Black women. Embedding liberationist theological ideas within a creative milieu is a theological approach for which I owe a great debt to the work of feminist theologians such as Heather Walton and Nicola Slee.[30] Walton's attention to the constructive role creative writing can play as a conduit for undertaking radical, liberationist theological reflection has been enormously influential in my own work. Of particular import is Walton's exploration of how creative writing in the form of journalling can be a means of narrating one's inner life and its concomitant religious and spiritual subjectivities.[31] While my use of Christian drama as a means of undertaking Black theology predates my engagement with Walton's formal academic work, her significance lies in the permission it offered me as I sought to refine this particular mode of liberative theologizing in my later works, after *Dramatizing Theologies*.

---

[29] See Reddie, *Dramatizing Theologies*, pp. 91-9.

[30] See Heather Walton, *Literature, Theology and Feminism* (Manchester: Manchester University Press, 2007); Nicola Slee, *Fragments for Fractured Times: What Feminist Practical Theology Brings to the Table* (London: SCM Press, 2020).

[31] See Heather Walton, *Not Eden: Spiritual Life Writing for this World* (London: SCM Press, 2015).

A relatively rare species—Lay Methodist theologians

Perhaps the most intriguing connection between Heather Walton and me lies in our so far unexplored identity as lay Methodist academic theologians. British Methodism, with its emphasis on social activism and praxis, has never been a site for producing a plethora of academic theologians in the UK. In addition, the theologians that have become most prominent have often been ordained, which is an interesting anomaly for a denomination that has often seen itself as one that has a high regard for lay leadership. I would state quite confidently that Heather Walton is one of British Methodism's most distinguished lay theologians, alongside the likes of Tom Greggs, Morna Hooker, Clive Marsh, Judith Lieu, Esther Reed and David Clough. And yet I suspect that not many within the current leadership of the church will be aware of the Methodist identity of this leading member of the British and Irish Association for Practical Theology (BIAPT) and former distinguished President of the International Academy of Practical Theology (IAPT). Heather Walton should be a revered name on the lips of all Methodists, as a leading feminist theologian and a pioneer in democratizing how theological reflection is undertaken using resources of writing and reflection that are open to all people, especially ordinary women.

I first became aware of Heather Walton through her 1985 publication *A Tree God Planted: Black People in British Methodism*. This landmark publication was a large qualitative research project exploring the lived experience of Black people of the Windrush Generation in British Methodism. The title refers to a quotation from one of the participants who states that Black people are like a tree that God has planted to bear fruit, and they will not be removed from the space and place in which God has placed them. This book was for many years the definitive rendering of Black people's experience within British Methodism. When I commenced my doctoral studies in 1995, *A Tree God Planted* was mandatory reading.

It is tempting to re-read Heather Walton's vast and impressive canon seeking to detect the benign influence of Methodism across the multifarious ideas and themes that punctuate her work. I suspect that like me, Walton is more liberationist than Methodist, not that these two entities are mutually exclusive, of course. What I mean to suggest is that from my reading of her work I have not detected a huge number of references to Methodism or formalized reflections on the ways in which being a Methodist has been instructive in her formation as a formidable and highly successful academic. In that regard, I would probably say that I was more of a Methodist theologian than Heather Walton, given the ways in which my narrative-based approach to theology has incorporated aspects of my familial religious upbringing. To be clear, this is not to suggest that there has not been any influence of Methodism in her work. In the final analysis, this is a question best answered by Heather herself than by speculation on my part.

This final section has been included because it remains the most ambiguous and even tenuous of all the many connections that exist between Heather and me. And yet, it is this Methodist connection that first brought her to my attention when she authored *A Tree God Planted*, and we first met when she was a tutor in Oxford at the then Methodist run and owned Westminster College.

I have a plethora of reasons for which to give thanks to Heather Walton and her towering scholarship. In our mutual love of utilizing creative writing as a means of undertaking liberative forms of theological reflection, Heather Walton has been for me an important interlocutor. Her work has inspired me and will continue to inspire others for many years to come.

1 1

Life in the liminal:
The ecotonal theology of Heather Walton

L. Callid Keefe-Perry

Heather Walton has consistently engaged with themes of liminality and emergence throughout her career. Her work explores the transformative potential of spaces and practices that exist on the margins of theological discourse, often operating within what can be termed "ecotonal" zones. These are transitional areas where different modes of inquiry and interpretation converge, leading to innovative theological reflection that is equal parts productive and provocative. Walton's turn to "theopoetics" and "theology through creative practice" especially emphasizes the importance of these liminal spaces in fostering new forms of theological understanding and expression. This chapter offers a comprehensive examination of how Walton employs the motif of liminality to reshape practical theology, focusing on her engagement with marginalized voices, creative practices and interdisciplinary dialogue.

The concept of an *ecotone*, borrowed from ecology, refers to a transitional zone between two distinct biological communities, where they meet and integrate.[1] Consider the ecotone between a salt marsh

---

[1] I'm grateful to my wife, Kristina Keefe-Perry, for this metaphor. Before she was a minister and pastor, she was an academic in the field of geography. My source for additional information about this is Marjorie Holland, Paul G. Risser and Robert J. Naiman (eds), *Ecotones: The Role of Landscape Boundaries in the Management and Restoration of Changing Environments* (New York: Chapman & Hall, 1991).

and an upland forest. In this transitional zone, you might find plant species that are adapted to both the wet, salty conditions of the marsh and the drier, shaded environment of the forest. These species might exhibit unique growth patterns or reproductive strategies that allow them to thrive in the ecotonal environment. Similarly, animals that inhabit this ecotone might have specialized feeding behaviours or habitat preferences that allow them to take advantage of the resources available in both the marsh and the forest. The ecotone, therefore, becomes a site of increased biodiversity and ecological novelty, as species from different communities interact and adapt in response to the unique conditions of the transitional zone.

Walton's scholarship operates in the ecotonal spaces between traditional theological discourse and creative practice, giving rise to new ways of understanding what constitutes theological knowledge. Like the salt marsh–forest ecotone, Walton's work inhabits a transitional zone where different disciplines and ways of knowing converge, such as theology, literature, poetry, visual art and embodied experience. In this ecotonal space, Walton engages in a creative and generative dialogue between these different fields, allowing them to interact and inform one another in unique and transformative ways. Her work challenges the boundaries of what counts as "theology" by drawing on the insights and practices of other disciplines, opening up fertile ground for theological reflection that is attuned to the complexities of human life.

This chapter traces the development of Walton's ecotonal theology across three key phases of her career. First, I examine how Walton's early writings laid the groundwork for her distinctive approach by exploring the transformative potential of liminal spaces and experiences. From her initial reflections on race, class and gender in theological research to her groundbreaking work on desire and embodiment, Walton consistently sought to unsettle dominant paradigms and attend to the generative power of marginality. Next, Walton's middle-period works deepen her engagement with embodied experience, particularly women's experiences. Through exploring eroticism, maternal ambivalence and testimony, she expands theological "in-betweenness" to include political and aesthetic dimensions. Finally, I consider Walton's more recent writings on theopoetics and theology through creative practice, which represent the culmination of her ecotonal approach. By advocating for a mode of theological reflection that embraces ambiguity, multiplicity and the generative power of artistic expression, Walton offers a compelling vision for the future of practical theology. She calls us to become "poets of the broken form", dwelling in the liminal spaces where new possibilities for understanding and transformation might emerge.

Throughout this analysis, I argue that the concept of the ecotone provides an illuminating framework for understanding the nature and significance of Walton's contributions to practical theology. Like the transitional zones between distinct ecological communities, Walton's work thrives in the spaces between established disciplines, discourses and practices. By inhabiting these "in-between" spaces, she generates new insights and adaptations that challenge and enrich practical theological reflection. In our current context of ecological, social and spiritual upheaval, her ecotonal vision offers vital resources for re-imagining the role of theology in a world in need of creative transformation.

Liminality and emergence in Walton's early work

Just as ecotones in nature foster biodiversity and adaptation, there are theological "in-between" spaces that invite an evolution of traditional narratives and a richer, more embodied understanding of desire and spiritual experience. Walton's commitment to inhabiting spaces of tension and discomfort is evident from the very beginning of her academic career. Her earliest published works, *A Tree God Planted: Black People in British Methodism*[2] in 1985 and *White Researchers and Racism*[3] in 1986, both demonstrated a willingness to grapple with complex ethical and methodological issues in theological research.

In *White Researchers and Racism*, Walton arrives at the position that white researchers should not, despite good intentions, interview

---

[2] Heather Walton, *A Tree God Planted: Black People in British Methodism* (London: Methodist Publishing House, 1985).

[3] Heather Walton, *White Researchers and Racism* (Manchester: Faculty of Economic and Social Studies, University of Manchester, 1986).

Black people due to the myriad pitfalls inherent in such cross-racial research. She frankly acknowledges the limitations of her own research experiences, stating that she wrote "as a white person about the impact that black people were making upon a white institution rather than being able to transcend the barriers of racial identity and examine a 'multiracial situation' as I had hoped".[4] This early work reveals several key aspects of Walton's approach that would come to characterize her later scholarship.

First, it demonstrates her willingness to critically examine her own positionality and the power dynamics inherent in academic research. Second, it shows her dedication to engaging with marginalized voices and experiences. Third, it highlights Walton's openness to dwelling in spaces of uncertainty and tension, resisting the temptation to offer easy solutions to complex problems.

Moreover, these early works showcase Walton's emerging interest in the intersection of lived experience and theology. By addressing issues such as race relations in the church, community life in working-class neighbourhoods, and personal experiences of illness through a theological lens, Walton began to develop the foundation for what I call her later "ecotonal" approach.

In her 1994 article "Theology of Desire", Walton explores how the Song of Songs functioned as a subversive text that challenged and reshaped the Genesis narrative of the Fall.[5] She argues that the Song of Songs presented a garden that was open and unguarded, in contrast to the closed garden of Eden from which humanity was expelled. The lovers in the Song transgress binary gender divisions and hierarchies, blurring the boundaries between male and female, self and other. Walton suggests that this liminal space of erotic desire and ambiguity offers a powerful alternative to traditional theological interpretations of sin, shame and separation from God. She argues that the Song of Songs subverted conventional notions of sin and redemption through its celebration of erotic love and its blurring of sacred/profane distinctions. The lovers "eat

---

[4] Walton, *White Researchers and Racism*, p. 16.
[5] Heather Walton, "Theology of Desire", *Theology & Sexuality* 1:1 (1994), pp. 31–41.

each other, pass into each other, echo each other", confounding binary oppositions in ways that pointed toward an integration of flesh and spirit, humanity and divinity.[6] For Walton, the Song reveals a divine presence that permeated the material world, a "God as garden, as origin and mother, as fruit to be eaten, as love to be made".[7] This incarnational vision challenges the clear dualisms and hierarchies that have long structured much Christian thought.

Similarly, in her 1999 article "Passion and Pain: Conceiving Theology Out of Infertility", Walton reflects on her own experiences of infertility and how they had shaped her theological perspective.[8] She describes her time in a hospital "for wombs" as a liminal space where the bodily realities of women's lives—miscarriage, abortion, infertility—converged in ways that challenge abstract theological discourse.[9] Reflecting on the space between infertility and a decision to adopt, she later wrote, "There are places of pain our debates have not yet reached into and I am not adequate to bring them to the table. But in the light of them all the other questions I am wrestling with begin to appear shallow and of less consequence."[10] By inhabiting and attending to these liminal spaces of embodied pain and ambivalence, Walton suggests that theology could begin to grapple more authentically with the complexities of human experience. There are many times when sure claims and certainty are not the balm that is sought.

While "Passion and Pain" explored the liminal spaces of women's embodied experiences, Walton's article "Theological Reflections Upon the Style and Spirit of the New Labour Party", published that same year, expanded her critique to the realm of political theology.[11] She argued

---

[6] Walton, "Theology of Desire", p. 34.

[7] Walton, "Theology of Desire", p. 35.

[8] Heather Walton, "Passion and Pain: Conceiving Theology out of Infertility", *Contact* 130:1 (1999), pp. 3–9.

[9] Walton, "Passion and Pain", p. 8.

[10] Heather Walton, *Writing Methods in Theological Reflection* (London: SCM Press, 2014), p. 75.

[11] Heather Walton, "If This Political Party Were a House: Theological Reflections upon the Style and Spirit of New Labour", *Political Theology* 1:1

that Christianity had yet to adequately respond to the "materialism of contemporary life under capitalism", often condemning the pleasures of domestic life and material culture.[12] Drawing on the work of Walter Benjamin, Walton suggested that everyday objects and commodities could function as "transmitters of religious power", mediating spiritual longings and utopian energies.[13] By attending to the aesthetic and imaginative dimensions of material culture, she contended, theology could develop more constructive and transformative engagements with the "concrete realities" of human experience.

In her 2001 article "The Wisdom of Sheba: Constructing Feminist Practical Theology", Walton employs midrash to explore the power relations implicit in male-centred theological thinking.[14] She critiques the ways in which dominant theological traditions have rendered women "the silent objects of superior understanding", obscuring the bodily ambiguities of women's lives.[15] Through the figure of Sheba, Walton envisions a feminine wisdom that stands in contradiction to patriarchal theological conventions. She argues that feminist practical theology must refuse to collude in discourses that present women as "benevolent, nurturing creatures", acknowledging instead the profound ambivalence of women's experiences of fertility, sexuality and motherhood.[16] By attending to the "uneasy, painful relations" in which "powerful emotional force is located", Walton suggests that theology can begin to harness the "destructive energy of women" for the project of political transformation.[17] This liminal, embodied wisdom challenges practical theology to grapple more authentically with the complexities of human experience.

By attending to the "dark and dismal work" of constructing "memorials" to the suffering and resilience of women and other marginalized groups,

---

(1999), pp. 11–18.

[12] Walton, "If This Political Party Were a House", p. 16.
[13] Walton, "If This Political Party Were a House", p. 17.
[14] Heather Walton, "The Wisdom of Sheba: Constructing Feminist Practical Theology", *Contact* 135 (2001), pp. 3–12.
[15] Walton, "The Wisdom of Sheba", p. 3.
[16] Walton, "The Wisdom of Sheba", p. 8.
[17] Walton, "The Wisdom of Sheba", p. 9.

she argues, practical theologians can begin to develop more inclusive and liberative forms of theological practice; ones that "contemplate the horrors we can no longer afford to ignore".[18] In doing so, Walton suggests, practical theology can become a more authentic and transformational discipline, grounded in the concrete realities of human experience and the ongoing struggle for justice and liberation. This ecotonal sensibility, one that embraces the creative tension and heightened diversity of liminal spaces, is central to Walton's vision of a practical theology that can transform both individual and collective consciousness, particularly among those who have been marginalized or oppressed.

Across these early writings, Walton consistently affirmed the transformative potential of liminal spaces—erotic, embodied, material— to reshape theological discourse and practice. By inhabiting the tensions, ambiguities and contradictions of human experience, she suggested, we open ourselves to new possibilities for encountering the sacred and re-imagining our relationship to self, other and world. By attending to what was unspoken, unspeakable or marginalized within dominant theological discourses, she opened up new possibilities for encountering the sacred in the midst of the passion and the pain of human existence.

The evolution of Walton's theology

Walton's middle-period works demonstrate a consistent concern with the theological significance of embodiment, particularly of women's experiences, which she situates within ecotonal zones of theological reflection. These are transitional spaces where the sacred and the profane, the personal and the political, intersect and create opportunities for transformative theological insight. In her 2005 article "Sex in the War: An Aesthetics of Resistance in the Diaries of Etty Hillesum", Walton explores how the erotic functions as a space of freedom and creative resistance amidst the horrors of the Holocaust.[19] Walton argues that for Hillesum,

---

[18] Walton, "The Wisdom of Sheba", p. 10.
[19] Heather Walton, "Sex in the War: An Aesthetics of Resistance in the Diaries of Etty Hillesum", *Theology and Sexuality* 12:1 (2005), pp. 51–61.

sex represented "a contrasting space to the space of war", a "vivid moment which transcends the total warfare in which she lived".[20] By attending to the embodied particularity of erotic experience, Hillesum constructed an "aesthetics of resistance" affirming beauty and intimacy in the face of destruction. Walton suggests that this liminal eroticism, dwelling in the tensions between flesh and spirit, points towards new possibilities for theological meaning-making.

Similarly, aesthetics plays a significant role in her 2007 book, *Literature, Theology and Feminism*.[21] In that volume, Walton deepened her exploration of the intersections between feminist theology and literature, emphasizing the role of poststructuralist theory in re-imagining these connections. Walton's engagement with the works of Julia Kristeva, Luce Irigaray and Hélène Cixous highlights the potential of literature to challenge and expand theological discourse. Walton critiques the conventional feminist theological use of literature, which often assumes a straightforward continuity between women's writing and feminist theological thought. She argues that this approach tends to instrumentalize literature, using it to serve predefined theological agendas rather than allowing the disruptive and transformative power of literary texts to challenge and reshape theological thinking. Walton advocates for a more nuanced and critical engagement with literature, one that recognizes its capacity to disturb and provoke, rather than simply support, feminist theological projects. She wants a deeply fleshy theology that exists in tension rather than one which abstracts and settles all debate:

> I want us to leave home and walk around in the wild places exploring all that can be experienced there. I want us to read more widely, all sorts of books, including those we have previously dismissed as indulgent, difficult or strange.[22]

---

[20] Walton, "Sex in the War", p. 52.
[21] Heather Walton, *Literature, Theology and Feminism* (Manchester: Manchester University Press, 2007).
[22] Walton, *Literature, Theology and Feminism*, p. 169.

By attending to the literary strategies employed by theorists, Walton demonstrates how feminist theology can benefit from a more adventurous and experimental approach to reading and interpreting texts.

Walton stresses the need for feminist theologians to embrace the challenges posed by literature, asserting that "it is a particular weakness of feminist theology that it is reluctant to contemplate irredeemable loss and the complicity of the divine in human tragedy".[23] This recognition of the shadow aspects of existence invites a more profound and honest theological engagement. By embracing the tensions and ambiguities inherent in these "in-between" spaces, Walton's work points towards a more dynamic and responsive form of theological reflection, attuned to the complexities of contemporary life. As Walton suggests, "Applying the insights of deconstruction we will identify the ways in which the binary schema through which meaning is generated can disclose how power functions within theological thinking."[24] Resistance to either–or thinking can yield a more nuanced approach to theological reflection, one that has a greater place for the ambiguities of life.

This emphasis on the theological importance of ambiguity is also evident in Walton's 2010 article "You Have to Say you Cannot Speak: Feminist Reflections upon Public Theology".[25] There she expressed deep reservations about dominant approaches to public theology, which often fail to address "the political ambiguity of the church as bearer of tradition or the equally ambiguous challenges of the way we live now".[26] Drawing on the work of Rebecca Chopp, Walton points towards the need for a "poetics of testimony" in public theology, one that can give voice to silenced suffering and "imagine future possibilities and restore what has been lost".[27] This focus on embodiment and political critique represents a significant deepening of her engagement with liminality.

---

[23] Walton, *Literature, Theology and Feminism*, p. 7.

[24] Walton, *Literature, Theology and Feminism*, p. 19.

[25] Heather Walton, "You Have to Say You Cannot Speak: Feminist Reflections upon Public Theology", *International Journal of Public Theology* 4:1 (2010), pp. 21–36.

[26] Walton, "You Have to Say You Cannot Speak", pp. 25–6.

[27] Walton, "You Have to Say You Cannot Speak", p. 35.

By attending to the ambivalent, transgressive potential of women's bodily experiences, she explores the theological meaning of liminal spaces in more explicit and far-reaching ways. With Walton, the erotic, the maternal, and the abject "in-between" zones become vital sites of revelation and transformation, challenging dominant paradigms and gesturing toward new possibilities, lifting up the need for a public theology that can dwell in the fissures and openings of a fractured social landscape, constructing provisional, contested meanings out of suffering and hope. Attuned to both the joy and terror of transcendence, this expansive liminality marks a significant development in Walton's thought.

Throughout these middle works, Walton presses more deeply into the disruptive and transformative potential of liminal experience. By foregrounding embodiment and sociopolitical location as key hermeneutical lenses, she opens up new avenues for engaging the sacred at the margins and interstices of human life. This persistent probing of threshold spaces—erotic, maternal, political, aesthetic—lays groundwork for Walton's later articulation of theopoetics and "theology through creative practice", while also revealing the growing sophistication and scope of her ecotonal imagination.

Divine bricolage: Walton's theopoetic vision

As we have seen, Walton's middle-period works deepened her engagement with the theological significance of embodied experience and the transformative potential of liminal spaces. This ecotonal sensibility finds its fullest expression in her later work on theopoetics and the relationship between theology and the arts. Throughout her writings on this topic, Walton emphasizes the importance of maintaining a dialogical and mutually informing relationship between these two fields, resisting any attempt to collapse their distinctive contributions into a single, undifferentiated discourse. This approach to theology and the arts, one that honours the unique qualities of each domain while exploring their potential for integration and transformation, is a defining feature of Walton's scholarship.

Ever since Ed Farley's *Theologia: The Fragmentation and Unity of Theological Education*, published in 1983, practical theologians have been wrestling with the ways in which the field's origins have been tied to the desire for academic institutional authority and recognition, sometimes resulting in the replication of systems of unbalanced power dynamics in theological knowledge production. In some cases, this has led to a kind of positivism in which empirical research and quantitative data analysis are held up as the height of theological interdisciplinarity. Walton has long resisted this approach. For example, In her article "Poetics" in *The Wiley Blackwell Companion to Practical Theology*, she argues that poetic modes of expression can serve as a powerful tool for challenging dominant theological discourses.[28] She suggests that that artistic expression can give "voice to the inexpressible without losing a genuine sense of it".[29] By attending to the embodied and affective dimensions of human experience, she suggests, poetics can enable practical theologians to develop more authentic and contextual forms of theological reflection, ones that honour the particularity of individual and communal narratives while also exploring their transformative potential.

I was a doctoral student when *The Wiley Blackwell Companion* was published. My advisor handed me a photocopy of the poetics chapter, telling me she thought I should read it, that Walton—along with Pamela Couture—were the people whose work most resembled what I wanted to contribute to the field. Most compelling about Walton then and now is her willingness to interrogate a system even when it has served her well. That is, even as a career academic she has nonetheless continued to ask if theological education has been living up to the role it might play in the *church*. In particular, Walton has questioned the consequences of theological projects keen on establishing "boundaries, separations, and divides", especially when they are erected between immanence and

---

[28] Heather Walton, "Poetics", in Bonnie J. Miller-McLemore (ed.), *The Wiley Blackwell Companion to Practical Theology* (Hoboken, NJ: Wiley-Blackwell, 2011), pp. 173–82.

[29] Walton, "Poetics", p. 175.

transcendence or the sacred and the secular.³⁰ In this regard, she is quite resonant with the work of Grace Jantzen, whose scholarship and use of the "sensible-transcendent" routinely appears in Walton's footnotes. Where Walton sharpens the critique is as it pertains to the discipline of practical theology in particular.³¹

Walton accepts that immanence and transcendence "can never, in a non-modern, hybrid world, be separated out and purified".³² Instead, she suggests that practical theologians ought to be "the people whose vocation it is to deal with the fact that life is complicated, ambiguous, and impure—and our challenge is to respond to this in faith".³³ However, the disruptive and revelatory nature of these "impure" experiences is too often tamed by means of pressing them into existing theological frameworks:

> When it comes to theology, apparent differences also conceal a greater unity than might be supposed. Although many feminist theologians do eschew doctrinal forms of normativity, a strong conviction concerning the goodness of embodiment prevails among us... It is a positive and generative theological paradigm that holds the commerce of everyday life in high regard. In turn this sustains an impulse to apprehend the lifeworld within a theological perspective and imagine a kind of harmony within it... Feminist practical theology is just as inclined to see daily life through a theological lens as empirical theology... and tends towards a benign understanding of theological practice.³⁴

---

[30] Heather Walton, "We Have Never Been Theologians: Postsecularism and Practical Theology", *Practical Theology* 11:3 (2018), pp. 218–30, at p. 223.

[31] I'm grateful for Wren Radford's book *Lived Experiences and Social Transformations: Poetics, Politics, and Power Relations in Practical Theology* (Leiden: Brill, 2022) on this topic. It is an excellent resource on the topic of the experiential in practical theology and Walton's scholarship features significantly throughout.

[32] Walton, "We Have Never Been Theologians", pp. 223–4.

[33] Walton, "We Have Never Been Theologians", p. 224.

[34] Walton, *Writing Methods*, p. 176.

For Walton, even though they disagree on a number of presuppositions, empirical and feminist practical theologians are inclined to "capaciously receive the insights of lived experience and seek to comprehend them within a higher sacred frame".[35] That is, rather than allowing the complex ambiguity and swirl of daily life to be accepted as polyvalent, there is a tendency to only attend to the things that map well into our pre-assigned categories.

Challenging this tendency to subsume lived experience within abstract theological frameworks, Walton calls on practical theologians to recognize everyday practices as significant praxis in their own right, rather than always seeking to relocate and name such fragments within existing theological paradigms. While resonances and connections can certainly be made, Walton resists the notion that such practices only gain meaning through integration into a "higher sacred frame". Her ecotonal sensibility instead dwells in the tensions, ambiguities and excesses of lived experience that may unsettle established theological categories. By allowing the particularities of embodied life to stand on their own terms, even when they don't neatly align with dominant theological discourses, Walton opens space for fresh insight to emerge from the liminal zones between theory and practice, the sacred and the mundane. As in a thriving ecotone, diversity and difference become generative forces for new growth, rather than problems to be resolved through assimilation into a totalizing framework.

Drawing upon the work of scholars such as Catherine Keller, John Caputo and Richard Kearney, Walton presents theopoetics as a way of engaging with a sacred that embraces ambiguity, multiplicity and the transformative potential of liminal spaces. In her 2017 Presidential Address to the International Academy of Practical Theology, Walton dedicated her talk to advocating for the role of theopoetics in practical theology.[36] There she claimed that theopoetics "commits us to engage with theo-making, across all levels: in the heart of God, in the world all around us as it groans in travail and births in glory, in our political

---

[35] Walton, *Writing Methods*, p. 176.

[36] Heather Walton, "A Theopoetics of Practice: Re-forming in Practical Theology", *International Journal of Practical Theology* 23:1 (2019), pp. 3–23.

and everyday lives".³⁷ She invites other practical theologians into this groaning and birth:

> Rather than an encompassing theory of everything providing the motif for our theopoetics, we would probably better proceed as bricoleurs, makers and remakers. Practical mystics and mystics of practice. Making our poetics out of tragedy and the sweetness of everyday life. Speaking faith and making love out of traditions that are fragmented and yet re-forming. I call upon practical theologians to become poets of the broken form.³⁸

Walton further develops this theopoetic sensibility in her 2019 article "Theopoetics in a Blazing World", where she engages with the writing of Siri Hustvedt to explore the profound ambivalence of human creativity.³⁹ Through Hustvedt's visceral portrayal of a woman artist's struggle for recognition, Walton challenges practical theologians to abandon "hygienic" models of creativity in favour of an approach that acknowledges its birth in "processes of abjection, pollution, rage and violence".⁴⁰ Walton's engagement with Hustvedt pushes practical theology to confront the shadowy aspects of creative making and their implications for theological reflection.

This resistance to collapsing disciplinary boundaries reflects an ecotonal sensibility, one that recognizes the value of diversity and difference in the pursuit of new understanding. While acknowledging the ways in which multiple disciplines and genres can inform and enrich each other, Walton resists any attempt to collapse their distinctive features into a single, undifferentiated mode of expression. Rather, she performs her argument: inhabiting the liminal space between theology and life writing allows each to challenge and transform the other in dynamic and unpredictable ways:

---

[37] Walton, "A Theopoetics of Practice", p. 11.
[38] Walton, "A Theopoetics of Practice", p. 22.
[39] Heather Walton, "Creativity at the Edge of Chaos: Theopoetics in a Blazing World", *Literature and Theology* 33:3 (2019), pp. 336–56.
[40] Walton, "Creativity at the Edge of Chaos", p. 352.

> I have brought you to a place in which you may recognize God and know yourself. This hospital is the same place exactly as the whole universe. When you see this you can smile at the small stories of human freedom and divine judgment which are told for children. They are charms recited to protect against the passion and the pain. There are darker, deeper tales to tell.[41]

This willingness to wait in discomfort not only emerges in her constructive work, but also permeates even her analytic sensibilities.

Walton dwells intellectually in the in-between spaces where different ideas and interpretations meet. This ecotonal approach is particularly evident in her examination of the novelist Marilynne Robinson's work, where she navigates the tension between admiration and irritation, critique and appreciation.[42] For instance, Walton openly acknowledges her discomfort with Robinson's nostalgic longing for a return to rigorous theological scholarship, a sentiment she initially perceives as conservatively magisterial:

> Robinson's work nurtures deep nostalgia. So when she writes and speaks phrases that irritate me such as "I would like to see a revival of real no-nonsense scholarship and the emergence of rigorous theologies," or when she berates the churches for an "uncoerced abandonment" of their former riches of theology and tradition, I tend to rebel against a lurking magisterial conservatism I think I identify here.[43]

Despite this irritation, Walton allows herself to explore the deeper analogical potential in Robinson's perspective, finding a "radical vision" intertwined with the nostalgia.

---

[41] Walton, "Passion and Pain", p. 7.

[42] Heather Walton, "The Children Are Always Lost: Marilynne Robinson and the Poetics of Theology", in Håkan Möller and Ola Sigurdson (eds), *Marilynne Robinson and Theology* (Stockholm: The Royal Swedish Academy of Letters, History and Antiquities, 2021), pp. 29–48.

[43] Walton, "The Children Are Always Lost", p. 45.

This capacity to hold and explore conflicting feelings demonstrates the ecotonal nature of Walton's analysis. She recognizes that alongside Robinson's call for traditional theological rigour lies a dynamic, imaginative approach to doctrine. Walton writes: "But maybe I should listen and read more subtly. Alongside this nostalgia lies a radical vision, one that is linked to the integral poetics I have explored here."[44] By inhabiting the space between critique and appreciation, Walton uncovers the creative potential within Robinson's theological vision, which treats doctrine as a form of "giant and intricate poetry" capable of revealing profound spiritual truths without fixing them into rigid propositions. Walton's analytical moves thus remain deeply ecotonal, blending critique with constructive engagement, and allowing new theological insights to emerge from the interplay of different perspectives.

Walton's ecotonal approach to theological analysis also informs her recent efforts to develop the PhD in Theology Through Creative Practice at the University of Glasgow. Through this program, Walton has been further exploring her position regarding the ways in which the arts can play a more substantial role than just a representation of theological ideas. As Walton puts it, our artistic expression of sacred mystery "isn't simply communication of the mysteries, it is an embodying of them".[45] At the 2023 Symposium for Theology Through Creative Practice, she offered an articulation of her vision of the program as a vital space for re-imagining the sacred in a time of profound cultural and ecological crisis. Walton elaborated on the emergence of "theology through creative practice" by tracing three genealogies that converge in the current moment.

The first genealogy explores the historical tension between theology and poetics, exemplified by Jacques Maritain's contrast between theology's abstract, eternal concerns and poetry's engagement with the contingent and singular. Walton argues that this "productive falsehood" has generated profound insights by facilitating encounters between theological traditions and artistic expressions. "This supposed tension

---

[44] Walton, "The Children Are Always Lost", p. 45.
[45] "Heather Walton on CTI Workshop with Marilynne Robinson," YouTube video, 2:02– 2:12. <https://www.youtube.com/watch?v=BrVzonrCFzo> (accessed 31 October 2024).

between these opposing worlds is of ancient origins and has been very productive in the development of Western thought."[46] The second genealogy situates theology within the broader humanities, tracing the impact of the "cultural turn" of the 1990s and the subsequent "creative turn" of the early 2000s. These developments saw disciplines increasingly incorporating artistic and creative practices to address crucial issues, paving the way for the emergence of arts-based research methodologies. "Research through creative practice infected history, geography, classics. It began to appear everywhere and now, at last, even theology has tested positive", Walton wryly observed.[47]

The third genealogy examines the role of art in contemporary society, particularly in the context of neoliberal economics and the climate crisis. While acknowledging the assimilation of the arts into the "creative economy", Walton insists on their enduring potential for resistance and transformative engagement. "I will make a wager of faith in the continuing ability of creative practices to resist co-option and to continue to voice their challenges."[48] Citing thinkers like the novelist Amitav Ghosh, Walton argued that creative practices are essential for developing new ways of seeing and responding to the urgent crises of our time. "To say that an imaginative failure lies at the heart of the climate crisis is to make a very contestable claim", she acknowledges, referencing the work of Ghosh. "However ... what our priority should be ... is to develop the imaginative capacity to see differently."[49] For Walton, the possibility of this new sight is an opportunity to invite others to this work.

Her genealogies lead the way for other practical theologians to join her in this risky, generative work of "making theology" anew—a task that is not only intellectually compelling but also ethically and

---

[46] Heather Walton, "Opening Comments at the 2023 Symposium for Theology Through Creative Practice", University of Glasgow, 14 May 2023.

[47] Walton, "Opening Comments at the 2023 Symposium for Theology Through Creative Practice".

[48] Walton, "Opening Comments at the 2023 Symposium for Theology Through Creative Practice".

[49] Walton, "Opening Comments at the 2023 Symposium for Theology Through Creative Practice".

existentially urgent in a world on the brink of ecological collapse. At the same time, Walton brings a critical lens to the turn towards theology through creative practice, calling for a "hermeneutics of suspicion concerning the institutional politics that will be in play".[50] She recognizes the labours and challenges involved in carving out a space for creative modes of theological reflection within the academy, from negotiating new assessment criteria to advocating for the scholarly contributions of artistic ways of working. Ultimately, however, Walton's commitment to theology through creative practice is grounded in a deep sense of its necessity and urgency in the face of climate destabilization. For Walton, cultivating new aesthetic modes of theological reflection—ones capable of grappling with grief, loss and the challenges of living "amongst the ruins"—is a vital task for practical theology in this moment.[51]

Attending the 2023 Symposium for Theology Through Creative Practice in Glasgow, I had the opportunity to witness firsthand how Walton's vision has taken root in the lives and work of her doctoral students. The gathering was a vibrant testament to the generative power of her ecotonal approach, as participants seamlessly wove together rigorous theological reflection with a stunning array of creative practices. In one moment, I found myself engaged in a substantive academic conversation about the implications of Walton's genealogies for contemporary practical theology; in the next, I was marvelling at an exhibition of original prints, discussing the fashion industry and listening to moving performances of poetry and experimental music. Novels and films were alongside research papers and funding proposals. The effect was a palpable sense of intellectual and artistic energy, a community of scholar-practitioners fully committed to "making theology" in all its diverse and embodied forms. Far from an abstract set of ideas, Walton's ecotonal vision had become a living reality, shaping a new generation of practical theologians who might be at home in the studio, the library and the streets.

---

[50] Walton, "Opening Comments at the 2023 Symposium for Theology Through Creative Practice".

[51] Walton, "Opening Comments at the 2023 Symposium for Theology Through Creative Practice".

The transformative potential of Walton's ecotonal theology

My hope is that viewing Walton's theological approach through the lens of an ecotone offers insights into both the nature and significance of her work. This ecological metaphor not only illuminates the unique characteristics of Walton's scholarship but also reveals why her contributions are particularly vital in our current theological and cultural landscape.

The concept of an ecotone provides a framework for understanding Walton's distinctive approach to practical theology. Just as ecotones are characterized by increased biodiversity, heightened tension and the emergence of novel adaptations, Walton's work has thrived in the liminal spaces between established theological discourses, disciplines and practices. This ecotonal perspective highlights the interdisciplinary richness of Walton's theology, which integrates insights from literature, feminist theory, poststructuralism and the arts. Like the diverse species that coexist in an ecotone, these varied influences generate novel theological insights that transcend the boundaries of any single field.

Moreover, Walton's work embodies the productive tensions and "edge effects" characteristic of ecotones. Her theology embraces the creative tensions that arise from inhabiting liminal spaces, challenging binary thinking and hierarchical structures within theological discourse. Walton's turn to theopoetics and theology through creative practice exemplifies the emergent quality of ecotones, opening up new possibilities for encountering the sacred in contemporary contexts. Just as ecotones reveal complex relationships between different ecosystems, Walton's interdisciplinary approach forges connections between seemingly disparate realms of human experience and knowledge, such as theology, embodiment, creativity and social justice. Her work offers a holistic vision that resists reductive categorizations and demonstrates the transformative potential of dwelling in these in-between spaces.

In an era of increasing global complexity and rapid change, Walton's work offers a model for engaging with ambiguity and contradiction without resorting to simplistic solutions. As traditional theological paradigms struggle to address contemporary challenges, her ecotonal approach demonstrates how inhabiting liminal spaces can generate creative responses to issues like climate change, social inequality and the erosion of meaning.

Furthermore, the ecotonal metaphor itself resonates with Walton's own deepening ecological awareness, suggesting how theology might learn from and contribute to our understanding of interconnected systems and the value of diversity. This alignment between Walton's methodological approach and broader ecological thinking underscores the timeliness and relevance of her work in addressing the complex challenges of the twenty-first century. As part of the "Hope Against Hope" initiative during the 2021 UN Climate Change Conference in Glasgow, Walton gave a talk that is demonstrative of her broader career:

> Spiritual traditions have sometimes been a source of false comfort contributing to passivity and inertia in addressing the climate crisis. However, we also claim that spiritual resources—our stories, our communities, our rituals, our visions—can become vital resources in the struggle for the planet's future. We seek a hope that is true but does not deny how difficult the days ahead shall be.[52]

While she notes "false comfort" and "passivity and inertia", she is simultaneously unwilling to dismiss spiritual resources entirely. Instead, she envisions their potential transformation, even if what comes ahead will be difficult. This balanced perspective embodies the productive tension characteristic of ecotones, where different elements converge and adapt. Walton's call encapsulates her broader theological approach— one that dwells in ambiguity, embraces complexity and seeks creative responses to contemporary challenges.

As we have seen, Heather Walton's ecotonal theology offers a compelling model for practical theological engagement in our time of profound uncertainty and change. By inhabiting the liminal spaces between disciplines, traditions and lived experiences, her work generates

---

[52] Heather Walton, "Hope Against Hope", YouTube video, <https://www.youtube.com/watch?v=6b65dz3enFE> (accessed 31 October 2024).

new insights and possibilities for transformative practice. Practical theologians today are called to cultivate an ecotonal sensibility in their teaching, research and public witness. This might involve experimenting with new forms of contextual reflection that integrate the arts and humanities, or developing modes of congregational life and social action that thrive in the tensions between different communities and worldviews. It certainly demands a renewed commitment to listening to voices from the margins and learning from the wisdom of those who have long dwelt in the "wild places" of human experience.

While Walton's work provides a rich foundation for this task, it also invites further exploration and development. How might her insights be extended through engagement with other emerging paradigms, such as new materialism or decolonial thought? What are the implications of ecotonal theology for the formation of practical theologians and the transformation of theological education? These are the kinds of questions that Walton's legacy calls us to grapple with. As Walton writes, "I call upon practical theologians to become poets of the broken form." May we have the courage to take up this call, to dwell in the liminal spaces where God's transforming presence is at work, and to risk new ways of "making theology" for the sake of a world in need of healing and hope.

12

It's another day to love you

Pamela Couture

Friday 28 July 2024 had not begun well. Late for an eye injection, my husband Jim, a normally conservative driver, passed a state patrol car going 73 in a 55 zone and got a $200 ticket. I told him, Go to court. You were going to the Mayo Clinic; they will probably reduce it. After the injection, we hurried back to Memorial Hospital in Black River Falls for an MRI on his leg, an appointment he'd missed ten days earlier. When we arrived, the nurse told us the MRI had been cancelled and that his family doctor, Dr Susa, wanted to talk with us. "Yesterday's x-ray shows a likely malignancy in the femur and it must be investigated immediately." In the last month, Jim's leg had been increasingly painful, and in the last week, he'd gone from walking without assistance, to using a cane and then a walker. This morning, he needed a wheelchair. We headed home to wait for follow-up the next week. Early in the evening a storm blew through. About 1:00 a.m., Jim attempted to get out of bed, slid between the bed and the bedroom wall, and pinned his leg at a painful 33-degree angle. He moaned in agony and couldn't move. I called 911 and after ten minutes ran to the end of the driveway to flag down the paramedics who normally arrived in twelve. For the next half hour, I ran back and forth, to check on Jim in the bedroom and to peer through the dark to wave down the paramedics. After 45 minutes, the ambulance arrived: the storm caused their delay. We were at the edge of my greatest fear: Jim could not come home. I could not handle him on my own.

The meditations below narrate our experience of my husband's cancer, de-differentiated chondrosarcoma, the most aggressive form of an already aggressive cancer, through the artwork that surrounded us on our journey. Despite the foreboding on 28 July, Jim's disease progression and death was, overall, not traumatic. It was filled with imagery, irony, humour, hard direct conversations, and much love through prayers, calls, text messages and visits from around the world. Each of these helped us meet each unfortunate transition with a measure of equanimity. The Mayo Clinic, particularly, tries to create a restorative atmosphere through art. Patients, their families and friends, and the hospital staff see it on a regular basis. In addition, one piece of art is on the wall of the meditation room at Memorial Hospital, Black River Falls, Wisconsin, and some are our own.

Orthopedics

River Bottom Mosaic hangs on the wall of the fourth floor at St Mary's Hospital at the Mayo Clinic. The collection of tiles, glass, agates and river rocks leads one's gaze from the external third on each side, set in a flaming orange, depicting the shore and more easily identifiable surface

Figure 1: Zen Series—River Bottom Mosaic by Sheryl Turoila (Brooklyn Park, MN). Handmade ceramic tiles, stained glass, agates and river rocks, 20 x 26.1.5 inches

and active components of the river's edge, toward the cool blue centre where the river flows mysteriously, quietly, calmly in its less disturbed depths.

It captures the experience of crisis that causes a patient and their family to wade into the waters of disease and treatment and the calm that may result when they are fully immersed in it.

The flaming orange experience of crisis began that night. Fear: does this begin the time when I need institutional help to care for my husband, a six-foot, 260-pound, 84-year-old man? Memory loss: Dr Mabry, the orthopaedist who previously replaced Jim's hip and knee on his right side, had discovered the tumour. But who was that orthopaedic oncologist who followed the tumour for 18 months? Time frozen: over that weekend, the staff at Memorial Hospital in Black River Falls worked to control Jim's pain and transfer him to an appropriate service in Rochester, but the Mayo hospitals, St Mary's and Methodist, had no beds. Fear accelerated: Jim needed to get a good diagnosis and treatment plan as fast as possible. Time accelerated: when I finally remembered his orthopaedic oncologist was Dr Rose, I was at home and called Memorial Hospital with the information—by the time I got to the hospital half an hour later, Jim had been admitted to Dr Rose's service with a bed at St Mary's. He was taken by ambulance to Rochester that morning. I attended to my own logistics: could I stay in the room with him? Not on orthopaedics, I was told. I dropped the dogs for boarding, readied the camper, packed my things for who knew how long, drove to Rochester and found the one parking lot where I could park an oversized vehicle. Jim was already undergoing tests and more tests, mostly under the watchful eye of Dr Rose's conscientious resident, Dr JJ.

Late in the day on Tuesday, Dr Rose himself came to Jim's room. He pulled out a chair and sat down for a long conversation. He explained the test findings in detail. The tumour had eaten through the femur. Normally, he would replace the femur, but Jim's former hip replacement allowed no place to attach it. Therefore, Jim required a surgery that would replace his hip, knee and femur. The surgery would be seven to eight hours and could be scheduled for Thursday. He showed us the surgery and the hardware. Oh, no. But how could Jim recover from this? And what kind of fortitude would be required for Jim to withstand the pain of a total hip, knee and femur replacement all at once? Jim struggled with heart and kidney function: Dr Mabry had said his hip replacement should be his last big surgery.

Jim had previously asked Dr JJ whether he could lose his leg; Dr JJ assured him it was unlikely. Now Jim asked Dr Rose about the option that had been his greatest fear: "What about amputation?"

"Funny that you should ask that," Dr Rose replied, "because Dr Mabry raised the same possibility." A simple surgery, easier recovery, and the likelihood of full function with a prosthesis and rehabilitation. Jim had swum us into the blue depths of the river: a viable way forward, a treatment plan, a direction back to the life we were enjoying. Though we continued to discuss the merits of the two options, with the option of amputation, I felt immediate Calm. Centeredness. Determination. Conviction. Even Vocation—a total commitment to direct our lives and our marriage toward a common goal. We had swum to the mystery of the river.

The day of his amputation was his court date for his speeding ticket. I called the clerk of court and explained. I faxed his "not guilty" plea handwritten on a piece of notebook paper from the Mayo Clinic business office to allow the proceedings to move to the district attorney's office.

Rehabilitation

Several months after his rehab, I asked Jim what one word he associated with the rehabilitation floor, Generose 4: "Work," he said. Daily I pushed Jim in his wheelchair to the gym past a series of pictures: a beaver stretches her brown body long across the water, a branch in her mouth. Only its end shows above water, but beneath, a full bough creates drag, pressing against the beaver's progress. Autumn leaves fall in the air and sink in the water, adding urgency to the task of the beaver readying her lodge for winter. The beaver, a loon fishing, a fish sneaking up on a frog on a tall grass—their activities directly correspond with Jim's physical work.

I was taken with this series, but Jim less so. Months after he left Gen 4, we returned to view its artwork. He had marvelled at the Botanical Plate Series. Twelve plates, each with the rough edge of a fan of leaves in relief, each a different design, each painted with contrasting colours,

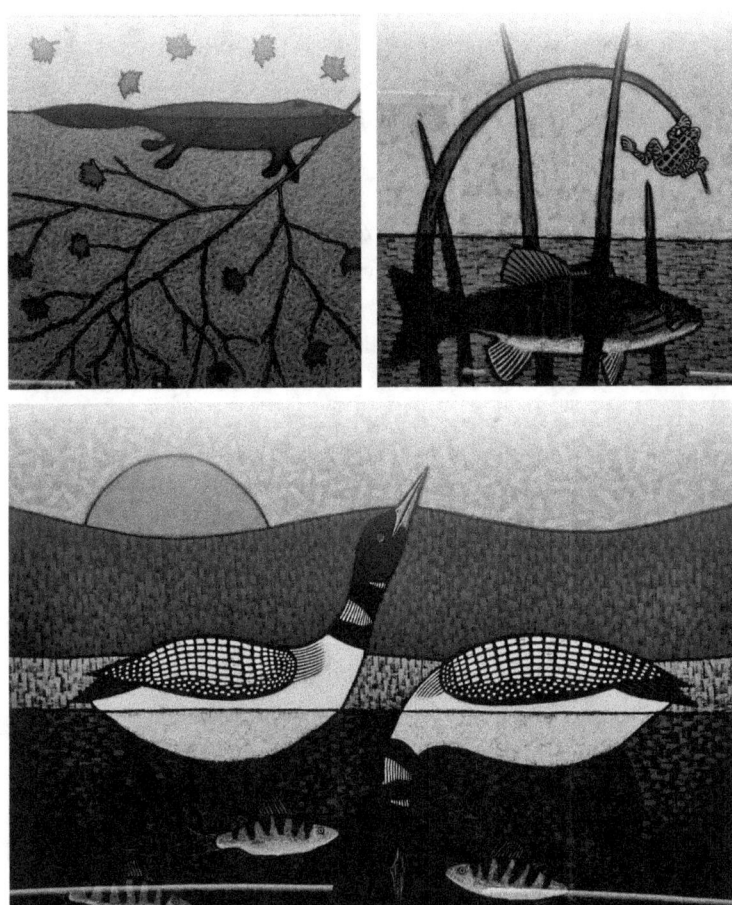

Figure 2: Animals working: Iris, Opeongo Sunset, Seasonal Work by John Ovacik (Chelsea, Quebec). Glicee

represented various flora and their parts. "I was fascinated with them, how intricate they are, how much work is involved."

Jim's rehabilitation began the morning after his conversation with Dr Rose. Dr Andrews from the prosthesis rehab team stopped by to show him a video about life with a prosthetic, discuss the world of artificial limbs, and describe the various forms and places of treatment. Her conversation opened a future for him: by the following summer he should be able to walk across the yard, descend three stairs, and cross the dock to launch his mini-pontoon boat; he should be able to mount the two stairs into our RV; he should be able to learn to drive again and perhaps even play golf. He set a goal: "I'm going to walk by Christmas and dance with my wife at New Year's." He announced he wanted to do intensive rehab at Mayo, where, to qualify, a patient must demonstrate that they have the willpower and physical strength to sustain three hours of occupational and physical therapy a day.

Jim had never been particularly disciplined about athletic activity, but he was determined to strengthen his residual leg, his upper body and his core muscles. His first hospital physical therapist prescribed exercises using pink bands tied to his bed. After the amputation, he stood, with the help of a walker and the physical therapists, on his residual leg. I was poised with the camera on video, cheering him on, announcing how many seconds he stood, each time. Each physical therapy visit he asked, "Do I qualify yet?" The answers were always provisional—"Physical

Figure 3: Botanical Plate Series by Chris Silverston (Muizenberg Capetown, South Africa). Ceramic

therapy in Gen 4 is intense." Four days after his amputation, Dr Smither, the head of rehab, gave us the good news that Jim would be transferred to Gen 4 that day for two weeks of intensive physical therapy. Then Jim would be sent home in time for us to take a long-awaited cruise to Alaska with friends. He would return immediately after the trip, the second week in October, for two weeks of prosthesis training.

At that time, I was following the journey of a graduate school friend whose husband had metastatic cancer. Our future held so much hope for a return to the life we were enjoying! I felt dizzy thinking about the unimaginable unknown involved in facing an advancing cancer like Beka and Len were.

During this time, the day arrived for a conversation with the district attorney about his traffic ticket. "You can pay $200 for speeding and three points on your licence or $260 for a speedometer not working and two points on your licence." I said, "You aren't driving anyway—take the $200." An hour later, he got a call from the district attorney, who dropped the charge, and a week later, a letter. "We determined it is not in the interest of justice to pursue this matter."

Domitilla Internal Medicine

The walls of the internal medical floor in the Domitilla Building communicate stark absence. St Mary's Hospital has a marvellous art collection, but Jim's floor in Domitilla had little art on its wall. It also lacked a family room with coffee, tea, vending machines, a microwave and a place to talk. The nursing staff were overworked—in part because they did for families what on other floors families did for themselves. But the walls of this floor reflected the stark absence in Jim's face for the hours he spent there, septic and unresponsive.

Jim entered rehab with gusto, up on his residual leg, strengthening it in the parallel bars. Two days into his therapy, he became feverish, his blood pressure plummeted, and the rapid response team was called. By the time he was transferred from rehab back to the hospital, he was unresponsive. His eyes were open but vacant, his face lacked personality, he could not respond to instructions or lift his arms. His face looked shrunken, skin against skull. Against the drab background of floor and patient, the senior resident, Dr Farrier, and his team sprang to life, treating symptoms and searching for the cause of the infection that was sapping Jim's life force. Talk to him, listen to music, they advised.

    I sat by his bedside and held his hand. Now I know what he will look like when he is dead. I knew sepsis could kill him. Or worse... that he would not die and would remain in this vegetative state. I named a truth: death is an opportunity. The next morning, both the orthopaedic resident and I thought he could have stroked in the night, and he was sent for brain imaging. A little after 10:00 a.m., when the internal medicine team was rounding, Jim had his Lazarus moment. Absence became presence. His personality filled his face and he came back to life, talking. Over the next day his cognition returned, though he could not remember his ordeal. Some antibiotic was treating some infection... but what was it? The search for explanation continued. I advocated: he needs physical therapy to rebuild his strength. When he was finally transferred back to Gen 4, with the loss of strength caused by sepsis and a week in bed, they estimated three weeks till his release.

    I had begun a regular posting of updates to family and friends on the platform Caring Bridge. When Jim's cognition returned, I read to him all of the well wishes from family and friends. He wept. The next day he had enough strength to dictate his own message:

> Greetings to my loyal friends and family. Jim here. I feel well enough tonight to be able to dictate this message to you and express my profound gratitude for the prayers, thoughts, and many messages of support that you have provided to us. Pamela has just been fabulous in assisting me through this difficult time. I can't thank her enough. She is dedicated, loyal, loving, and has performed many tasks. The doctors have welcomed me back to the rehab unit and shared with me that they will be working with me very hard to get me back on the road to full recovery. I'm encouraged that we've been asked to select a local company to provide the prosthetic and to work with me through the training. That's gonna take a while but that's OK. It's something to look forward to. The people at the Mayo Clinic have been simply

outstanding. I have been provided with care beyond my ability to be able to describe it. It brought me back from a very dark and difficult place to where I am strong and confident and enabled me to face rebuilding. It's a huge task in front of me for the next two to three weeks. It's a huge development and one that has me extremely elated about its implications. I wish I could speed up the timetable but that's not possible. However, I can promise you that I will do everything possible to gain the strength that I need and the skills to face a new reality. My grandson Alex suggested that I take up hopscotch as a hobby once I'm out of hospital. I thought that was a very insightful suggestion. I'll be here at Mayo Clinic for another two, maybe three weeks maximum. Then we will be home for our trip to Alaska and then back here for two weeks of intensive work, getting the prosthetic fitted and getting the workout. My objective is by Christmas to be walking without having to use a cane or walker and be able to dance with my wife at New Year's. I don't know when I will see all of you again but when I do, I will do all I can to express my deep gratitude for your love and support. It's really overwhelming and it has sustained me for three days of lying in a hospital bed with IVs out of both arms. I pray God's blessing on all of you. Don't give up praying for me and pulling for me. I need your prayers and your support and so does Pamela. A final word to my children David and Kathryn. They've just been wonderful and standing behind me and supporting me. God bless you all. Good night, Jim

After sepsis, Jim's rehab extended to three weeks, and then a fourth, when I contracted Covid. On 23 September, after my five-day isolation period, my brother and sister-in-law drove from St Paul to Rochester to Hatfield to bring Jim home—five days shy of two months after diagnosis. He made his first transfer from wheelchair to the car. They arrived back in Hatfield, three hours later, in pouring rain, and Jim made his first transfer from the car back to the wheelchair.

We were mostly ready, except I was still miserable from Covid. Our house already had a ramp, and an occupational therapy consultant had helped me purchase the best equipment for the bathroom. Family and neighbours rearranged our house: in our great room friends stored unnecessary furniture and rearranged the rest for wheelchair accessibility. In the bedroom, our handyman and his mother built an open air, accessible closet. Neighbours heard on the radio about a free hospital bed someone was giving away and other neighbours drove to a town an hour away to get it. We had a used hospital bed for Jim on one side of the room and a cot for me on the other. In his study, my daughters organized his clothes and built accessible drawer units; they cleared the path to make his desk accessible for a wheelchair. I continued to isolate in the camper; our handyman slept with Jim in our room and helped him during the night.

Black River Falls Memorial Hospital

The motto of Black River Falls, Wisconsin is "The Northwoods Closer to Home". At the end of the medical floor of Memorial Hospital, a picture-window-sized bas-relief sculpture is carved in frosted glass. It depicts a peaceful Northwoods scene. A weaving waterway is surrounded by pines, lined with tall grasses and leading to a waterfall. A heron watches over the river. On one side, a doe drinks from it while a buck stands majestically by; on the other, two foxes romp. Overhead, a tree branch shows the change of seasons: from the branch union it extends summerish laden with apples and cherries, then springlike dressed with dogwood blossoms, and finally, wintry with icicles extended from the branch on which a cardinal perches.[1]

Sepsis and Covid had depleted our energy; we cancelled our Alaska cruise. Jim continued physical therapy locally until a backache impaired his mobility. The pain led to an emergency room visit, where the ER doc asked—has he had a PET scan? I was sure he had, as I knew that Dr Rose's team had looked for mets and found none. He was admitted and given intensive physical therapy and pain relief for a week, without success. Dr Miller, the medical director, ordered further tests.

---

[1] <https://krauskiartglass.com/pages/medical/brmh-jb/brmhindex.html> (accessed 31 October 2024).

When I visited, Dr Miller came to the room. He sat, but he always sits when he visits a patient: it's one of his calling cards, part of his patient care, to make sure you know that you are the only person he is thinking about right now. Over the years, we had grown to care very much for Dr Miller with his gentle style. And as a generalist, he had solved problems that evaded the specialists.

He said to me, "I came in earlier, but I wouldn't have had this conversation without you." He looked at Jim with his direct, honest, unemotional but empathic gaze, and said, "I have some bad news. The pain in your spine is from a tumour that has grown in your L3 vertebra." He allowed time for us to absorb the bad news and adopt his matter-of-fact attitude toward it. Despite the amputation with seemingly clean margins, the cancer was spreading. He held us in the kind of peace communicated by the glass sculpture on the wall. We agreed that he would call Dr Rose.

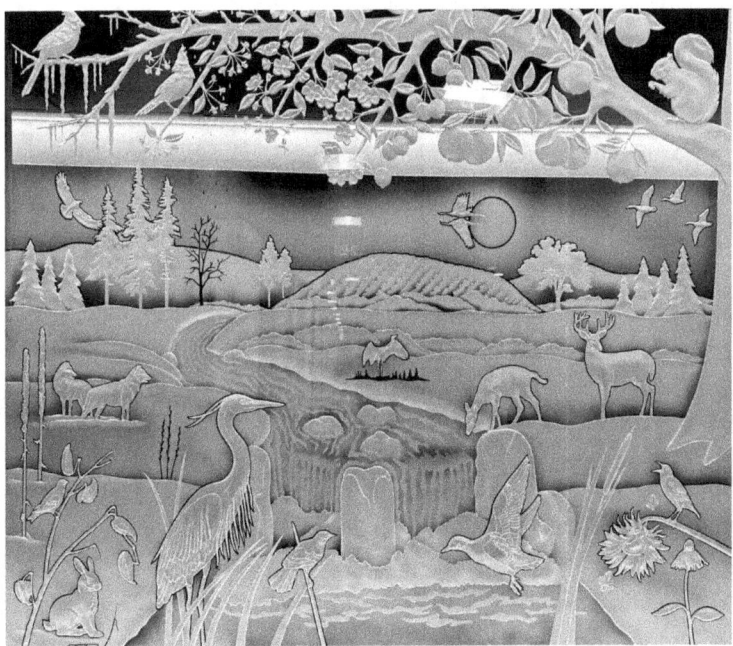

Figure 4: No title, by Robert and Mary Krauski, Krauski Art Glass (Hartland, WI)

Later than afternoon he returned. "I caught Dr Rose on the way to the airport. He knows your body very well—he says you would not survive the surgery required to remove the tumour. He wants to transfer you to a unit for directed radiation." Jim prepared for his second transit to Rochester via ambulance.

At a follow-up appointment with Dr Rose, he showed us the x-rays of Jim's spine taken before his surgery. "We looked for any metastasis exactly at this place; it wasn't there." Surgically, however, Jim's cancer treatment had ended. Over the coming months, as the future we had imagined disappeared, we did ask the question: was the amputation worth it? Yes, within short order it provided pain relief and good mobility with the use of various forms of mobility equipment—gait belt, slide board, shower bench, bariatric commode chair—mobility that allowed us more time in the privacy of our own home. And as the months of the future shortened, I had the increasing sense that every day counted. Our summertime life, laden with apples and cherries, was yielding to the time when the leaves turn to their reds, yellows and golds.

At this appointment Jim told Dr Rose, "Every day is a gift. I just want one more day to love my wife." This phrase became our greeting each day: "It's another day to love you." But the approaching winter, with snow and ice hanging in the trees, would have its own kind of beauty.

Mayo Clinic
Radiation Clinic

Mixed Media Art Quilt
Japanese paper, silk, metal leaf
(3) 30h x 30w, (2) 30h x 6w inches
Lucinda Carlstrom
Atlanta, Georgia

In the radiation clinic hangs a quilt with lines of trapezoid fabric cuts in various shades of white, blue, green, gold and black, each line outlined in dark blue. On larger squares, autumn leaves in green, yellow and orange are topstitched, following the vein of the leaves, onto gold backgrounds.

This craft is perhaps one of my favourites because Jim and I had recently travelled to Quebec in the autumn, and I found the greens, yellows, oranges, golds and reds among the evergreens so nourishing. This very precise craft mirrors the exact placement and dose of radiation that targeted the tumour in Jim's L3 vertebra.

His radiation on 9 November, an antidote for pain but not a cure, worked immediately! It allowed Jim to prepare for his highly anticipated appointment on 16 November: the fitting of his prosthetic. For that procedure, Jim needed the strength to stand in parallel bars for 20 minutes on his residual leg while the mould for the prosthesis socket firmed. Two weeks later, Jim was scheduled to return to rehab for two weeks to learn to walk—two one-hour physical therapy sessions a day. He practised valiantly, walking the 30 feet of the parallel bars, watching himself in the mirror, but by the end of two weeks, was not cleared to walk with a walker at home. We anticipated flying to a gathering of my daughters and grandsons in Eagle, Idaho, over Christmas—a trip I looked forward to very much, as most recent family trips had visited his side of the family. We left his right "leg" behind. Jim was wheelchair-bound, and he needed accessible accommodations.

Jim flew by himself from Boise to Portland, Oregon to visit his son's family while I travelled to the mountains with mine, where four teenage grandsons toasted Jim with his favourite Angry Orchard blackberry hard cider around the campfire. In Portland, Jim's son, David, worked with a nearby retirement home where his mother had lived to get the necessary accessibility equipment for Jim to stay with them. When Jim returned to Eagle, Idaho, we checked into an accessible room at the Homewood Suites. A competition of gingerbread houses by the elevator made us smile; we voted for the wigwam gingerbread house with candy buffalo in the yard. We went to Christmas Eve services at the megachurch my grandson was attending, which Jim, who favours high church liturgy, enjoyed. We almost made it to Christmas.

But early Christmas morning Jim was wracked by pain—a kidney stone? Paramedics took him to the emergency room, where we received more news: the L3 vertebra had crumbled. He stayed hospitalized on pain meds for the next 36 hours till we were due to fly home. On Christmas morning, in front of the fireplace and the Christmas tree during our family gift exchange, Zoey, my daughter's shorthaired English pointer, climbed on the couch and tenderly laid her head in my lap. They say dogs know. This one did. On the day after Christmas, the whole family gathered at the hospital to see us off. The grandsons decided they needed to bring Jim donuts, as he had often brought to them. They drove to the best gourmet donut shops—all closed for the holiday—and finally found an open Krispy Kreme.

That week Jim was scheduled for an ablation and vertebroplasty—further radiation of the tumour, followed by a cementing of the crumbled bone. He commented to the radiation doctor, "I think this is my last Christmas."

"Why would you say that?" she answered. "You aren't dying." But autumn leaves scattered by birds flying south were falling.

Oncology Clinic

> Oncology Quilts
> No further identification.

The nurse calls "James Glass".

I push the wheelchair to the door of the clinic. He responds, "April 3, 1939."

She says, "You know what I was going to ask." Of course, he's been asked hundreds of times. She turns and leads us through the door. My gaze is diverted by the vivid colours of a full-length quilt hanging on the wall to the left. On a solid blue–green background, eight rows of five hearts, each of a different hue of purple or pink and one yellow, mostly solid but a few patterned, are wrapped in hot pink ribbons like arms gracefully holding the heart. Each time we enter the clinic, the nurse pauses a moment while Jim and I pay homage to the quilt. On the way out, I look closer: each heart is signed with the name and age of a patient: Karen, breast cancer, 3 years; Susan, breast cancer, 26 years . . .

Jim's PET scan before our trip at Christmas showed that the cancer had metastasized to his lungs, spleen and liver. Dr Okuno, Jim's oncologist, believed it was now time to try chemotherapy. His goal was to slow the cancer or arrest it, and because Jim had myelofibrosis, an underlying disease of the bone marrow, Dr Okuno would begin with a three-quarters dose of one drug, and if that went well, proceed to the second drug with which the first is usually given. The first dose was scheduled for 27 December, the same day as Jim was due for dermatology biopsies, as he had a long history of skin cancer. That day, I did think, why worry about squamous and basal cells (though Jim also had had two melanomas) in the presence of chondrosarcoma? Was it Jim's denial of how vicious sarcomas are? Or was it his need to continue living life as he had, and derm checks and cancer removals were simply part of that life? Jim wanted to keep the derm appointment, and he needed to be in control of his treatment. As the day progressed, the biopsies kept bleeding. That night we discovered that his platelet count had dropped precipitously.

At his oncology visit a few weeks later, Dr Okuno told Jim he could not proceed with the planned chemo treatments. "If we give you another one, you could bleed out." Various treatments could extend Jim's life with quality—blood transfusions, thoracentesis to drain the fluid building up in his chest, and ongoing physical therapy to keep him as mobile as possible.

At another hospitalization, Jim was admitted to the cardiac unit, as fluid was filling his chest cavity on the right side. The palliative care team was asked to visit with us. The previous November our rector from our church in Canada had come to Wisconsin to plan Jim's funeral; we updated our advance directives; we talked about the moments as they occurred that reminded us of Jim's impending death—for example, when, in one of the oncology waiting rooms, a newly cancer-free patient rang a bell to indicate a successful treatment, Jim said, "It makes me sad to know I will never ring that bell." Among other things, the palliative nurse wanted to talk about a DNI/DNR (do not intubate, do not resuscitate) order. I wasn't ready for that conversation. I knew compressions and electric shocks could leave my frail mother worse than before, but Jim's body still looked strong. Every month, every day mattered.

As we always did in moments of confusion, we called Dr Hook to find out what he thought. He talked us through the science of the situation so we could come to our own conclusion. "If your heart stops on the street and paramedics revive you, you have about a 25 per cent chance of being discharged from the hospital. If you are in ICU, you have a 40 per cent chance. If you have multiple morbidities, you have about a 48 per cent of having significant neurological deficits. Then the next of kin is in the very difficult place of having to decide to withdraw life support." After we heard that, Jim signed the DNI/DNR with my support. Dr Hook knew how to use science to clarify and calm.

The pulmonary team was called. Two pulmonary fellows very carefully inserted a chest tube to drain the fluid in Jim's chest. It was not the painful procedure Jim expected. "You are very good—very careful—very precise," he told the doctors. "I didn't feel it at all." Dr Dante Schiavo came by on Saturday afternoon to check on Jim and said, "I was so glad you commended the fellows. They are doing so well I didn't even scrub in. I knew they could do it on their own with a few words of guidance."

Jim often reversed the bad days and exhaustion of medical staff. He was remembered for his gratitude—he thanked everyone from the most prominent doctor to the night shift personal care assistant. He tried to speak very personally about how he had experienced their care, and he often bought gifts for the nurses' children. In this time, he had to receive the gifts of those around him, as they created disability accommodations that supported his determination and celebrated his small, daily "hurrahs" of success.

But now Jim had a pensive look on his face. "Doctor, may I ask you a question? How does this all end?" Dr Schiavo sat for the next 45 minutes and talked to Jim about death from cancer, pouring alabaster oil on his soul, wrapping pink ribbons of care around his heart.

Our Rochester home
Gifts from our international friends

By early January 2024, I thought often of Luke 7:36–50, in which Mary Magdalene washes Jesus' feet with her tears and expensive oil. Jesus is dining in the home of a Pharisee, who objects. (In the version I learned growing up, the Pharisee says, this expensive oil could have been sold and the money given to the poor. I saw the Pharisee's point.) Through a story Jesus leads the Pharisee to realize that human generosity is met with God's. The anointing is preparing Jesus for his death. The passage communicates tenderness and grace—once more, God's reversal of the values of living by the world's rules and standards. Over the previous fall, I began to want to make decisions by the standards of *kairos*, rather than *chronos* time. For example, in Hatfield I decided that I did not want to spend the rest of our nights sleeping across the room from one another. I purchased a king-sized bed with automatic lifts and a solid hickory bedstead with spindles—these together allowed Jim to manipulate himself in and out of bed as he had in the hospital bed, but it also provided the proximity we needed. It had become our custom to watch movies together and discuss them, holding hands; this time was restored to our lives. It was the first of several major purchases that prepared us for the holy week to come.

When we realized the increasing number of specialists and appointments Jim would have at the Mayo Clinic, we decided to purchase a three-bedroom, three-bath accessible townhome in Rochester. In November, while he was in prosthesis training, I signed a contract on a property and began to look for furnishings that were necessary to augment what we could bring from Wisconsin. We needed another king-sized lift bed and two queens for visitors. On 2 January, while Jim was having his ablation and vertebroplasty, I signed the sale documents with the title company in the waiting room at the clinic and the beds were delivered shortly.

That week Jim's son David came and chose and installed televisions. Friends from Seattle flew in and helped us settle. Ian did household tasks, while Leah and I picked out a grey couch that matched the grey kitchen and grey and yellow countertops across the room. The entire first floor had wooden floors, easy for the wheelchair, but the living room needed a rug to create the space. After much searching online, I found a rug with African animals. "It's the only one that has anything to do with us," Jim said. We had spent many years working on various mission and research projects in the Democratic Republic of Congo, Liberia and Kenya, and we decided to decorate the living room with gifts from our friends in Africa and from my students.

My nephew Will, who was in physical therapy school, and his fiancé, Michael, visited from St Paul. Will discovered he could use the physical

*Figure 5: Our Rochester home: Gifts from our
International friends (Pamela Couture)
Copper bas relief scene of a hunter
Copper bas relief scene of a mother with her children
Copper bas relief scene of mother, father and
children around a campfire
Gold map of Congo on tanzanite background
Statuary from Congo, Tanzania and Ghana
Praying woman in the shape of a cross from Korea
Tapestry square from Fiji*

therapy skills he was learning with Jim. We hired Michael as our painter and decorator, to turn a bland space into a home in record speed. Regular visits followed. We needed a colour that made the African art objects "pop". Michael painted different swaths of colour on the walls; at one point Jim came home from an appointment and kidded, "You fucked up my walls!" Over the next few weeks, Michael painted and hung pictures.

The second week in January, during a polar vortex, Jim's daughter, Kathryn, and grandson, Alex, visited for the weekend from California. They threw snowballs and we all played NFLopoly. Longtime friends from San Diego, Calli and Joe Allen, visited for the day, and Joe built the electronic fireplace for the living room. Jim's cousin Bill Billings, "the closest person I have to a brother", visited multiple times from Chicago. My nieces from St Paul and their families visited Jim in his hospital room with their children, whom Jim had loved, and then had a family dinner at the new home. Multiple friends from around the world kept in touch with Jim by text message or phone calls or Caring Bridge.

Jim, Kathryn and David were die-hard Kansas City Chiefs fans. When the Chiefs played in the Superbowl at the end of January, Kathryn and David flew in to watch the game as a family. We ordered the Famous Dave's platter with barbeque ribs, chicken and corn muffins. The Chiefs came from behind to win in overtime. It filled the house with joy. Our friend Brooke came for a week from Virginia and friends from St Paul and Hatfield visited. My brother and sister-in-law brought my 92-year-old mother from memory care in St Paul. Michael's parents visited; in fact, his father, an endocrinologist, recognized that Jim's oxygen saturation was low, leading to one of Jim's hospitalizations. In those two months, we made the new house into a home with warmth and family and friends from near and far.

In those two months, in the midst of these visits, we called paramedics four times and Jim was hospitalized repeatedly. My experience of time was changing. Time was no longer linear, like days one after another on a calendar. Rather, time was in slow motion, as if we were living in a fullness of time that was multidimensional. Time was literally embodied, marked by what the body was doing, or not. Time was deeply intimate and emotional, palpable, so that it could be felt in the belly. At the same time, time was transitional, as we prepared for the continuation of our relationship in a different spiritual way, apart from our usual bodily presence with one another. Instead of saying, "Where did the time go?" as we do in parts of our lives like academic semesters that rush by, time seemed overfilled, and a few days seemed like a very . . . long . . . time. It took long-term memory to recall last week. Experiencing time in this moment was surreal.

Every day was another day to love each other; every day mattered.

At the end of February, during one hospitalization, Jim seemed to be dying, and the doctors recommended that we call in the children and our rector, Stuart Pike. They were planning to come at the end of March for Jim's 85th birthday party. "I think we should cancel the birthday party," Jim said. David and his wife, Michelle, his daughter Kathryn, and our rector arrived, and Jim stabilized. He woke up one morning, and with his usual morbid humour, said, "So am I still dying? I just want to know what the plan is." He lived that day, and the next, and the next . . .

With the family present, the Mayo Clinic palliative care team conducted a small bedside ritual that recognized Jim's 35 years as a military chaplain, presenting a statement, pins and a flag. Before Stuart left to catch his plane, he blessed Jim and said all of the Anglican prayers for the dying except the final one. Kathryn gripped her father's hand and said her goodbyes; David and Michelle tearfully did the same. Jim revived, and the hospital suggested that I could take him home with hospice care.

Will planned to spend the week with us over his spring break, and Michael spelled Will when he had to work so that someone was always with us. On Sunday, Dr Hook and his family came for dinner, and we ate cod au gratin, one of Jim's favourites, seated around Jim's hospice bed, which was now facing the television and the artwork in the living room. The next night we watched *Rustin* together, a movie about the planning for the March on Washington. Jim relived where he had stood and saw footage of the orange buses on which he rode to Washington. Hospice aides and nurses came by daily. On Thursday morning, his aide gave him a bed bath. He kissed her hand in gratitude, and she said she would return the next morning.

We started to watch one of his favourite movies, *Out of Africa*. I held his hand on one side, and he reached out for Will on the other. But he shortly fell asleep. After that, he wasn't responsive to our touch and pulled his hands closer to his body. I loaded laundry in the washer, right off the living room, and switched to *Grey's Anatomy* on the television to entertain myself. Shortly after dinner Will and Michael took the dogs for a walk, and Jim's breath seemed more laboured. Remembering that hearing is the last sense to go, I thought that he probably didn't want to leave this life listening to the washing machine noise in the background and *Grey's Anatomy* on TV. I found solace in the disciples who could not attend to Jesus constantly while he was praying in Gethsemane. "Alexa, play Handel's *Messiah*." I readjusted his BIPAP and called the hospice, who decided to send a nurse over. Then I called our rector and got him on FaceTime. "I think it's time to pray the last prayer for the dying." I laid the phone next to Jim's good ear. The beautiful prayer commending Jim to God ended, and Jim gave one last, heavy shudder, almost as an Amen, and he was gone.

In the immediate time to come I realized how much crucifixion theology stresses forgiveness of sins, and yes, Jim would say that shouldn't be overlooked. He was a person with a deep sense of guilt who needed regular reminder of his forgiveness. But we so often forget that Jesus' last words on the cross are not, "My God, my God, why haven't you forgiven me?" but "My God, my God, why have you forsaken me?" First, Jesus experienced being left by the disciples; then he thought that the one he called "Abba" had also abandoned him. I felt the meaning of crucifixion as the promise of presence. If the crucifixion has a one-and-for-allness to it, may it also be that people should die in the presence of love—God's love and that of the community. If it takes a village to raise a child, it also takes a village to keep vigil when an elder dies, and that village may be represented by those who are present, those who communicate through the range of today's technologies, or those who are present through artwork on the walls of our homes.

In the days to come, I also felt the meaning of resurrection as the explosion of love. The *philia* of the doctors—particularly Dr Hook, Dr Rose, Dr Okuno, Dr Miller and Dr Schiavo—in the very direct conversations they had with us. The *ludos* behind Jim's sense of humour, always lifting the mood of the medical personnel in his room. The *agape* of our family and friends, who travelled sacrificially and became a village surrounding Jim and me. The *eros* that bound Jim and me physically and continues to connect us spiritually. Jim never missed an opportunity to let me know that he loved me, and love filled my chest, crowding out intense sorrow and grief. In the surround-sound of love, Jim and those around him made the experience of his death a good experience for me—the highest compliment I can pay.

In birth and death, we become very focused on the physical processes of life, and those processes, and the fact that they end, remind us, "It's another day to love you." For the marriage of Will and Michael, I wrote:

The human being breathes about 7.5 million breaths per year.
The first breath, a cry.
The last breath, a sigh.
How many kinds of breath in between?
The quick breath of surprise,
The held breath of worry,
The slow breath of trust,
The ragged breath of vulnerability,
The panting breath of sex,
The heaving breath of play.
How many times will you breathe in your
    marriage, in how many ways?

The human heart beats 35 million heart beats a year.
The first beat, anticipation.
The last beat, rest.
How many kinds of beats in between?
The regular beat of routine,
The elevated beat of accomplishment,
The rapid beat of life out of control,
The sloshy beat of failure,
The beats that sync
When two chests snuggle close.
How many times will your heart beat in your
    marriage, and in how many ways?

May your marriage have millions of chances for your lungs to breathe and hearts to beat. When the breathing is rough and the beating is hard, may you have another, and another, and another chance to breathe and beat well.

But breath is spirit and heart is love, and when breaths and beats cease, may the spirit and love of your marriage carry you on.

13

The great derangement in literature and practical theology: Following fiction into the other-than-human world

Bonnie J. Miller-McLemore

Of the some thousand books I left behind when I moved out of my Vanderbilt office in 2020, Heather Walton's work survived the purge. That I still have her *Writing Methods in Theological Reflection* and *Not Eden: Spiritual Life Writing for the World* among the handful of books on my study shelves says something about the importance of her scholarship, not just for me but also for the discipline of practical theology.[1] This essay offers an opportunity to reflect on that value and bring her work into conversation with questions about practical theology, modern fiction and our climate catastrophe that have lingered beyond my exodus from the academy.

Amitav Ghosh, recipient of India's highest literary honour in 2018, issued an arresting critique of his novelist peers and myopic Westerners, deranged in our capacity to imagine the forces of nature and hence the reality of climate collapse. Departing from his acclaimed role as storyteller and novelist, he narrates a bigger tale in his 2016 book *The Great Derangement: Climate Change and the Unthinkable*, analysing

---

[1] Heather Walton, *Writing Methods in Theological Reflection* (London: SCM Press, 2014) and *Not Eden: Spiritual Life Writing for the World* (London: SCM Press, 2015).

modern literature, history and politics to reveal a massive occlusion of nature's intelligence, unpredictability and destructive power. Our era, he declares, "which so congratulates itself on its self-awareness, will come to be known as the time of the Great Derangement", remarkable for its concealment of environmental demise and delusion about our planetary self-importance.[2]

Ghosh's words seem especially relevant in a book that honours Walton, a practical theologian unique in her love for the creative arts and literary imagination. Her corpus suggests that practical theologians should heed his critique of modern literature. The chapter moves from Walton's argument for a deeper engagement with the arts to Ghosh's portrait of the "great derangement", to a more exploratory final section on contemporary novels that lift up other-than-human beings that we ignore at our own peril. In essence, it argues for greater engagement not just with the literary world but with the natural world.

Making a place for literature and the arts

In two early books, *Imagining Theology: Women, Writing and God* and *Literature, Theology and Feminism*, Walton pioneered research on the significance of literature in feminist theology.[3] In the years since then, she has expanded this literary appreciation into her study of practical theology and everyday life. Throughout this time, she has been singular in insisting on alternative ways of knowing through artistic means, what she captures through the words *poesis*, *poetics* and *theopoetics*. She encourages practical theologians to expand their religious imagination and methodological horizons through narrative, literature and creative non-fiction.

---

[2] Amitav Ghosh, *The Great Derangement: Climate Change and the Unthinkable* (Chicago, IL: University of Chicago Press, 2016), p. 11.

[3] Heather Walton, *Imagining Theology: Women, Writing, and God* (London: T&T Clark, 2007) and *Literature, Theology and Feminism* (Manchester: Manchester University Press, 2007).

Although *Writing Methods in Theological Reflection* is not the snazziest title, it is one of the more inventive books in practical theology, from its introductory and explanatory chapters to its illustrative essays. Each of three parts on autoethnography, journalling and life writing contain four chapters, in which the first describes a particular method for writing self-reflexively and the next three offer examples from her own practice. The final Part Four returns to larger questions about theology, *phronesis*, wisdom and poetics or the "devices through which authors create their texts".[4] The book helps those searching for their vocation in ministry, but it is also useful for those who wish to advance research in practical theology. It makes space for first-person singular in theological writing (beyond trite lines that locate the author) and, as important, it re-imagines where theological knowledge lies and how students, scholars and religious professionals alike might go about discerning and articulating it. She offers a way of seeing everyday things made invisible under the reign of dominant epistemologies, things one cannot measure through number or comparison. Or, in her words, she pursues "forms of expression that are more able to bear the weight that theology does not seem able to carry at the current time ... 'things' about which direct speech seems currently not possible".[5] In doing so, she engages in a kind of empirical theology but in a different way than conventionally understood via scientific methods of quantitative and qualitative research.

There is in Walton's writing a call to integrity—to be fully present and to make that presence available. It is not unusual for her to begin an essay with a richly crafted portrait of a living moment. "I went to church last Sunday", begins a journal article.[6] Readers feel the sun slanting through stained glass and the warmth of the community, and then the mood sours as the preacher calls congregants to protest the "rotten" consumptive world around us. Her presidential address for the International Academy of Practical Theology (IAPT) in 2017 began with rumination about the need for a second holy week to live into the "strange season of the empty

---

[4] Walton, *Writing Methods*, p. xxiv.
[5] Walton, *Writing Methods*, p. 161.
[6] Heather Walton, "We Have Never Been Theologians: Postsecularism and Practical Theology", *Practical Theology* 11:3 (2018), p. 218.

tomb", and included slides of Botticelli's *Madonna and Singing Angels* and Picasso's *Guernica*.[7] She spoke of a conversation with Don Browning in a Chicago café where Tillich hung out and where she first thought she just might become a practical theologian. I loved it, but apparently a few IAPT colleagues were less enamoured. When I heard this, I was reminded of an earlier IAPT conference in 2011 when she read the first section of a paper that began with this line—"My daughter was laying pink cheeked and sweetly asleep in bed"—and a European peer suggested she drop the opening and get straight to her academically recognizable analysis.

Unfortunately, as Walton argues, practical theologians have regarded *poesis* as inferior to two other poles in Aristotle's triumvirate on knowledge, *phronesis* and *theoria*. In the 2011 essay, published in a conference volume and republished in *The Wiley Blackwell Reader in Practical Theology*, Walton shows how a literary approach complements and extends a practical theology grounded solely in the social sciences, ethics and philosophy.[8] *Poetics* refers to more than the means by which authors create texts. It includes knowing through making, artistic creating and craft knowledge. She advances *poesis* as a persuasive mode of knowing through both creative writing and theoretical argument, engaging, for example, neglected figures in practical theology such Henri LeFebvre and Bruno Latour.

All this to say: literature can give new life to practical theological knowing. Recently, a doctoral graduate reminded me that I had encouraged her to keep a novel by her side as she worked on her

---

[7] Heather Walton, "A Theopoetics of Practice: Re-forming in Practical Theology", IAPT Presidential Address, 23 April 2017, Oslo, Norway; published in the *International Journal of Practical Theology* 23:1 (2019), pp. 3–23.

[8] Heather Walton, "Desiring Things: Practical Theology and the New Materialisms", in Rein Brouwer, Ruard Ganzevorst and Bonnie Miller-McLemore (eds), *City of Desires—A Place for God?* (Berlin: Lit Verlag, 2013); and Heather Walton, "Desiring Things", in Bonnie J. Miller-McLemore (ed.), *The Wiley Blackwell Reader in Practical Theology* (Hoboken, NJ: Wiley-Blackwell, 2019), pp. 117–26.

dissertation on immigrant and queer experiences. She is now teaching a course that features novels, memoirs and short essays by Latinx writers, convinced that such sources are essential to a fuller engagement with the struggles of Latinx peoples. Her first assignment pairs Walton's introduction on "Reflective Theological Writing" in *Writing Methods* with Gloria Anzaldúa's "Speaking in Tongues", giving students a side-by-side display of linear theory and liberative practice with the hope of encouraging them to write from their minds *and* hearts.[9] In a class my graduate took, I also used Walton's work to embolden students to engage more fully in their writing and learning, grateful for her example and blessing.

The derangement of modern fiction

What if modern fiction has a serious flaw that distorts perception, however? This is a crucial question, one that I'm not sure Walton or other practical theologians have considered. But her scholarship on the literary arts suggests we should heed Ghosh's words and warnings. He's a prolific fiction and non-fiction writer, including his most recent book *The Nutmeg's Curse: Parables for a Planet in Crisis*. I focus here on *The Great Derangement*, where his critique of modern literature is most succinct.

Ghosh writes in a style that Walton would value, painting pictures and performing textual analysis. *The Great Derangement* contains case example, personal story and close reading of critical research and cultural movements. Its three parts progress from "Stories" of climate change and modern novels to the "History" of Western imperialism to the "Politics" of denial. Part I, which comprises almost half the book, is most relevant here, but its themes of literary delusion are connected to arguments

---

[9] Walton, *Writing Methods*, pp. xi–xxxiii; Gloria Anzaldúa, "Speaking in Tongues: A Letter to 3rd World Women Writers", in Cherríe Moraga and Gloria Anzaldúa (eds), *The Bridge Called My Back: Writings by Radical Women of Color* (New York: Kitchen Table: Women of Color Press, 1981), pp. 165–73.

in Part II about Western empire as a driver of climate change and the political disincentives to addressing the challenges in Part III.

So, what does Ghosh mean by the "great derangement" and what might practical theologians learn from his analysis? Derangement appears in many forms, but its essence is a persistent distortion in Western culture that makes our climate crisis unthinkable. The deranged modern mind is exemplified in phenomena like colonial cities such as Mumbai, Singapore and New York City built right on the shoreline, foolishly defying the power of the surrounding seas. Before colonial expansionism, people lived far inland out of respect and legitimate fear of raging water. But today, as sea levels rise and storm intensity increases, the most expensive properties of wealthy landowners sit precariously and stupidly on the coast.

Modern literature has had a central hand in sustaining this delusion of human power and importance. Literary journals and critics have failed to take climate change seriously, relegating it to more suspect, borderline genres like science fiction and fantasy. "When novelists do choose to write about climate change," Ghosh says, "it is almost always outside of fiction."[10] He draws a contrast between patterns of modern realist fiction and climate events of today. Modern fiction exiles "catastrophism" to the margins and portrays it as "un-modern". Novels take place in contained settings, remain confident in the predictability of bourgeois life, and see nature as "moderate and orderly". Yet, the realities of our era reveal unpredictable "forces of unthinkable magnitude".[11] At the very moment when collective action is crucial, modern literature lifts up the singular hero and breaks things down into smaller and smaller parts, obscuring a reality made evident by climate chaos—the earth's interconnectedness across time and space. It is *uncanny*—the word Ghosh chooses to capture the eerie "strangeness of what is unfolding around us"—that right when "human activity was changing the earth's atmosphere ... the literary imagination became radically centred on the human", on the "individual moral adventure", and on interiority rather than people "in the aggregate".[12]

---

[10] Ghosh, *Great Derangement*, p. 8.
[11] Ghosh, *Great Derangement*, pp. 20, 22, 63.
[12] Ghosh, *Great Derangement*, pp. 30, 66, 77.

The "irony of the 'realist novel'", therefore, is that the "very gestures with which it conjures up reality are actually a concealment of the real".[13]

Today, by contrast, the improvable has become provable. The earth, which has seemed so inert, turns out "to be vitally, even dangerously alive", like the memorable scene in *The Empire Strikes Back* when Han Solo discovers the asteroid he thought he had landed on is monstrously alive. Contrary to the mistaken view of only three centuries, our surroundings force upon us, as they have on Ghosh himself, "the urgent proximity of nonhuman presences".[14] He describes some of his own moments of recognizing the uncanny. "In these encounters we recognize something that we had turned away from ... the presence and proximity of non-human interlocutors ... an awareness that humans were never alone."[15] In fact, he speculates, the earth may have its own agenda, "about which we know nothing", intervening to reveal the arrogance of humans who have attributed all intelligence to ourselves while denying it to everything else. Maybe people will finally realize that the earth does not "exist solely, or even incidentally, as a stage" for our star performance.[16]

Ghosh's argument carries these thoughts into wider spheres in Parts II and III. Our economics and politics are also deranged, he maintains, predicated on the myth of global industrial development for everyone of a kind the earth simply cannot sustain. The problem, of course, isn't just capitalism and its ever-expanding desires but also the power politics of Western empire. Imperialistic preservation of Western dominance "lies at the core of the climate crisis", Ghosh insists, made more difficult "because it remains largely unacknowledged".[17] Western politicians and corporate entrepreneurs gesture toward addressing the crisis, but the real plan is preservation of the status quo. Moreover, climate debate remains Eurocentric when in fact Asian participation is crucial. As he argues, "No strategy can work globally unless it works in Asia and is adopted

---

[13] Ghosh, *Great Derangement*, p. 23.
[14] Ghosh, *Great Derangement*, pp. 3, 5.
[15] Ghosh, *Great Derangement*, p. 30.
[16] Ghosh, *Great Derangement*, pp. 5, 6, 31.
[17] Ghosh, *Great Derangement*, p. 146.

by large numbers of Asians."[18] Ghosh could be accused of offering few solutions, but he does suggest the need for a dramatic shift in collective consciousness and action and, of particular interest here, an urgent need to change the stories we tell.

Possibilities and perils of non-anthropocentric literature

Other practical theologians have offered a thorough-going critique of the anthropocentrism of a field predicated on promoting human wellbeing,[19] but few have suggested fiction as a viable handmaiden in this overhaul, perhaps for reasons Ghosh points out—novels that break the modern fixation with individual adventure are the exception. To think about the Anthropocene, he argues, requires a move beyond language to images and away from logocentrism that the academy may not be able to make. But to think like a forest is to think in images.[20]

In an essay on "Making Literature in the Anthropocene", Episcopalian priest Amy Peterson expresses a similar desire for new sources. "For the past few years," she says, "I've been looking for literature that ... transforms my understanding of what it means to be human in (is *in* the

---

[18] Ghosh, *Great Derangement*, p. 90.

[19] For a review of the work of practical theologians who have questioned the field's anthropocentricism, see Bonnie J. Miller-McLemore, "Climate Violence and Earth Justice: A Research Report on Practical Theology's Contribution", *International Journal of Practical Theology* 26:2 (2022), pp. 329–66. For a few outstanding examples, see Pamela R. McCarroll, "Listening for the Cries of the Earth: Practical Theology in the Anthropocene", *International Journal of Practical Theology* 24:1 (2020), pp. 29–46; Cláudio Carvalhaes, *Rituals at World's End: Essays on Eco-Liturgical Liberation Theology* (York, PA: Barber's Son Press, 2021); and Lisa Dahill, "For the Life of the World: Toward the Next Ten Years of *Spiritus*", *Spiritus* 10 (2010), pp. 287–92.

[20] See Ghosh, *Great Derangement*, pp. 81–4. He draws on Eduardo Kohn, *How Forests Think: Toward an Anthropology beyond the Human* (Berkeley, CA: University of California Press, 2013), who calls for a "decolonization of thought" beyond language and concept.

right preposition? A human *with*? or *of*?) the world. I've been watching for writers who reckon with the Anthropocene by attending to and even animating the nonhuman world in their work."[21] However, her review only touches briefly on a couple of novels (Madeleine L'Engle's *A Wind in the Door* and Robin Sloan's *Sourdough*) and two poets—Mary Oliver, an obvious and popular choice, and the less-known Jorie Graham.[22] But Peterson asks a question Walton might welcome and another that Ghosh implies: what is the "role of the artist in the Anthropocene?" and "who speaks, and who listens, in our literature?"[23]

Ghosh himself acknowledges literary exceptions. In a review in *The Guardian*, he surveys several books but unfortunately focuses mostly on non-fiction (e.g., Elizabeth Kolbert). He mentions Annie Proulx's memoir *Bird Cloud* and novels by Barbara Kingsolver and Richard Powers. But his remarks are descriptive and too abbreviated to be of much help.[24] His comments on exemplary fiction in *The Great Derangement* are equally limited. He flags Ian McEwan's *Solar* but only in a footnote and says in passing that Kingsolver's *Flight Behavior* and Liz Jensen's *Rapture* capture the "uncanniness and improvability, the magnitude and interconnectedness" of today's environmental upheaval.[25] There are novels, he admits, like John Steinbeck's *East of Eden*, that were ahead of their time in situating the "human within the nonhuman" and several non-Western novelists who have featured the collective and the nonhuman.[26] He spends the most time on *Cities of Salt* by Jordanian

---

[21] Amy Peterson, "Making Literature in the Anthropocene", *Image*, Issue 103, <https://imagejournal.org/article/article-anthropocene/> (accessed 31 October 2024), emphasis in the text.

[22] Poetry has largely managed to evade the modern evasion of nature, Ghosh observes, partially because it is awash in imagery (*Great Derangement*, pp. 26, 69).

[23] Peterson, "Making Literature".

[24] Amitav Ghosh, "Life stories: Books about a planet in peril", *Guardian*, 14 October 2019, <https://www.theguardian.com/books/2019/oct/04/books-make-sense-wounded-planet-amitav-ghosh> (accessed 31 October 2024).

[25] Ghosh, *Great Derangement*, pp. 73, 165.

[26] Ghosh, *Great Derangement*, p. 80.

writer Abdel Rahman Munif, perhaps because his estimation of the book stands in sharp juxtaposition with John Updike's dismissal, one of the most stunning instances of myopic modernism in the entire book. Ghosh recognizes *Cities of Salt* as a novel of immense importance, the first to give full expression to the "Oil Encounter"—an encounter that has "almost no presence in our imaginative lives, in art, music, dance, or literature" but touches "every aspect of our existence". By contrast, Updike wrote a scathingly negative review four years before Ghosh's (unbeknownst to him), accusing Munif of being (ironically) "insufficiently Westernized". Updike goes so far as to say that with "no central figure", no individual hero battling the world, just "men in the aggregate", it hardly deserves to be called a novel.[27]

Even before reading Ghosh but definitely since then, I have had an interest in climate fiction. I don't have space or expertise to be exhaustive in my own review. But I can offer a sampling, sparked by Ghosh, Peterson and friends with similar interests. On his suggestion, I read *Cities of Salt* and was stunned by Munif's story of imperialist destruction and cultural upheaval all for the sake of extracting oil, a hidden and untold story, as Ghosh says, of Western greed, exploitation and violence, one I had understood in the most general sense, but not in the detail and horror Munif offers.

But let me start with where I left off recently in my reading. Native American author Tommy Orange's book *There There* begins with a prologue that is also unthinkable for most white Americans, and the racist unthinkability is related to the white Western inability to think climate catastrophe.[28] What Americans have done to Native peoples is horrendous and the suppression of these realities parallels the suppression of what we have done to the earth, decimating not just

---

[27] John Updike, cited by Ghosh, *Great Derangement*, pp. 76–7. In his bibliographic notes on p. 177, Ghosh says his review is reprinted in *The Iman and the Indian* (New Delhi: Penguin India, 2002) and *Incendiary Circumstances* (Boston: Houghton Mifflin, 2004). He doesn't give a citation for Updike's review, but it appears in "Satan's Work and Silted Cisterns", *The New Yorker*, 17 October 1988, pp. 117–20.

[28] Tommy Orange, *There There* (New York: Vintage Books, 2018).

women and children in massacres like Sand Creek in Colorado territory and hosting thanksgiving feasts predicated on the celebration of crushing victories over Native communities, but also destroying an entire way of life attuned to the earth, labelling it uncannily as "uncivilized". No wonder minoritized peoples declare, as editorialist Mary Annaïse Heglar does, that "climate change ain't the first existential threat".[29] One reason many Westerners are uncaring about climate change, Ghosh reminds readers, is that its first and greatest (initial) victims will be the poorest people in the southern and non-western hemispheres.

My own moment of awakening to the uncanny came late unfortunately, but I credit award-winning author Richard Powers with hastening my conversion. I've written in detail about his work elsewhere and will restrict my comments here, except to extol his insight into tree intelligence and his ability to portray this knowledge from the inside.[30] Trees become primary characters in *The Overstory*, but somehow he achieves this feat without unjustified and inappropriate anthropomorphizing, speaking through a variety of human characters—one who hears trees speaking, another who studies them and goes to court in their defence, two others who live in a tree to save it, a few who plant trees, and several who stage dramatic protests against tree loggers. Throughout the story, readers are reminded again and again that trees turn light, water and air into food, eating carbon dioxide and breathing oxygen; they form a vast underground network, their roots extending at least twice the breadth of their crowns above; they are our kin, sharing a quarter of the same genes, but they talk on a frequency we can't hear and live on an entirely different time scale than we can perceive, something one family captures by taking a picture of a resilient chestnut every month for decades and compiling a flip book. As one of the characters concludes, "*This is not*

---

[29] Mary Annaïse Heglar, "Climate Change Ain't the First Existential Threat", *Medium*, 18 February 2019, <https://zora.medium.com/sorry-yall-but-climate-change-ain-t-the-first-existential-threat-b3c999267aa0> (accessed 31 October 2024).

[30] Bonnie J. Miller-McLemore, "Trees and the 'Unthought Known': The Wisdom of the Nonhuman (or Do Humans 'Have Shit for Brains'?)", *Pastoral Psychology* 69:4 (2020), pp. 423–43.

our world with trees in it. It's a world with trees where humans have just arrived."³¹ We are less than a mere footnote.

Not all of the recent hoopla about tree intelligence is great, however. As the idea of trees relating with one another through fungi became common knowledge—especially popularized by German forester Peter Wohlleben and bestselling author Suzanne Simard³²—it has become trivialized and even cliché. Suddenly, in social media and beyond, we hear "trees are therapeutic", producing chemicals that bathe and soothe us. Strange how humans can turn almost anything into a story about us—that now people should get to the woods because it will improve our mental and physical health. Around the same time that I read Powers, I also read Annie Proulx's *Barkskins*, which seems like it deserves as much attention as her memoir for warning us about romanticizing trees and our interactions with them. *Barkskins* is a sweeping four-century epic about the massive deforestation of the North American forests and the annihilation of peoples who depended on them. As the woods toppled, the "wildness of the world receded, the vast invisible web of filaments that connected human life to animals, trees to flesh and bone to grass shivered as each tree fell and one by one the web strands snapped".³³ Colonizers assumed the forest and its creatures were infinite and, like the Native peoples, in need of taming or killing.

In discussing Powers above, I used the phrase *unjustified* or *inappropriate* anthropomorphizing for a reason. I'm grateful to novelist Sigrid Nunez for this nuance. The first line of her novel *The Vulnerables* begins with the narrator quoting from a book about which she can remember "almost nothing" except one line: "It was an uncertain spring." And that sets the stage for a novel about an author's mundane travails during Covid. It doesn't matter, as the narrator goes on to say, whether

---

31 Richard Powers, *The Overstory* (New York and London: W. W. Norton & Company, 2018), p. 424, emphasis in the text.
32 Peter Wohlleben, *The Hidden Life of Trees: What They Feel, How They Communicate: Discoveries from a Secret World* (Vancouver: Greystone Books, 2015); and Suzanne Simard, *Finding the Mother Tree: Discovering the Wisdom of the Forest* (New York: Vintage, 2022).
33 Annie Proulx, *Barkskins* (New York: Scribner, 2016), p. 12.

you can remember what happens in every novel you read, as she used to believe. Now she knows the "truth": "What matters is what you experience while reading, the state of feeling that the story evokes, the questions that rise to your mind, rather than the fictional events described."[34]

Nunez's *The Vulnerables* is true to form: there is no memorable storyline except perhaps the narrator's encounter with a barely tolerated apartment-mate who landed in the same space by unforeseen circumstances. And the narrator's ruminations are startling. After noting the unusual attraction to animals during the pandemic, she talks at length about the French documentary *My Octopus Teacher*. Filmmaker Craig Foster's zest for work had dwindled to nothing until he meets "an octopus living in an undersea kelp forest in the Western Cape, South Africa", and he "sensed he had something to learn from her". Together they form an incredible bond, finding ways to communicate, entertain and aid one another. Nunez's narrator questions the quick dismissal of Foster's film by scientists: "Anthropocentricism... Projection. Not really friendship, but rather the elimination of a fear barrier, and a familiarity that allows for greater intimacy."[35] This reaction makes no sense, she suggests, in a world that has repeatedly disdained the ability of beings in the natural world to think, relate and emote. Rather, "we should have made [anthropomorphism] our religion," she says. "Irrational, but then what religion is not." Maybe a little anthropomorphism would do us narrow-minded humans good.

This idea gave me new sympathies for novelists that fail to portray other creatures as deftly as Nunez and Powers—Shelby Van Pelt and her surprisingly popular (to my mind) first book *Remarkably Bright Creatures* and Elif Shafat's *The Island of Missing Trees*.[36] Shafat does a better job speaking in the voice of a tree than Van Pelt does for an octopus who becomes the hero of her story, giving his life to save the relationship between an estranged grandmother and grandson. Both Van Pelt and Shafat alternate chapters about human characters and chapters in which

---

[34] Sigrid Nunez, *The Vulnerables* (New York: Riverhead Books, 2023), p. 3.
[35] Nunez, *The Vulnerables*, p. 86.
[36] Shelby Van Pelt, *Remarkably Bright Creatures* (London: Bloomsbury, 2022) and Elif Shafak, *The Island of Missing Trees* (New York: Bloomsbury, 2021).

either the tree or the octopus expresses their thoughts and feelings: the tree's sentiments of bereavement in transplanted exile from Cyprus, brought to Britain during the Greek–Turkish war by an immigrant, and the octopus's sense of entrapment in an aquarium following his rescue from the ocean after a life-threatening injury. Perhaps isolating their voices in separate chapters lent an artificiality to their reflections that Powers avoids by creatively integrating trees into nearly every word and page of his novel.

Writer Brian Doyle offers yet another approach to other beings in his novel *Marten Martin*. Focused on the adventures of a community on Oregon's Mount Hood, the book follows a curious, courageous and wise pine marten named Martin from birth to maturity through the narrator's observation and speculation. For example, the narrator suggests that Martin "did not *think* about evidence and implication as we do; he absorbed the evidence and drew conclusions and implication in another way that we do not yet understand and perhaps never will. We would be very foolish and arrogant to conclude that our way of thinking is necessarily better or deeper than his."[37] Doyle's naming the marten Martin seems less contrived than Van Pelt's naming her giant Pacific octopus Marcellus.

Doyle's writing here and in two other novels, *Mink River* and *The Plover*, is based on his own naturalist love of the earth. He doesn't try to talk for other beings; instead, he reminds readers over and over how little humans really know. In *Martin Marten*, a trapper who tutors a young boy in the ways of the woods reiterates this message throughout the novel ("let's start by learning to be silent"). "The plethora and panoply of scents in [a pine marten's] talented nose alone are beyond our mutual eloquence," the narrator observes, "and you and I would have to invent lots of languages just to get *close* to a few of the things Martin knew without having words for them." "Perhaps the less we think we know," he concludes, "the wiser we are and the closer to actual understanding we get."[38]

---

[37] Brian Doyle, *Martin Marten* (New York: St. Martin's Press, 2015), p. 69.
[38] Doyle, *Martin Marten*, pp. 68–9, 86–7.

Doyle may not fit Ghosh's expectations when it comes to new climate fiction. In fact, Ghosh ignores a whole body of literature that attends to what the discussion section of *Martin Marten* calls the "subtle and complicated relationships between people and animals", like *Big Red*, *Old Yeller*, *Black Beauty* and so on, perhaps because many of these books are aimed at young people and sadly not considered serious fiction either.[39] Even *Martin Marten* is (mis)labelled "young adult fiction". I even wonder if Ghosh would revise his critique in light of this literature and in light of novels that have appeared in the years since his book.

We need to give greater credit to authors, including children's authors, who dive into the worlds of the more-than-human. Nunez spells out the goods that come with greater immersion in the natural world—gentleness; less depression; prevention of extinctions, other species' and our own, and the saving of the planet; and knowledge about the unique intelligences or "genius" of other beings. We also gain greater compassion for vulnerability stretched across the earth. The narrator refers back to Foster's testimony in his film: "You start to care about all the animals, even the tiniest ones, you understand how highly vulnerable animals' lives are, how vulnerable all lives are. You start to think about your own vulnerability and about death, your own death", a good practice in general but especially during these times of planetary extinctions.[40] The narrator concludes her thoughts on *My Octopus Teacher* with a real zinger: "It was the kind of story that makes me think I should have changed my life. Instead, I have wasted it", a feeling not uncommon for latecomers to the climate crisis.

We moderns have suffered a gross failure of the imagination, a sad inability to see beyond ourselves. Amazing that social scientists and activists recognize the crucial place of recognition when it comes to human sanity and flourishing but fail to see its place when it comes to the world around us. Humans denigrate other humans by denying their humanity, a horrendous pattern in the ongoing history of humankind.

---

[39] Discussion questions in *Marten Martin*, p. 308.
[40] Nunez, *The Vulnerables*, p. 87. For comments on dying in the Anthropocene, see also Bonnie J. Miller-McLemore, "'This is My Body': Christian Wisdom on Dying in an Age of Denial", *Practical Theology* 14:5 (2021), pp. 467–91.

But many of us, especially Westerners, have also failed to recognize the planet and thereby denied the aliveness of land, water, air, and their creatures, an equally tragic and devastating pattern of modernity.

How might theology follow contemporary fiction into the more-than-human world? I have grown impatient with theology done at grave distance from the land and creatures around us. At the moment, my conversation partners, the ones that will carry me past practical theology into a wider, scarier, unknown future (and not just my own but the planet's), are no longer so much the social sciences and theology but naturalist novelists and the natural scientists for whom love of the world carries far greater weight than figuring out why humans do the stupid (and for theologians, the evil) things we do. I now live among lodgepole pines, what one naturalist dubs a "fire forest" and what local fire fighters and public agencies call a "wildland urban interface", where human "structures ... meet or intermingle with undeveloped wildland or vegetative fuels".[41] I like to think of this interface more as a place where humans have intruded upon the territory of other beings and now need to deal with the damage we've done and learn to live less intrusively and with clearer limits and unpredictable vulnerabilities. This past winter I took a naturalist class focused on the Colorado's front range that met every Friday for nine weeks. We covered huge topics, each unit's immense breadth and depth reminding me a bit of the impossibilities of covering in a single semester several centuries of Christian history, the entire New Testament, or the basics of caregiving.

My biggest takeaway resembles Doyle's lesson: I have a naturalist certificate, but I have only *skimmed* a very small part of the surface, less than a fraction of what there is to know about the world we live in. Let's start with insects. According to entomologists, insects make up 80 per cent of the world's identified species, but there are more unknown species than known. A conservative estimate of unknown species: two million. It takes 12 bees to make one teaspoon of honey. We owe one third of our diet to pollinated plants and their pollinator insects. To get more particular: there are over six thousand species of dung beetles and seven

---

[41] U.S. Fire Administration, "What is the WUI?" <https://www.usfa.fema.gov/wui/what-is-the-wui.html> (accessed 31 October 2024).

thousand species of spiders. In Colorado alone, there are 1,000 species of bees. Nor is there just one kind of fly; and some flies mimic bees and wasps to protect themselves. Or take birds: birds have songs *and* calls, and any particular bird, say an American robin, has a huge array of both. All black birds do not look alike; we should at least know the difference between a raven and a crow. Or consider geology: geologists work on a timescale beyond everyday comprehension. I was totally unable to conceive of what they study—an earth that is four and half billion years old (the first 500 million years an ocean of lava for which we cannot fully account) and rocks, of which there is also an incredibly expansive variety. Over and over again, I simply couldn't fathom the number of species, colours, kinds, variety, age, capacities of the animals, rocks, birds, plants, trees and water that make up the world.

All to say: how very little I (we humans or at least we non-natural science or non-naturalist humans) know about the almost inexpressible diversity of creatures and land around us. As Doyle's narrator says about a second pine marten whose story he cannot fit into his saga: there are "a *billion* stories you could tell about the living beings on *just this side of the mountain*. The fact is that there are more stories in the space of a single second in a single square foot of dirt and air and water than we could tell each other in a hundred years. The word *amazing* isn't much of a word for how amazing that is." We cannot tell all the stories. But there is still hope, as the narrator concludes: "The more stories we share about living beings, the more attentive we are to living beings, and perhaps the less willing we are to slaughter them and allow them to be slaughtered."[42]

I finished this chapter near a tree line, camping amid pines and snowmelt on Guanella Pass, which in a few weeks will be abloom with flowers. I cannot count the number of insects buzzing by, released by the warmth of spring; nor can I identify the high-pitched song I heard or the small sparrow-type bird that just hopped by. But I will spend as many of my remaining days either as close to the more-than-human surrounding as I can get or working in whatever small way to preserve and appreciate the earth's bounty. And I will enjoy reading novels that are not just about human suffering and happiness.

---

[42] Doyle, *Martin Marten*, pp. 57–8, emphasis in the text.

Selected bibliography of Heather Walton's published writings

Books

Practical Theology beyond the Empirical Turn (London: SCM Press, 2025).

(With Zoë Bennett, Elaine Graham, Stephen Pattison) *Invitation to Research in Practical Theology* (London: Routledge, 2018).

Not Eden: Spiritual Life Writing for this World (London: SCM Press, 2015).

(With Avril Maddrell, Veronica della Dora, Alessandro Scafi) *Christian Pilgrimage, Landscape, and Heritage: Journeying to the Sacred*, Routledge Studies in Religion, Travel and Tourism (New York: Routledge, 2014).

Writing Methods in Theological Reflection (London: SCM Press, 2014).

Imagining Theology: Women, Writing and God (London: T&T Clark, 2007).

Literature, Theology and Feminism (Manchester: Manchester University Press, 2007).

(With Elaine Graham and Frances Ward) *Theological Reflection: Methods* (London: SCM Press, 2005).

An Ethnographic Study of a Moss Side Pub, Working papers in applied social research 12 (Manchester: Faculty of Economic and Social Studies, University of Manchester, 1987).

My Mother is Ill: An Experiment in Feminist Research, Working papers in applied social research 47 (Manchester: Faculty of Economic and Social Studies, University of Manchester, 1987).

White Researchers and Racism, Working papers in applied social research 10 (Manchester: Faculty of Economic and Social Studies, University of Manchester, 1986).

A Tree God Planted: Black People in British Methodism (London: Methodist Publishing House, 1985).

Edited books

(With Elizabeth Anderson and Andrew Radford) *Modernist Women Writers and Spirituality: A Piercing Darkness* (London: Palgrave Macmillan, 2016).

Literature and Theology: New Interdisciplinary Spaces (Farnham: Ashgate, 2011).

(With Elaine Graham and Frances Ward) *Theological Reflection: Sources* (London: SCM Press, 2007).

(With Andrew Hass) *Self, Same, Other: Re-visioning the Subject in Literature and Theology* (Sheffield: Sheffield Academic Press, 2000).

(With Susan Durber) *Silence in Heaven: A Book of Women's Preaching* (London: SCM Press, 1993).

Articles

"A theopoetics in ruins", *Toronto Journal of Theology* 36:2 (2020), pp. 159–69.

"Creativity at the edge of chaos: Theopoetics in a blazing world", *The Journal of Literature and Theology* 33:3 (2019), pp. 336–56.

Special Issue [Guest Editor] *The Journal of Literature and Theology* 33:3 (2019).

"Theopoetics as challenge, change and creative making", *The Journal of Literature and Theology* 33:3 (2019), pp. 229–32.

"A theopoetics of practice: Re-forming in practical theology", *International Journal of Practical Theology* 23:1 (2019), pp. 3–23.

"We have never been theologians: Postsecularism and practical theology", *Practical Theology* 11:3 (2018), pp. 218–30.

"Theology in the way we live now: A theopoetics of life writing", *Concilium* 5 (2017), pp. 13–24.

"'And a sword will pierce your soul also': reflections on the holy mother and the holy child", *Holiness: The Journal of Wesley House Cambridge* 2:1 (2016), pp. 93–103.

"The consolation of everyday things", *LIR* 4:15 (2016), pp. 137–52.

"Seeking wisdom in practical theology", *Practical Theology* 7:1 (2014), pp. 5–18.

"The course outline: Teaching theology through creative writing", *Journal of Adult Theological Education* 9:2 (2012), pp. 210–18.

"You have to say you cannot speak: Feminist reflections upon public theology", *International Journal of Public Theology* 4:1 (2010), pp. 21–36.

"Calls to preach: Constructing vocational theology", *Practical Theology* 2:1 (2009), pp. 63–74.

"Staging John Coetzee / Elizabeth Costello", *The Journal of Literature and Theology* 22:3 (2008), pp. 280–94.

"Sex in the war: An aesthetics of resistance in the diaries of Etty Hillesum", *Theology and Sexuality* 12:1 (2005), pp. 51–61.

"The gender of the cyborg", *Theology and Sexuality* 10:2 (2004), pp. 33–44.

"Advent: Theological reflections on IVF", *Theology and Sexuality* 9:1 (2003), pp. 201–9.

"Re-vision and revelation: Forms of spiritual power in women's writing", *Feminist Theology* 12:1 (2003), pp. 89–102.

"Extreme faith in the work of Elizabeth Smart and Luce Irigaray", *The Journal of Literature and Theology* 16:1 (2002), pp. 40–50.

"Speaking in signs: Narrative and trauma in pastoral theology", *Scottish Journal of Healthcare Chaplaincy* 5:2 (2002), pp. 2–6.

"The wisdom of Sheba: The construction of feminist practical theology", *Contact: The Interdisciplinary Journal of Pastoral Studies* 135:1 (2001), pp. 3–12.

"Mothers' Union: The maternal in feminist reading, writing and theology", *Modern Believing* 41:1 (2000), pp. 22–30.

"'If this political party were a house': Theological reflections upon the style and spirit of New Labour", *Political Theology* 1:1 (1999), pp. 9–16.

"Passion and pain: conceiving theology out of infertility", *Contact : The Interdisciplinary Journal of Pastoral Studies* 130:1 (1999), pp. 3–9.

"Theology of Desire", *Theology and Sexuality* 1:1 (1994), pp. 31–41.

Chapters in books

"Registering: Theology and poetic practice", in Ashley Cocksworth, Rachel Starr and Stephen Burns (eds), *From the Shores of Silence: Conversations in Feminist Practical Theology* (London: SCM Press, 2023), pp. 57–71.

"Rubble and dust: A sacrament of ruins in art and theology", in Bridget Nichols and Nicholas Taylor (eds), *The End of the Church? Conversations with the Work of David Jasper* (Durham: Sacristy Press, 2022), pp. 35–53.

"The children are always lost: Marilynne Robinson and the poetics of theology", in Håkan Möller & Ola Sigurdson (eds), *Marilynne Robinson and Theology*, KVHAA Konferenser (Stockholm: The Royal Swedish Academy of Letters, History and Antiquities, 2021), pp. 29–48.

"Between Ascension and Pentecost: A theology of adoption", in John Swinton and Brian Brock (eds), *A Graceful Embrace: Theological Reflections on Adopting Children* (Leiden and Boston, MA: Brill, 2017), pp. 205–16.

"Faith in ruins: fragments and pattern in the late works of Rose Macaulay", in Elizabeth Anderson and Andrew Radford (eds), *Modernist Women Writers and Spirituality: A Piercing Darkness* (London: Palgrave Macmillan, 2016), pp. 69–94.

"The history of feminist theology in the Academy: An autoethnographic research journey", in Lena Gemzoe, Marja-Liisa Keinänen and Avril Maddrell (eds), *Contemporary Encounters in Religion and Gender* (Basingstoke: Palgrave Macmillan, 2016), pp. 285–306.

(With Elizabeth Anderson and Andrew Radford), "Introduction: The intricate persistence of strange Gods", in Elizabeth Anderson, Andrew Radford and Heather Walton (eds), *Modernist Women Writers and Spirituality: A Piercing Darkness* (London: Palgrave Macmillan, 2016), pp. 1–20.

"Desiring things: Practical theology and the new materialisms", in Ruard Ganzevoort, Rein Brouwer and Bonnie Miller-McLemore (eds), *City of Desires—a Place for God?*, International Practical Theology (Berlin: Lit Verlag, 2013), pp. 131–40.

"Poetics", in Bonnie Miller-McLemore (ed.), *The Wiley Blackwell Companion to Practical Theology*, Wiley Blackwell Companions to Religion (Chichester: Wiley-Blackwell, 2012), pp. 173–82.

"When love is not true: Literature and theology after romance", in Heather Walton (ed.), *Literature and Theology: New Interdisciplinary Spaces* (Farnham: Ashgate, 2011), pp. 37–54.

"Jean Rhys, Elizabeth Smart, and the 'gifts' of the King James Bible", in Hannibal Hamlin and Norman W. Jones (eds), *The King James Bible after 400 Years: Literary, Linguistic, and Cultural Influences* (Cambridge: Cambridge University Press, 2010), pp. 318–35.

"My green bed", in David Marston (ed.), *Goldfish 2: The Second Anthology of Writing from Goldsmiths* (London: Goldsmiths, University of London, 2008).

"Our sacred texts: Literature, theology and feminism", in Dawn Llewellyn and Deborah F. Sawyer (eds), *Reading Spiritualities: Constructing and Representing the Sacred* (Aldershot: Ashgate, 2008), pp. 85–94.

"The feminist literary revisioning of sacred traditions", in Andrew Hass, David Jasper and Elisabeth Jay (eds), *The Oxford Handbook of English Literature and Theology* (Oxford: Oxford University Press, 2007), pp. 543–57.

"Literature and theology: Sex in the relationship", in Darlene Bird and Yvonne Sherwood (eds), *Bodies in Question: Gender, Religion, Text* (Aldershot: Ashgate, 2005), pp. 131–46.

"Women writing the divine", in Pamela S. Anderson and Beverley Clack (eds), *Feminist Philosophy of Religion: Critical Readings* (London: Routledge, 2003), pp. 123–35.

"Passion and pain: conceiving theology out of infertility", in David Willows and John Swinton (eds), *Spiritual Dimensions of Pastoral Care: Practical Theology in a Multidisciplinary Context* (London: Jessica Kingsley Publishers, 2000), pp. 196–201.

"Love relations: exploring the intimacy between women's writing and theology", in Liam Gearon (ed.), *English Literature, Theology and the Curriculum*, Theology in Dialogue (London: Cassell, 1999), pp. 338–47.

"Breaking open the Bible", in Elaine Graham and Margaret Halsey (eds), *Life Cycles: Women and Pastoral Care* (London: SPCK, 1993), pp. 192–9.

EU GPSR Authorized Representative:

LOGOS EUROPE, 9 rue Nicolas Poussin, 17000 La Rochelle, France

contact@logoseurope.eu

www.ingramcontent.com/pod-product-compliance
Lightning Source LLC
Chambersburg PA
CBHW061443300426
44114CB00014B/1807